CHILDREN OF THE SUN

CHILDREN OF THE SUN

The Cork Mission to South America

Leonard O'Brien

VERITAS

First published 2009 by
Veritas Publications
7/8 Lower Abbey Street
Dublin 1
Ireland
Email publications@veritas.ie
Website www.veritas.ie

ISBN 978 1 84730 199 4

Copyright © Leonard O'Brien, 2009
Photographs appear courtesy of Richard Mills

10 9 8 7 6 5 4 3 2 1

The material in this publication is protected by copyright law. Except as may be permitted by law, no part of the material may be reproduced (including by storage in a retrieval system) or transmitted in any form or by any means, adapted, rented or lent without the written permission of the copyright owners. Applications for permissions should be addressed to the publisher.

A catalogue record for this book is available from the British Library.

Cover designed by Niamh McGarry

Printed in the Republic of Ireland
by ColourBooks Ltd, Dublin

Veritas books are printed on paper made from the wood pulp of managed forests. For every tree felled, at least one tree is planted, thereby renewing natural resources.

Contents

Foreword – Bishop John Buckley	7
Introduction	9
Cork's First Missionary Outreach	16
The Archbishop and the Archdeacon	21
Journey to the Andes	29
Life in the Andes	35
Indian Achievement in the Andes	43
The Coast of Peru	48
Cork Chooses a Mission on the Coast	55
Trujillo: A Spanish Colonial City	59
The Mission Begins	67
Breaking the News in Cork	74
Opposition from Evangelists	79
Arrival of the Irish Nuns	85
The Mission Gets a 'Finished Look'	93
Life in a Shanty Town: Housing	99
Life in a Shanty Town: Surviving	104
Life in a Shanty Town: Sickness	110
'Invasion' from the Andes	114
Correspondence	120
Michael Murphy, Defender of the Poor	130

Building in an Earthquake Zone	134
Baptism: Revered but Postponed	144
My College and My Professor	148
Marriage or Living Together	152
Second Generation of Missionaries	157
Theology of Liberation	160
Feeding the Hungry	166
The Fall of the Inca	173
1975–1990: Years of Peace and Progress	181
Vocations to the Religious Life	184
The Mission in Crisis	191
Cork Priests in Chile	210
New Mission in Ecuador	215
Early Years in Manta	219
Two Ocean Currents	222
A New Dawn in Trujillo	226
Ecuador: An Undertaking Completed	230
The Last Years of the Mission	233
Epilogue: Mass of Thanksgiving in Cork	240

Foreword

It is now over forty years since Bishop Cornelius Lucey wrote a letter to the people of Cork informing them of his decision to establish a diocesan mission to South America. Little could he have known, or indeed imagined, the impact that decision would have. One thing he did sense very accurately was the support and prayers of the people, priests and sisters of Cork and Ross.

Primarily, the work of all who served in South America was to make Christ better known and loved. From this came a commitment to the material welfare of the people. The sacrifice of the priests and sisters was matched by the generosity of the people at home.

It took faith and courage to take on responsibility for a large and distressed area in South America. The mission survived terrorism, earthquakes and political turmoil. It is indeed unusual for a missionary project to last as long as that of the Cork and Ross South American mission. It is very important that this unique outreach, the most original ever undertaken by any diocese in Ireland, should be recorded for future generations.

I wonder if Monsignor O'Brien was aware of what he was letting himself in for when I invited him to write this history of our work in Peru and Ecuador. I warmly congratulate him on a work elegantly done. Despite his demanding pastoral duties, I think that the writing of this history was a labour of love for him. He eloquently captures not only the historical facts, but also, and indeed even more importantly, the spirit of the mission. The recounting of the success of this mission story in such a splendid narrative must have taken an enormous effort, no matter how gifted the writer. All the detail regarding major events in the mission's areas of South America is captivating.

The only guideline I gave Monsignor O'Brien when I invited him to undertake this task was: 'Keep in mind people who would know very little about the mission.' His style of writing strikes exactly the right chord for a popular history, one that is acceptable to the general public and eminently readable. He does not merely give the facts, he brings them to life. His anecdotal recollections make it easy reading. Monsignor O'Brien's book will be a rewarding and enjoyable experience and it is not always that such a harmony can be achieved.

We are all in his debt, not only the priests and sisters who served there, but all people who have an interest in the missionary work of the Church. I hope you enjoy reading *Children of the Sun* as much as I did. It deserves a wide readership.

+John Buckley,
Bishop of Cork and Ross

Introduction

Nostalgia – the homesickness of the ancient Greeks, the yearning of modern man for times past, an illness of sentimental minds, incurable because the past is past and can never be recaptured – enshrines some decades in a legend of wonder and awe. The 1960s stand out in the past century as an idealised era of youth and protest and hope for a new and better world. President Kennedy was the eloquent prophet of that golden age; Pope John XXIII lent it the warmth of his loving heart; the Beetles became its muse and the uninhibited youth of the time became at once creator and product of a new world. No matter that it was little more than a false dawn followed by the dreary '70s and '80s, when a new breed of student would swap protest for academic conformity, and the bland dominance of middle age would once again be re-established in every area of human life. In spite of the unrealised dreams, the '60s will live on in music and legend. In that magical decade the Catholic Church experienced its own new springtime with the aggiornamento of John XXIII, the Vatican Council, the vernacular liturgy and the new focus on the laity.

All over Ireland and in every area of human life, the fresh air of the '60s blew away the stale stagnation of previous decades marred and blighted by an economic war, World War II and the emigrant boat. Not everything, of course, was right in those years: children could still leave school at fourteen and, in the less prosperous areas of the cities, many did. However, jobs were plentiful. A familiar sight in Cork's north side was the groups of blue-overalled teenage girls heading towards the Sunbeam textile factory in Blackpool, linking arms, laughing and chatting, school days over, money in their pockets (three pounds a week) and the exciting dawn of adult life before them. Their fathers headed off towards the city's docklands where work awaited in the port or in the Ford and Dunlop factories.

The spirit of the new age influenced every aspect of the young Cork person's life. The older dance bands, whose musicians dressed in white tuxedos and bow ties and performed seated on stage, had given way to the new showband rockers, gyrating on stage to new rhythms of new music. Young lives were not yet touched by drugs or alcohol; the 'ballrooms of romance' boasted only a mineral bar.

The Catholic Church in Cork was also full of life and vigour, led by a new bishop who had taken over a few years previous from an old man of ninety-two. Nowhere was this new life more evident than in the eucharistic procession, held each year along the streets of the city. As the second city of Ireland, Cork had all the ambitious instincts of a younger son to surpass his senior in some field of endeavour other than size or age. In the field of sport – hurling in particular – Cork could justly claim a pre-eminence unmatched by anything that Dublin could attempt. Certain cultural areas such as literature could also be cited by Corkonians as fields of unique achievement, where Corkmen like Seán O Faoláin and Frank O'Connor surpassed any other Irishman in the crafting of the short story. John Stanislaus Joyce, garrulous father of James Joyce, saw himself as a 'professional' Corkman living in exile in the capital among lesser men.

In one rather surprising area of human endeavour, Cork city held unchallenged superiority. On a summer Sunday, every year since 1926, the city staged a procession of the Blessed Sacrament that far surpassed in attendance and civic unity any similar public expression of faith organised elsewhere in southern Ireland. This religious event owed its uniqueness to the fact that while other cities and towns staged processions at parochial level, in Cork every parish in the city participated in one huge demonstration of faith, sending in feeder processions of marching men to the city's central Daunt Square, where the marchers converged for the Sermon and Benediction of the Blessed Sacrament. Here a huge wooden

Introduction

platform some ten feet in height was erected to accommodate an altar, podium and seating for this central event of the day's devotions. The Monstrance was carried to this point by the bishop from the Cathedral in the north side, accompanied by the greatest pageantry, where the waiting parish delegations interspersed the decades of the Rosary with eucharistic hymns led by a leading local tenor.

Seen in the light of the later development of Cork and Ross as a diocese with a foreign mission, the eucharistic procession of 4 June 1961 has taken on a significance that no one on that day could have suspected or appreciated. The huge lay participation in the procession itself indicated the favourable disposition of Cork people to their faith, their spontaneity in giving it public expression and their loyalty to their bishop and priests. Also significant was Bishop Lucey's choice of preacher for the event, Bishop Thomas J. McDonough of Savannah, Georgia, USA, with whom he had set up plans for an informal 'twinning' arrangement whereby Cork, with its abundant vocations to the priesthood and religious life, would come to the aid of the Diocese of Savannah, then suffering from an acute shortage of vocations. For Bishop Lucey, this experiment became in effect a practice run for a much greater missionary operation that he would undertake in South America some years later. There was another reason that particular procession day was so significant: it was the day on which Bishop Lucey would invite Fr Michael Murphy, curate at the cathedral, to join the St James's mission to South America, run by Archbishop Cushing of Boston.

Sunday, 4 June 1961 was blessed with daylong hot sunshine tempered by a pleasant breeze. At 3.00 p.m. the main procession moved off from the cathedral, bound for Daunt Square, led by the men and boys of the confraternities bearing heavily embroidered banners, steadied against the breeze by long, white ribbons like yachts under spinnaker. Marching bands accompanied the hymns, interspersed with decades of the Rosary. After these came the religious orders: Christian Brothers, Presentation Brothers, Carmelites in black, Dominicans in white, Franciscans and Capuchins in brown. There were small boys strewing flowers before the large canopy, which was hung with cloth of gold brocade, beneath which the bishop carried the Blessed Sacrament in a golden monstrance. Adding more colour to the spectacle came the Lord Mayor and members of the City Council in their red robes, the university faculty in scarlet, followed by army, Gardaí and Slui Muire units in their different uniforms.

The *Cork Examiner* newspaper estimated that 40,000 men and boys marched from the cathedral, watched by as many women and children from the sidewalks or from the windows of business premises. At Daunt Square, and filling the Grand Parade as far as the south channel of the River Lee, thousands more awaited the arrival of the main procession. A photo of the scene published the following morning suggested a vast concourse of worshippers. When all the uniformed detachments had taken up position beneath the altar and the civic dignitaries were seated at their prie-dieux, Bishop McDonough of Savannah addressed the vast gathering, stating that it would be difficult for him to remember when he had been as touched as he had been that day, taking part in such a great demonstration of faith. His sincerity and vibrant style of preaching so impressed the gathering that in an unusual departure from the tradition of the time his final words were greeted with applause that filled the city's Sunday afternoon quietness.

When the procession had returned to the cathedral and the tired walkers dispersed, the banners were furled for another year. While the clergy disrobed in the sacristy, Bishop Lucey called Fr Michael Murphy and, with an inscrutable expression, asked him to come and see him that evening. The latter, wondering what had gone wrong in the day's proceedings that merited a 'carpeting' at the Bishop's Palace, ran his mind over the events of the day back in his rooms in the cathedral presbytery. As junior curate at the cathedral, Michael Murphy was in charge of the altar boys for the event. It was his responsibility to allocate to them the different liturgical duties involved in the eucharistic procession. 'Organiser of Altar Boys' – some responsibility, he reflected wryly, after ten years in the priesthood, the first six of which had been spent in Washington, DC, where all of his former colleagues were now pastors responsible for large parishes staffed by two or three assistants.

The cathedral altar boys were never happy with the arrangements for the procession because the important 'jobs' went to the students of Farranferris College, the minor seminary of the diocese. When Fr Murphy had given them their instructions they crowded around him, hands up as boys do in class, pushing and shouting: 'Me Father, me Father, it's my turn for a job, Father.' Altar boys tended to regard the youngest priest in the parish as their particular friend and, in his mid-thirties, Michael Murphy was by far the youngest priest on the cathedral staff, the others being in their late fifties or sixties, which was the usual age at the time for curates awaiting promotion to the office of parish priest. It was natural for young boys to relate to him because of his age, but he also appealed to them for another reason: his American background.

Unlike most Irishmen who had lived in the United States, Michael Murphy never affected an American accent, or 'twang' as it would have been popularly known. However, quite unconsciously, whether from living with American priests during his Washington days or attending movies which he loved, his vocabulary, turn of phrase and mode of expression had become totally Americanised, taken not merely from the speech of Americans but straight from the Hollywood script writers of the black and white movies of the 1940s. Phrases like 'I shoot from the hip, see' and 'Let's get this show on the road' were part of his speech. A hostile dog would be described as 'a mean-looking hound dog' and a priest on duty on a quiet Sunday afternoon would be referred to as 'the guy minding the store'. To Cork boys of the pre-television era, when cinema, dominated by Hollywood movies, was their window into a world of excitement, adventure and romance, his unconscious mastery of the movie idiom elevated him to the rank of Hollywood hero.

In appearance Fr Murphy had the physique to match his movie image. Nicknamed 'Tarzan' in secondary school, he had matured with the years into a Garry Cooper type. Tall by the standards of the time and well built with a slight droop of the right shoulder, he had the air of a western cowboy hero. Dressed in his black suit of designer cut, which he always wore, he could with the addition of a Panama hat have doubled as a Chicago boss in the days of Al Capone, or, toting a 'ten-gallon' Stetson, he could stand in for John Wayne. In later years, South American women would speak of him as the *'Irish padre un tipo de* John Wayne'.

At times Michael Murphy wondered why he had returned to Ireland at all. Usually young priests on temporary mission overseas counted the months to their return home where they could pay weekly visits to their parents and attend weddings of childhood friends. Fr Murphy's situation was different because his parents were dead and the family no longer occupied the farm where he had grown up – ties to his native place were few and fragile.

On the Sunday in question, Fr Michael Murphy left the cathedral presbytery on foot for the Bishop's Palace. He walked along St Mary's Road with the high, prison-like walls of the Peacock Lane Magdalen Laundry to his left. On his right there were blocks of ancient lanes built on a lower level so precipitous that one could touch the roofs of the house with an outstretched hand: eighteenth century lanes collectively known as 'Strawhill'. Strawhill housed families Fr Murphy knew by name from his twice yearly visits to collect 'the dues' (offerings of a shilling or two, which each family contributed to support the bishop and the priests of the cathedral).

The bishop lived in the 'Palace': a redbrick, 1930s building, large as a country mansion, set in wooded grounds at the top of a steep, shrub-lined avenue. The former bishop, who for much of his time had occupied rooms in the minor seminary nearby, had built this imposing residence for himself and his successors. Bishop Lucey, his immediate successor, now occupied the house, which was attended by two Bon Secours Sisters from the convent on College Road. One of these nuns answered the door and ushered Fr Murphy into a small room furnished with a mahogany table, some chairs and a glazed china cabinet housing a collection of silver trowels inscribed with the details of the foundation stones the bishop had laid. Bishop Lucey entered the room, sat at the other end of the table, joined his hands as though in prayer and spoke to his reflection in the polished mahogany. Getting to the point immediately, without any reference to the impressive procession of the afternoon, he explained that Cardinal Cushing of Boston had asked for some volunteers to work in South America with the Boston mission. Three priests had been selected, but now one could no longer go, so Fr Murphy was asked if he would be prepared to go instead, as he had volunteered previously.

Listening to the bishop, Michael Murphy recalled the picture of the three volunteers that had appeared in the newspaper and wondered which one had dropped out and why. Tactfully, he refrained from asking the question. Without hesitation Michael Murphy accepted the invitation and was told to get a United States visa and be ready to leave within a month for Cochabamba, Bolivia, to begin Spanish studies in the language school there run by the Maryknoll missionaries. The bishop rose, indicating the interview was over, offered his episcopal ring to be kissed and ushered the priest out into the warm evening sunshine.

It is not given to us to know the future and little did the bishop know that the young priest he had met with would one day succeed him as Bishop of Cork and Ross, when he himself would leave the Palace forever to work as a missionary in Africa's Turkana Desert.

Cork's First Missionary Outreach

The special relationship between Cork and Savannah, though brief – it lasted a mere five years – was of greater significance than its brevity would suggest, because in it we see the first manifestation of a missionary awareness in the mind of Bishop Lucey. In the first ten years of his episcopate, he had concentrated on an ambitious church-building programme and the fundraising drives needed to finance it, especially in the construction of the Rosary of Churches (the construction of five new churches surrounding the city, each dedicated to a Mystery of the Rosary). The response of the laity to his appeals for funds and the goodwill shown assured him of his acceptance as bishop by the priests and people of his diocese. Now, with the home front secured, so to speak, the time had come to look for new challenges beyond his ecclesiastical boundaries. Already Bishop Lucey had shown concern for the spiritual well-being of Irish emigrants in his Confirmation addresses and in his Minority Report for a Government Committee on Emigration, on which he sat. The choice of the Diocese of Savannah in Georgia as the setting for an outreach to the Irish diaspora was as unlikely as it was fortuitous.

In the summer of 1960, Bishop Lucey and his close friend and lifetime travelling companion, Fr John Barrett, Adm, from Skibbereen, flew to the United States where they were met in New York by a young Clonakilty priest on temporary mission, Fr Paddy Leader. They planned to rent a car and drive to San Antonio, Texas, where a distant cousin of the bishop, also Lucey by name, was archbishop. Fr Leader drove them to the outskirts of New York City and set them off on Interstate Highway 1, on the long 2,000-mile drive to Texas – a fairly daunting undertaking by two men in their fifties who had never before driven on American roads. Highway 1 would take them south into the state of Georgia where they would connect with Highway 80, turn west and travel on to San Antonio, Texas.

They made an overnight stop in Augusta, the city in Georgia made famous by the Masters Golf Tournament, some sixty miles from their planned turn-off onto Highway 80. Next morning they called to the nearby parish of St Mary on the Hill to say Mass. Here they were greeted by two Irish priests: Dan Bourke, a native of Tipperary, and Kevin Boland from Cork, who had been ordained the previous year at All Hallows College for service in the Diocese of Savannah. These two genial Irishmen insisted that the visitors break their journey and travel to Savannah to meet Thomas J. McDonough, who had recently been appointed bishop there.

And so the following morning after Mass they set out southwards for Savannah on Georgia State Highway 25: Kevin Boland driving his pastor's air-conditioned Chevrolet; the highway stretching straight ahead through the wide clearing between the motionless trees of the virgin forest. Traffic was light and along the margins of the forest there was no sign of life, except the occasional plume of smoke rising from the stone chimney of some clapboard shack where poor share-croppers lived. At the small town of Statesboro they joined Highway 80, which links San Diego, a city on the California-Mexican border 3,000 miles to the west, with the city of Savannah on the Atlantic seaboard to the east. For the visitors from Ireland this road trip was an unexpected introduction to the scenery of the Deep South, so different from the standard pictures of America, which show either city skyscrapers or open prairie. Nearing the coast the scenery changed: dense forest gave way to reed swamps bordered by live oak trees, trailing wisps of Spanish moss – the grey, cobweb-like parasitic growth that drapes every tree along the sea coast of the Deep South, providing a backdrop to a story of mystery and stillness.

Kevin Boland found that his Irish visitors knew little of Georgia and the South, apart from what they remembered from *Gone with the Wind*. He explained that the bloody events of the Civil War of 1864 were very much alive in the folk memory of a community who only referred to the disaster as 'the war between the States' and still hated the memory of the 'Yankee' General Sherman, who burned, murdered and looted on his march from Atlanta to Savannah – the song 'Marching Through Georgia' was never played south of the Mason-Dixon Line. Sherman, having laid the State to waste, was at least civilised enough to spare the beautiful, undefended Savannah from the fire and sword that had reduced Atlanta to a smouldering ruin.

Thanks to Sherman's mercy in this instance, Savannah, when they drove into its downtown historic quarter around the cathedral, appeared to them as no other American city. It was nothing like the canyon-like streets of New York, dwarfed by impossibly high skyscrapers that shut out the sun. Here, instead, were leafy trees, gorgeous camellias and perfumed magnolias in landscaped squares. Streets and squares were lined with town houses from another century. Their pink, white and ochre weather boards reflected the light of the Georgia sunshine; verandas with shingle roofs were supported by classical columns and topped with fretwork fascia boards, shading rocking chairs where old men and women snoozed in the midday heat behind railings of intricate ironwork.

Kevin pulled in beside the Chancery Office, a low building built of grey brick, shaded by huge oak trees. Inside, they were greeted by Bishop McDonough and his staff: the Chancellor and several secretaries, who left their desks and offices in high excitement to meet the visitors from Ireland, assuring them in their rich southern accents that they, too, were Irish. When Bishop Lucey inquired from which part of Ireland they had come, he was informed that it was over one hundred years since their ancestors had arrived.

At lunch in a nearby restaurant, Bishop McDonough talked excitedly about his huge diocese, greater in extent than the island of Ireland, yet staffed by only thirty priests. He talked enthusiastically about his plans for vocations: the setting up of a minor seminary; recruitment of secondary school boys in Ireland to study for the priesthood; and appeals to Irish convents to make foundations in Georgia. He gave his guests a short history lesson about the Catholics who had come to America after minor famines in Ireland in 1820 and 1830; how the Irish had sailed across the Irish Sea to Liverpool, where they had taken a ship for the Port of Savannah and on to the main shipping port for the cotton grown on the plantations in the southern states, bound for the Lancashire mills.

Most of the newly arrived Irish remained in the city of Savannah, where over one hundred years later they formed the bedrock of the city's Catholic community, estimated at 10 per cent of the total population. However, those who ventured into the interior of the State of Georgia found themselves without priests, nuns or the support of the Catholic Church, so that today many of the great Irish names like Murphy and McNamara are held by third generation Baptists. All of this made a huge impression on Bishop Lucey, especially the thought that faith had been lost through the lack of priests. He compared in his mind the size of his own diocese to that of Bishop McDonough's. To him it was a scandal that this part of the world, linked so closely with Ireland in the past, was now both forgotten and neglected by the Irish Church.

Here the Bishop of Cork and Ross found his first missionary challenge and he rose to it with enthusiasm and determination. During the months following his return to Ireland from that trip, which had become a turning point in his life, he took immediate steps to 'twin' Cork and Ross with Savannah. He appointed Fr Christy Walsh, curate at Ss. Peter and Paul, as the liaison man with Savannah. He invited Bishop McDonough to visit the senior Cork and Ross students in Maynooth to encourage them to spend their temporary mission in Georgia, which he did with success. Two newly ordained priests accepted the invitation to work in Savannah in 1961, four in 1963 and two more in 1964. The Ursuline Sisters and Presentation Sisters in Cork founded two convents in Georgia, which are still flourishing over forty years later. Many secondary school pupils entered Irish seminaries to study for the Diocese of Savannah, numbering over forty at one stage. Bishop Lucey's own thoughts on the project were aired in an article he wrote for *The Fold*, his diocesan magazine, in which he stated that with so many Irish now working in Savannah, Cork priests and nuns would 'not even lose their Cork accent' by living there.

This close linking between Cork and Savannah might have lasted many more years if events had not taken an unexpected turn when Bishop Lucey visited South America to attend the funeral of Archdeacon Duggan, a priest of his diocese who had volunteered to work there with Cardinal Cushing's mission and whose story will be told in a later chapter. Just as his unplanned visit to Savannah produced one Cork outreach, his unexpected visit to Peru resulted in a much grander undertaking. In the event, the Diocese of Savannah went on to become self-sufficient in vocations, but always remained grateful for the help given by Cork in a time of crisis. When the Cork mission to Peru opened up there were no more young priests free to go to Savannah for their temporary mission, and the loss was on the side of Cork. Few environments could have been more suitable for a young priest, fresh out of Maynooth College, which at that time was strictly cut off from the outside world. A year or two working in America provided an admirable finishing off of the excellent academic formation received at college. To live in Savannah, of all American communities, meant a daily exposure to old world politeness, to a world where men still stood up when a woman entered a room and where male dinner guests stood behind the chairs of lady diners to help them be seated before taking their seats themselves. Antebellum courtesy still survives in the Old South, even a century later, and a little of it rubbed off on men newly arrived from Ireland, where Victorian customs were rapidly dying out.

Over the years, the links with Savannah have continued at a social level and were further strengthened by the appointment of Kevin Boland – the same man who had first welcomed Bishop Lucey – as Bishop of Savannah in 1995.

The Archbishop and the Archdeacon

The opening of the Cork and Ross mission to Peru in 1965 meant that in future there would be few newly ordained priests available for temporary mission, and this brought to an end the 'twinning' arrangement with the Diocese of Savannah. This represented a major change in Bishop Lucey's mission policy. Up to now his concern was for communities of Irish extraction, it then changed to a policy of solicitude for the poor, regardless of their ethnic background. However, the basic strategy remained much the same: Cork volunteers would be concentrated in one place and, as far as possible, be under his personal control.

Neither Cork, nor indeed Ireland itself, ever had any ties with Peru, located as it was on the west coast of South America, home to Native Americans, conquered by the Spanish and run as a Spanish colony until the eighteenth century when it won its independence. As happened in North America, liberation from the mother country made little difference to the indigenous people, who still remained subservient to the European settlers and their descendents. Argentina was the only South American country with an Irish community among its colonisers. Peru had none. Why then, one might ask, did Bishop Lucey pick a country unknown to Irish people, where the language was Spanish and spoken English was unknown even among the educated classes? The answer to that conundrum lies in an unlikely friendship that developed between Cork's archdeacon, Tom Duggan, and Boston's Cardinal Cushing.

In the 1950s, Archdeacon Duggan was sent to America to raise money for the Cork church-building fund. In Boston he met Cushing and both men became friends. When Bishop Lucey invited Cushing to bless one of the newly built churches in Cork, he asked Duggan to make the arrangements for the visit, which involved the granting of the freedom of the city of Cork to the visiting bishop and the conferring of an honorary degree by the university. Archbishop Cushing was driven in an open car from the railway station to City Hall for the civic reception, at which these honours would be conferred.

We may chuckle sympathetically today at the innocence of Corkonians, who in their thousands braved a downpour to wave to a passing American bishop, but at the time, Cushing was an international superstar and that is what people did in those days to share in the reflected glory of the great and the good. Irish people knew of Boston's archbishop from the pages of *Time Magazine* and from the Kennedy legend, which had been building up around the handsome young senator from Massachusetts and his radiant wife. Cushing was Kennedy's bishop and, in a sense, both fed off each other's fame. Both were Catholic, both Bostonian, both Irish. As the Kennedy star ascended so did Cushing's. When a Catholic was elected to the White House for the first time in history, Protestant America in all its shades, from High Church Episcopalian to fundamentalist southern Baptist, waited suspiciously for Roman Churchmen to insinuate themselves into the political life of Washington, expecting diplomatic Italians or wily Irishmen to tamper with the separation of Church and State. In fact, nothing of the sort occurred. Instead, Cardinal Cushing broke on the Washington scene: neither a diplomat nor an intellectual, but a huge Irishman of patriarchal proportions; a man larger than life, sonorous, human, witty, sincere, with a craggy head that might have been chiselled from Mount Rushmore. To the Kennedy family he was a father figure, celebrating their weddings, Baptisms, and burying their dead, forgiving their failings, non-judgemental, above controversy, yet strong in his faith while respectful of the faith of others. He was a man without enemies; more a figure of fun than of division.

Genetically linked with County Cork – his father came from Glanworth in the north of the county – his generosity to Cork City was legendary. Several times he contributed to the church-building fund

The Archbishop and the Archdeacon

and each contribution amounted to about a quarter of the total cost of each church. Cushing's friendship with Archdeacon Duggan continued for years: he stayed in the archdeacon's house in Ballyphehane; invited him to accompany him to Rome when he received the red hat from John XXIII; took him to Bolivia as part of the Papal entourage on a visit as Papal Legate. Their letters were always brief and to the point, but it is evident from Cushing's letters to Duggan from 1958 onwards that he had developed a new interest in South America, where he was setting up a missionary society dedicated to St James the Apostle. The concept of a missionary society permanently attached to a diocese with the bishop as its superior was quite new. In the past, missionary societies were run as separate entities under their own superior, quite independent of the diocese. When the Maynooth mission to China was founded it became known as the Columban Missionary Society, with its independent structure. The idea of linking foreign missionaries with European dioceses came from the Encyclical of Pope Pius XII, *Fidei Donum*, published in 1957. This was a short but important Encyclical Letter concerning an urgent situation facing the Church in Africa. It was a call to action in favour of Third World Churches made to the whole Church. What marked it out as a highly original document was the proposal that diocesan priests in Europe and North America could be sent on temporary mission to Third World countries that were in need of priests. Pius XII wrote: 'A form of interchangeable assistance is adopted by some bishops who give permission to one or other of their priests to leave their diocese for a time, and place themselves at the disposition of bishops in Africa.' (*Fidei Donum*, 73) This new thinking inspired many dioceses in the developed world to share their priests with Third World countries.

In South America, the country that benefited most spectacularly from the so-called *Fidei Donum* priests was Peru. In the decades following the Encyclical, as many as one hundred and fifty religious congregations from other countries went there and 68 per cent of all diocesan priests who went to Latin America went to Peru. Much of the credit for this must go to Archbishop Romolo Carboni, Apostolic Nuncio to Peru, who actively promoted the system of lending diocesan priests to the missions.

Half a century later it is still probably too early to evaluate the work of the *Fidei Donum* priests. To some lifetime missionaries, like the members of Maryknoll or the Columbans, the experiment may seem idealistic in the way it put amateurs in the mission fields. To others it may seem a successful emergency solution to meet an emergency situation. For good or ill the system had one positive outcome: the temporary missionaries returned home with a love for the people they served and an awareness of the needs of the Third World, which they passed on to their parishioners in the developed world.

Cardinal Cushing attributed much of the inspiration for the Society of St James to Fr James Hennessy, a priest of the Diocese of Boston, who worked as a missionary in Buka, New Guinea. He went there some years before the Second World War. He was taken prisoner by the Japanese in March 1942. In July of the same year he was sent to Japan aboard the Montevideo Maru, which was sunk off the Philippines with the loss of all prisoners on board. The Cardinal saw Fr Hennessy as an example of a diocesan priest who died on the foreign missions.

Another priest who had a profound influence on the foundation of the Society of St James was Fr Frank Kennard of the Diocese of Portland, Oregon. When he read of the Pope's concern for the state of the Latin American Church he went, with the blessing of his bishop, to work alone in Peru, basing himself in Apurimac, one of the most deprived mountain areas, where there had been few priests since the turn of the century. He travelled from village to village on foot or on horseback under the most primitive conditions imaginable. The Papal Nuncio of the time was so impressed with this priest's great work that he encouraged him to write to other North American bishops asking them to send more priests to Peru. Cushing was one of those who wrote back. When Cushing finally met Kennard he invited him to address the junior clergy of Boston in 1958, seeking volunteers for missionary work in Peru. Those who volunteered were the first members of the Society of St James.

The priests from Boston set up a base in Lima, the capital of Peru, which became known as the Centre House. The original building proved too small and a new premises was found in a comfortable area of Lima overlooking the Pacific Ocean in Barranco. New arrivals studied Spanish from this base and priests on respite from service at high altitude used it as a haven of relaxation. Here batteries were recharged, retreats were made, old friendships renewed and, in summer time, the beaches around Lima enjoyed. Then, after a few weeks, the men from Boston returned to the primitive conditions and isolation of their Andean outposts.

Cardinal Cushing was a man who espoused projects on the grand scale and he wanted nothing less than a grand scale for his newly founded mission to South America. He did not limit its membership to his own men from Boston, but invited priests from other dioceses and other countries to join in his great venture. It was no surprise in the light of the help he was giving to the building of Cork City's new churches that he approached Bishop Lucey for volunteers. Bishop Lucey responded by sending out three volunteers in July of 1961, among them Fr Michael Murphy, curate at the cathedral.

The departure of the three priests received little publicity, as in those years Ireland was still sending young priests off in droves to the missions. It was a time when priests and nuns always wore clerical dress, even when travelling, and groups of religious were a familiar sight on trans-Atlantic liners leaving Cobh and on the new jet planes departing from Shannon Airport. The archdeacon's departure for the missions was quite different from that of three young, little-known priests. Mission work was for the young and the fit, not for a man of seventy-one. Besides, he held a prominent, if mainly honorary, position as archdeacon of the diocese, in addition to his demanding post as parish priest of St Patrick's on Lower Road, considered to be the most prestigious parish in Cork. The local press found his volunteering an interesting story and covered it enthusiastically, filling out their reports with stories of his previous escapades as a chaplain to the British Army in two world wars.

Archdeacon Duggan's life was both colourful and unusual. Even his family history was enriched – his grandfather had been dismissed from his teaching position in the garrison village of Ballincollig for his Fenian activity. For continuing with these secret and seditious activities he was tried, found guilty and sentenced to ten years' penal servitude, which he served in a western Australian penal colony, never to return home. This man's grandson, Tom Duggan, whom he never met, was ordained a priest for the Diocese of Cork in 1915. Two years later, after post-graduate studies, Fr Duggan volunteered for a military chaplaincy with the British Forces and arrived in Flanders in the autumn of 1917, just a year before World War I ended. In March of 1918, German forces launched the 'Big Push', with a heavy bombardment of the First Royal Munster Fusiliers, who were in the front line with Duggan as their chaplain. All that day he was attending the wounded at an Aid Post in St Emile until he was taken prisoner by the Germans, who transported their prisoners of war all the way to the city of Mainz in the south of Germany, where they remained until they were repatriated a few days before the armistice of November 1918.

On his return to Cork, Fr Duggan taught classics in the diocesan seminary, Farranferris, until the outbreak of World War II in 1939. By then he was forty-nine years old and the age limit for army chaplains was forty. Through devious lobbying of old army comrades, he succeeded in securing an appointment as chaplain to the Durham Light Infantry, based in Oxfordshire, from where he travelled with them to France in January 1940, taking up position on the Belgian border as part of the British Expeditionary Force.

All was quiet until 10 May when the Germans launched the Blitzkrig and the British failed to hold the line and were driven back to Dunkirk, where they mounted one of the greatest rescues of a defeated army in history. Extracts from the battle history *Into Battle With the Durhams* by P.J. Lewis and I.R. English make reference to Tom Duggan's courage during the shelling of the retreating army:

> Padre Duggan then established an unofficial Aid Post in a house in the main street of Carvin where he worked untiringly all day, tending the wounded and showing a complete disregard for the German shelling, which was most accurate and caused a lot of damage in the town.
>
> Next day, headquarters was set up in the chateau of Les Moeres. Here Duggan achieved his greatest fame.

The Archbishop and the Archdeacon

The shelling of the area of the chateau was intense; casualties came in fast. A regimental Aid Post was established in the cellars of the chateau which was soon blazing above their heads. Assisted by the redoubtable Padre Duggan they did some excellent work. Throughout the afternoon the figures of Padre Duggan and Cpl. Fletcher, the stretcher bearer sergeant, could be seen wherever the shelling and casualties were the heaviest. Journey after journey was made by the two men to the cellars of the chateau, where the padre's cheerful humour was like a tonic to the long lines of men who lay on the floor waiting to be evacuated. He seemed quite oblivious to the heavy shelling, and his coolness, energy and courage undoubtedly calmed as well as kept up the morale of the wounded men in his care. Padre Duggan was awarded the Military Cross.

From these brief glances at the life of this colourful and brave priest, one can see how difficult it was for those close to him to dissuade him from becoming a missionary at the age of seventy-one. Both Cardinal Cushing and Bishop Lucey tried and failed. On his visit to Peru and Bolivia at the invitation of Cushing, he had seen at first hand the miserable conditions under which the poor of these countries lived. He was realistic enough to know that he would be of little use as a missionary because of his age, but he did feel that his gesture might inspire younger priests to follow his lead. What he may not have realised was the influence his sacrifice would have on the lay people of Cork, who would later, when Cork founded its own mission, support the venture enthusiastically.

Archdeacon Duggan arrived at the St James' Centre House in Lima, Peru, on 7 November 1961; by 17 December he was dead due to a heart attack. Writing of this event in the biography of Duggan, Carthach MacCarthy provides some details: 'Some visitors arrived and were received by Tom. They had brought some Irish newspapers which they forgot to leave behind them when they were going away. Tom discovered the loss very quickly and ran into the street to intercept them but their taxi was already on its way.' This little incident took on wings in the telling, ending up as a most dramatic tale of Tom forgetting his breviary in a local bus, running after the bus and collapsing on the pavement. The story may well have some foundation in fact and the excitement may have triggered off the cardiac attack, which necessitated a visit from the doctor next morning, during which 'he went out like a light'.

His unexpected death made a huge impact on the people of Cork, some of whom had known him personally from his time as parish priest of Kinsale and Ballyphehane. Many more knew of him from the publicity his recent departure had generated. Looked at from the publicity angle, his death so soon after his arrival in Lima could not have been more well timed. His burial in Lima brought together Cardinal Cushing, Bishop Lucey and Lima's archbishop and the Papal Nuncio to Peru, Archbishop Carboni. But for this funeral, it is unlikely that Cork's bishop would ever have visited South America. What he saw there of the poverty and sub-human living conditions affected him profoundly in his plans for a Cork missionary outreach. His evolving commitment to the poor of the Third World must have been nurtured by the words spoken by the Nuncio at a dinner he gave for the visitors after the funeral: 'Catholics in the more fortunate parts of the world have a great responsibility to investigate, study and help solve the serious problems that beset their co-religionists in other parts of the world.' There was no doubt that these remarks were directed at Bishop Lucey and, in the following years during the Vatican Council, Carboni continued to reopen the subject.

Perhaps the most persuasive influence of all was the encouragement that Bishop Lucey would get from his own priests working with the men from Boston in South America. They spoke for the younger priests of Cork and Ross and the bishop knew that if they gave their support his brave undertaking of 'going it alone' would succeed.

Journey to the Andes

January of 1962 marked not only the beginning of a new year, but also the beginning of a new era in the history of the Diocese of Cork and Ross. With the appointment of the three Cork priests to their new parishes in South America, a forty-year presence of Corkmen working in Latin America in pastoral ministry would begin.

The excitement of 1961 in the lives of these three priests was over: their departure from Ireland; the challenge of learning a new language in the Spanish school of Cochabamba, Bolivia, for two of them; Michael Crowley's first taste of Peruvian life on the coast at Monsefú (he had learned Spanish some years before in Spanish Harlem, New York); the final dramatic weeks of Archdeacon Duggan's eventful life, ending with his burial in Lima; and the visit from Bishop Lucey to attend his funeral. For Michael Murphy, Michael Crowley and Paddy Leader, all that personal upheaval was over as they began the day-to-day life of a foreign missionary working in a new language in the exotic world of the Peruvian Andes.

All three were, for the moment, appointed to parishes in the mountains and their location would impress on them the reality that the country of Peru was divided into two totally distinct worlds: a modern world on the Pacific coastline where transport and communications were reasonably up to the standards of the twentieth century; and another world from another age, the Andean world cut off by impossible terrain from modern civilisation, home to a population whose customs, dress and often language had not changed for thousands of years. Living in such a remote and primitive environment the priests would experience extreme hardship, but would also gain an insight into the mentality of the native people of Peru – the people that they, and the many Cork missionaries who would follow them, would serve on the Pacific coast for over a generation. The high Andes was the world from which the poor migrants would come to the shanty towns, or *barrios*, on the coast. Only by living among them in their native mountain environment could the missionaries ever develop an understanding sympathy for a primitive people struggling to adapt to the harsh modern world to which they had migrated. The Andean experience would teach them many lessons, such as the physical difficulty for Europeans of survival at altitude and the psychological risks of isolation and loneliness. In the planning of the Cork and Ross mission yet to come, all this experience would prove invaluable.

In January 1962, the three Cork priests received their appointments in the southern Peruvian Andes at Limatambo and Abancay. The long journey made by road to their remote assignments was an unforgettable introduction to life in the Andes. They travelled in a Ford V8 pickup truck driven by a priest from Boston who had been in Peru since the foundation of the St James mission in 1958. As they stocked up the truck for the journey with drums of petrol and boxes of provisions, a newly arrived American who knew little, if anything, about conditions in the interior of the country assured them there was no need for such provisions and that 'there are gas stations all the way to Limatambo; there's even a supermarket in Limatambo'. Wisely they ignored that advice.

After driving south along the Pan-American Highway with a grey mist blanketing the dreary sand dunes of the coastal desert, they turned to the left into the foothills of the Andes that rose from the desert floor, their folds filled with drifts of sand blown by the ocean winds of centuries before. Soon, as the road began to climb around the foothills, the climate changed as they rose out of the mist into sunshine that warmed the fresh mountain air. A stop at a lay-by where roadside traders had set up their stalls was a first introduction to the new and exotic world in which they would spend the next three years of their lives. The stalls were constructed of straw matting supported by eucalyptus poles, open on three sides, the roof shaded the fruit and vegetables laid out on rickety tables or piled on the ground beneath: green and purple grapes; mounds of water melons, olive green and larger than a football; yellow melons twice the size of rugby balls; unfamiliar fruits of varied colours like mangos; and bright tomatoes stacked on wooden boxes.

A young woman, brown-skinned and bare-shouldered, smilingly offered her wares helped by her children, black-haired with gleaming teeth, while a small child watched contentedly from his perch on a pile of empty boxes. Mountain women journeying to the coast had left the large trucks in which they travelled to purchase some fruit. In dress and grooming they contrasted so sharply with the young woman tending her stall that one could hardly believe they were of the same nationality or race. The women from the Andean countryside wore traditional dress that went back to Inca times, before any European had set foot on the American continent. Their black hair was parted down the centre and gathered above the ears in two plaits that reached below the shoulder. Over brightly coloured garments they wore a shawl woven in scarlet, blue and green, tied over their backs in such a way that a young child wearing a colourful knitted cap was held in a sitting position almost on the mother's shoulders. Older women whose children had grown up still wore these makeshift backpacks to carry their belongings. A flounced knee-length skirt in scarlet or black completed their dress. The differing feminine fashions of the stall-holder and the customers highlighted the clash of cultures that is Peru: traditional and modern; mountain and coastal; Indian and European.

The trucks that waited nearby were like cattle lorries of indeterminate vintage – indeterminate because they had been adapted to uses the Michigan designers had never anticipated. The steel bubble-like cab, then in fashion, had been replaced with a timber and glass cabin built to the width of the body of the truck, providing seating for four men. The truck's body was enclosed by timber sides with a top deck added, which was surrounded by partly open crates and furnished with seats on which rows of travellers sat motionless, their white sun-hats visible in solid ranks above the sides. Over the cab a steel-railed deck was packed with boxes and bundles. These trucks were the ocean-going liners of the mountains with passengers seated on the top deck, while the body of the truck was packed with bags of potatoes or Indian corn bound for the markets of Lima, or carrying cattle and donkeys destined for the slaughter houses on the coast. 'Tomorrow's hamburgers', commented the American priest as he admired an aged donkey.

The road had been carved from the cliff leaving a rough shelving wall on one side and on the other an unprotected drop to the river far below. This unprotected abyss constituted the greatest threat to life in mountain travel in Peru. Whenever a truck slipped over the brink to tumble down the steep mountainside, the carnage was appalling when the top deck passengers were thrown in all directions, while those trapped in the driver's cab were doomed to certain death. Years later, Michael Murphy would recall the horror of seeing a woman's body dangling by her clothes from branches on the far side of the abyss, unreachable from above or below, her body prey to the vultures floating on the rising air currents of the canyon. Though beautiful, the Andes also possessed an air of menace.

The priests drove onwards and upwards, sometimes along what appeared to be level stretches along valleys with hills rising on either side, at other times when the steep climbs came they zigzagged up the mountainside through impossibly sharp turns. The valley below receded with every new level that was reached, the truck in second gear, the scent of eucalyptus trees wafting through the open windows, filling the cab with a medicinal fragrance reminiscent of a Turkish sauna, until a new level was reached and new hills rose around a new valley. Close up, the colours of the terrain were dappled brown and earthy; in the middle distance the slopes were mauve shading to lavender; while the far distant peaks were a delicate violet merging with the sky.

Once they stopped above a deep gorge where an almost dried-up stream meandered through the gravel bed of what would become a wide river when the rains came. A family group were picnicking by the stream. From another pass, they viewed a wider and deeper valley laid out in rice paddies in geometrical shapes irrigated from the stream. The paddies of young rice were emerald green while those from which the crop had been lifted were dark brown. In this watered and productive valley no land was wasted, even that which reached up the steep hillsides was stepped in terraced fields where potatoes and Indian maize grew. They stopped to eat at a small village where four palm trees flanked a dry fountain on the plaza in front of a small colonial church, which they noted was locked up and shabby. They ate rice in a bar giving onto the square where they chatted with the lady who served them about the parish life of the village: 'No. There was no Padre living here.' She could never recall a time when one did live here: 'He did come every year for the festival from farther away. What noise, during the festival! Such crowds! Such fireworks! What a grand procession when the image of the patron was carried through the streets!' She took a faded black and white picture from the wall and showed them the procession. The statue of the patron was carried on a carved wooden frame with shafts that rested on the shoulders of the men of the village. A band of ragged musicians marched before the patron with a priest in surplice in their wake. Crowds pressed from all sides. 'Would they be coming for the festival next year?' she asked. No, they were going to Limatambo. 'Limatambo? That must be farther away along the Sierra.' She did not seem to have heard of that town.

This short conversation was instructive in that it put a human face on the tragic state of the Church in Peru, which counted its membership in millions, yet was unable through lack of vocations to provide more than a sacramental service for more than a few days each year, when a priest came to visit the small forgotten towns and villages lost in the folds of the Andes. In each village's annual festival to honour its patron saint, Mass would be celebrated, children baptised, couples married and the graves of those who had died during the year without priest or sacrament would be blessed.

The Irish priests discussed this situation with their American driver as they drove on through endless hours and changing light, as mid-day brilliance gave way to the lengthening shadows of evening until they reached the final altitude of 12,000 feet and gazed down on their destination in the valley below. Its low houses and church bell-tower and dome brightly lit by the evening sunlight, the jagged hills rising all about it, mottled with the shadows of drifting white clouds. The downhill drive to the town on the valley floor carried them around sharp bends and zigzags, through groves of Australian eucalyptus. On a hill beyond the town huge letters written in white stone proclaimed *'Viva El Peru'*. Through dusty streets they reached the church. They had arrived. The long journey from their former parishes in Cork – the North Cathedral, the Lough and Blackrock – was finally complete.

Life in the Andes

The Andean town of Abancay was to be home to two of the Corkmen, while the third, Paddy Leader, was assigned to another mountain town, Limatambo, some distance away. Of the three missionaries, Michael Murphy was to remain in this region for the longest time: from the beginning of 1962 to the middle of 1964. His correspondence with Bishop Lucey, though somewhat limited, gives an insight into his state of mind during that period. The letters convey a sense of urgency in his missionary work because of the limited time given to him to remain with the Society of St James, counterbalanced by frustration at the many obstacles he encountered to the effective carrying out of that work.

His field of pastoral activity was divided between two separate areas: the parish of Abancay where he lived in an urban setting, and the far-flung missionary outposts that he visited on horseback for the celebration of local festivals. Because of the rare and somewhat superficial contact with those distant communities, it was to be expected that the faith would have shallow roots, but in the case of the urban parish the equally shallow grasp of Catholic living came to him as a surprise. There Mass attendance was minimal and reception of the sacraments practically negligible, in spite of the continuous presence of residential priests. As a man who during all his life put his faith in the effectiveness of lay activity in the Church, Michael Murphy established a branch of the Legion of Mary in the hope that that would improve religious practice, especially among men and boys who seldom entered a church.

As a man of vision, he found the obstacles to the realisation of his hopes intolerably frustrating. Not least among the forces that impeded a missionary programme was the geography of the mountain parish, which was prone to natural disasters. In the early days, he experienced landslides that cut off communication for months on end, as well as earthquakes with their continuing aftershocks, which threatened the poorly-built presbytery with collapse. During these periods of seismic instability, he and his colleagues spent nights sleeping in the car rather than risk entombment in collapsed masonry. He found both the standard of accommodation and diet dangerously inadequate, remarking that during the rainy season, when communication with the outside world was at a standstill, the can opener was relied upon daily. A believer in the Napoleonic dictum that an army marches on its stomach, he was conscious of the fact that priests who lived on canned rations and spent the night sleeping in cars would be unlikely to function effectively as spiritual and social leaders.

Michael Murphy, in his letters to his bishop in Ireland, expressed particular concern about Paddy Leader's health, whose initial housing in Limatambo was of some type of temporary structure that proved both unsafe and inadequate to the needs of a European, reared without the immunity acquired from infancy by the native people of the Andes. He remarked that Paddy had lost weight and his hair had turned prematurely grey. Later he would advise Paddy to return permanently to Ireland before completing his time with the mission. His concern for his colleague was justified some years later when Paddy died suddenly as a curate in his native Clonakilty at the age of forty-six. Michael's own ill health and blood disorders in later life may well have been connected with the years he spent in the Andes, where the production of red blood cells is affected by altitude. Altitude sickness or 'sorroche' manifests itself on first arrival by headache, feelings of nausea and breathlessness – symptoms that would be alarming but for the fact that everyone is well prepared for its onset by veteran travellers at high altitude.

The sickness is easily explained: at an altitude of 12,000 feet, the air is so thin that simply breathing enough of it to stay alive is exhausting. The thin air permits water to boil at a low temperature. An egg could be bubbling around in a pot for several minutes and still remain uncooked. Motor radiators can boil away their coolant unknown to the thermostat since the water is not increasing in temperature while evaporating. No red light comes on as the radiator empties and many an engine has been ruined by the driver's ignorance of the danger. New arrivals at high altitude adapt to the new breathing conditions in a few days through an increase in their breathing rate and an increase in the production of the red blood cells that carry oxygen from the lungs. However, in the long run, this over production of red blood cells can have an adverse and even lethal effect on the body, especially if one is disposed to cardio-vascular disease.

Michael Murphy also expressed in his letters dissatisfaction with the command structure of the St James Society at the time. This critical opinion seemed to have been shared by the other members of the Society working in the mountains. They felt that decisions for the day-to-day running of the mission should be made locally by people familiar with the challenges peculiar to the Andean environment, rather than by a superior based in the coastal city of Lima. During their annual January gathering in the Lima centre house, they had their complaints accepted by the Society and it was decided that a local superior should be appointed to take charge of the Andean branch of the operation. In the light of Michael Murphy's subsequent promotion to bishop, it is significant that he was elected by his colleagues to this new position.

Of all his experiences in Abancay, the one that Michael Murphy mentioned most frequently in later life was that of visiting the remote villages attached to the parish. The travel on horseback, the sleeping conditions, the food, the discomfort, all left a lasting impact on his imagination. In carrying out this pastoral visitation of village festivals he was following in the tradition established by the earliest Spanish missionaries. Distance in any country is always relative to the size of that country. 'Nearby' in America might mean a distance of fifty miles, while in Europe it might mean two miles. In the Andes, distance is measured in hours rather than miles because of the near impassability of the terrain. The vastness of the American continent is brought home to us when we recall that Mexico is as far from the tip of Chile as Dublin is from Bangkok. Peru alone extends over an area greater than Spain, France and half of Germany put together. For the missionary in the interior of Peru, the distances he would have to travel would be daunting enough on level terrain where the population lived for the most part in towns and cities, but when the people are scattered in tiny villages across almost impassable mountains the challenge becomes enormous. In the Andes, one may come upon two little huts by the roadside, two more five miles further on and perhaps five more after five miles and one hour of hazardous travel by mule. This diffusion of the population is necessary because the native cannot abandon his few animals grazing the mountain peaks or travel impossible distances from a town to cultivate his stony fields, which seem to hang from the sky. If religion is to be brought to the Peruvian mountain man then the priest has to go to him. This is exactly what the first Spanish missionaries did, thereby setting a pattern of visitation that still holds today, four centuries later. The visit was tied to the feast day of the patron saint of the village. Which saint was to become patron of the village was decided mainly by accident, depending on the day of arrival of the first missionary after the Spanish conquest.

The priest would set out on the first day of September and celebrate the birthday of the Blessed Virgin in one village, thus establishing Our Lady as patron of that community, which ever afterwards celebrated its festival on 8 September. Next he would pass on to another village for the Feast of the Holy Cross, a week later. A third village would be dedicated to St Matthew on his feast, a fourth to St Michael, a fifth to St Francis, a sixth to the Holy Rosary, and so on through October and November. Each year the missionary priest in the Andes follows this pattern of visiting his people. The newly arrived Cork priests had to accustom themselves to doing these journeys on horseback accompanied by a guide from the host villages, to sleeping in accommodation that varied from basic to rudimentary, to surviving on food that was abundant if strange, and to drink water of uncertain purity.

Life in the Andes

The journey from one village to the next was always undertaken, if at all possible, early in the morning when the sun was gentle and the mountain air fresh. The road underfoot varied in proportion to the remoteness of the village: always unpaved, the track might be wide enough for wheeled traffic. More often than not it narrowed to a footpath, which could, on the corners of high peaks, be alarming in its precipitous height. The horses, accustomed to the route, walked steadily and sure-footedly, but there was always the thought that the track might suddenly crumble beneath their hoofs where rains had washed away the clay, or falling boulders from above had smashed its stone foundation.

The monotony of each trip was broken by the sight of a mud-walled hut with a tiled roof built up against the slope, with a donkey, two cows and a few children playing on stony soil. As the village drew nearer, more people appeared walking the track or riding a donkey on their way to the festival. The men walked in front, followed by a woman with a child on her back wrapped in a coloured shawl, the woman spinning thread from sheep's wool onto a hand-held spindle as she walked. Husband and wife never seemed to converse.

The village was always transformed for the festival from a dusty, sleepy backwater into a vibrant funfair: the plaza in front of the colonial church transformed into streets of canvas stalls housing the traders that followed the festivals. Strings of light bulbs lit up at night while the tantalising smell of barbecued meats and pungent spices floated up on smoke from white-hot charcoals. All day and night music throbbed from loudspeakers or was performed live from parading bands. Inside, the church which had been locked up for twelve months now exhaled incense and the smell of burning candle wax rose from the shrines banked with candle flame beneath the image of the patron saint. This was taken down from above the carved wooden altar reredos to stand on the *anda* or ceremonial litter, which when fitted with long shafts would bear the saint through the streets of the village on the central day of celebration. This *anda* was profusely adorned with palm branches, flowers and coloured ribbons, the statue itself fully clothed in embroidered brocade cloaks. In this atmosphere charged with devotion, the priest would offer Mass in the mornings, sit for hours in the confessional, baptise children, some as old as five or six years of age, and perform marriages for couples whose children they might have baptised at the same ceremony.

After four centuries, the Christian faith brought by the early Spanish missionaries was still alive, even in the most remote hamlets of the Andes, with special emphasis on devotion to the Eucharist, the Blessed Virgin and the saints. However, this annual explosion of religious fervour tended to hide the serious shortcomings in the depth of the conversion from the old paganism to Christianity. Rather than apportion blame for the serious failings in the deepening of the faith, one should attempt to appreciate the difficulties the Spanish faced in their task of evangelisation. For the sixteenth century, Spanish missionary challenges were particularly insuperable: there was the problem of language and the geographical distribution of the population they were attempting to convert. The missionaries preached in Spanish because they had no understanding of the native Indian tongue. They communicated through native interpreters who had little if any understanding of what they were translating. An example of the confusion which resulted was the attempt to expound the mystery of the Blessed Trinity to the Inca king, Atahualpa, who had been captured by Pizarro, leader of the conquistadors. The Indian translator explained that there were three Gods plus one other, giving you four in all. While he could translate numbers and names he had no theological grasp of the idea of the Trinity. Even though the missionaries did ultimately master the Quechua language and the Indians learned the Christian doctrine by rote, the latter had no understanding of concepts like the Trinity or the virginity of Mary. In a word, they were baptised without receiving instruction in the faith.

When the second and third generations of missionaries arrived, they found the native Indians already converted to Christianity and made the mistake of assuming they knew the tenets of the faith. On this false assumption they went on to give instruction in moral precepts while neglecting the basic evangelisation, which they had never received. There was little opportunity for the modern missionary to correct this situation during his visit to the village festival. Even if the round of festivals left more time for leisurely instruction in the faith (which, of course, it did not) the missionary still had to contend with the problem of language and the cultural differences between a European Catholic with over a thousand years of Christianity behind him, and the native Indian coming from thousands of years of idolatry.

Processions on the great central day of the festival always began not so much with a bang as with a series of explosions, rather like the pounding of a trench by heavy artillery in World War I. The man in charge of the fireworks, known in Spanish as '*el pirotecnico*', was a key player in the celebration of festivals; on the central day he excelled himself and often practically blew himself up in the process. Fireworks were strung out like clothes on a line about the plaza and could be detonated in sequence by a trailing fuse that carried fire and flame first along the lines and then high into the sky where, in the bright sunlight, nothing more than puffs of white smoke were visible. During the progress of the bearers of the saint the fireworks expert walked a little ahead with a sheaf of bamboo, each armed with a home-made cartouche. He always smoked a cigarette, the glowing end of which he used to ignite the small fuse attached to each firework. Then, holding the bamboo aloft, he held on until the explosion was about to burst, letting go at the last minute to let it soar skywards. Sometimes a damp firework fell prematurely to the ground, the fuse sizzling menacingly, scattering the participants in all directions with the threat of imminent explosion in their midst. Sometimes he held on too long and the explosion was likely to open his thumb or forefinger like a rose.

Music from brass bands built up expectancy to emotional heights for the great moment when the statue appeared through the open double doors of the church, to the cheers and applause of the crowd. Children in fancy traditional dress whirled and danced, soon to be joined by groups of older women in full traditional costume dancing the *huayno*, a rhythmical dance to the time of throbbing Andean music. The statue bearers were under the orders of an experienced member of the brotherhood responsible for the organisation of the festival. His great moment came when he drilled the bearers so that they moved in perfect rhythm, stepping sideways, first to the left then to the right, thus prolonging forward movement in a kind of quivering dance that made the image of the saint appear to move from side to side in a lifelike fashion, yet keeping a grace and dignity remote from the dancing throng beneath. This must have been how the Inca emperor, king and deity, progressed through his mountain dominions hundreds of years before.

For hours the pageant continued to the throb of music and the bursting fireworks echoed through the built-up plaza of the village. Though the teams of bearers changed at regular intervals, at no time did the *anda* touch the ground, so perfectly were the bearers drilled in the complicated manoeuvre of transferring the load from one group to the next. Eventually the cortege returned to the church and the statue was placed beside the altar, while the plaza outside was transformed into a whirling mass of dancing men and women, beating the ground with their feet as they hammered out the steps of a dance that must have gone back thousands of years to the time of their ancient ancestors. Here, more than in any other situation, the foreign missionary felt like a stranger in a strange land.

At the end of the festival there was one more solemn ceremony to bring the annual festivity to a close: the statue of the patron was lifted from its flower-adorned stand and raised up to its niche above the high altar where it would remain for another year. Once again the small church filled and overflowed onto the plaza. The music took on a more sombre note and old men were often seen to cry with emotion as the days of celebration came to an end. Perhaps they wept for the steady passage of their lives, recalling how briefly the years had passed since they danced as children before the same saint so many years before. Next day the crowd had scattered to their homes far away up in the hills or down in the valleys, the church was locked up, the priest departed and religion became an interior relationship between the Indian and his God for another year.

Indian Achievement in the Andes

At the end of 1966, Fr Denis O'Donoghue, a priest of the Diocese of Cork, completed his contract with the missionaries of St James and left the high Andes to join the fledgling Cork mission in Trujillo on the Pacific coast. His departure brought to an end the personal connection between Cork and Ross with the mountainous areas of Peru and Bolivia. For the next thirty-five years or so the Cork missionaries would work with the poor of the coast, but almost all of those people were either born in the mountains or were sons and daughters of migrants from the mountains. The founders of the new coastal mission, thanks to their personal contact with the people of the hills in their native environment, already had a great sympathy and understanding of a migrant people who had lost so much of their hereditary culture in their exchange of an ancient way of life for a modern world in which they were strangers. That sympathy and understanding was passed on to later arrivals on the Cork mission and was reinforced by visits to the mountains, which was always part of the introduction of the newly arrived priests in Peru.

In their migration from the mountains to the coast, the Peruvian people had lost much of their dignity. Their mountain culture had evolved over centuries and was ingrained in their spirit and coloured their view of the world. On the coast they found themselves in a new environment where that culture no longer existed, and familiar pursuits such as sowing and harvesting crops and caring for animals were gone forever. Even the women's traditional dress in all its glorious colours changed from being a symbol of prestige to a badge of shame. The Irishmen's awareness of the native Peruvians' achievement in the mountains over the centuries gave them a respect for the people they served and an appreciation of the magnificence of their culture forever preserved in the stones of Cusco, the mysterious beauty of Machu Picchu and the farming achievement in the terraced mountainsides of the high Andes. The ancestors of the migrants, barely existing in hovels in the coastal desert, had tamed and cultivated some of the most inhospitable terrain on earth. The achievement of the Peruvians in their mountains remains one of the wonders of the world.

When the Spanish conquistadors arrived in Peru they found a highly organised society presided over by the all-powerful Inca. The Inca Empire, however, was itself a relatively recent development in the country's history, going back a mere century and a half when it gathered together the remains of earlier civilisations that flourished in different areas of the country, long before the rise of the Incas as a governing class. The natives of the mountainous regions had over the centuries developed a way of life that was to an incredible degree intelligently adapted to the landscape in which they existed. Self-sufficiency was essential to the survival of a people in such isolated terrain. Over centuries the South American Indians had achieved a balance between production and necessity that guaranteed an abundance of food without damaging ecological balances. To the Indian, the art of agriculture was of supreme interest. They not only developed many different plants for food and medicinal purposes, but they understood thoroughly the cultivation of the soil, the art of proper drainage and correct methods of irrigation and soil conservation by the use of terraces constructed at great expense. Most of the cultivated fields in the Peruvian Andes are not natural; the soil has been assembled, put in place artificially, and still remains fertile after centuries of use. Anyone who grows plants or flowers in window boxes will understand the principles of terraced farming. For a successful window box display, a box is constructed strong enough to contain the soil with which it is filled. In that fertilised soil the seed is sown and the plants or flowers can germinate, grow and mature. Many of the hills were too steep to be tilled, so the Peruvians cut down a slice from the slope, built a stone

Indian Achievement in the Andes

wall strong enough to contain the soil, even when floods swept down the mountainside, and filled the cavity with soil, levelling it off to make a flat terrace on the side of a slope in which they sowed their seeds. While the first terrace built around the base of a mountain might contain many acres, the succeeding terraces diminished in size as they ascended to the mountaintop, until the uppermost was only large enough to accommodate a few rows of Indian corn.

Looking at terraced hillsides around Machu Picchu, one can only marvel at the patience, ingenuity and doggedness of a people who constructed them at such enormous cost of time and manpower so many centuries ago without the help of machinery. It fairly staggers the imagination to realise how many millions of hours of labour were required to construct those great agricultural terraces, which are still in use. It was, however, an investment in infrastructure that justified itself over the centuries in providing an everlasting source of land suitable for crops. The crops that were produced on these terraces are familiar to us today: corn on the cob and potatoes. The latter crop must surely constitute the most significant contribution that Peru has made to the world. Centuries ago the Indians discovered a plant with a pea-sized tuber that grew wild on the upper levels of the Andes, which proved to be edible. This they cultivated and developed to the stage where today it is one of the most widely used vegetables in the world. Tradition claims that the potato was first brought to Europe by Sir Walter Raleigh of Youghal, and later brought back across the Atlantic to North America by Presbyterian emigrants from Ireland. Few in the modern world realise as they look at McDonald's golden arches, which frame chip shops everywhere, that they have the Peruvian Indians to thank for that wonderful eating experience. The natives of the Andes developed more varieties of maize than any other people in Central or South America. They were the first to learn the advantages of certain medicinal herbs, particularly quinine, long known as a specific in the treatment of malaria. They discovered the effects of cocaine, which they extracted from the coca leaf, but only allowed it to be used by those engaged in strenuous activity.

Among the animals that the ancient Peruvians domesticated, the llama is best known and has in effect become a symbol of the country, invariably appearing in its tourist literature accompanied by natives in traditional dress. Larger than a sheep, this animal belongs to the camel family, with the same aptitude for survival in extreme conditions, ranging from arid desert to frozen mountainsides. The Andes level off at a height of 13,000 feet into barren, windswept table lands known as Puno, from which rise the cone-shaped, snow-covered peaks, and here the llama can survive without water on moss and stunted grass. In the pre-Spanish world, without horse or mule the Peruvian used the llama as a beast of burden, even though it could carry no more than seven stone and travel at a walking pace.

A smaller breed of llama was the alpaca, best known for its fine wool. However, the finest wool of all came from a wild cousin of the llama, the vicuña, which roamed in total freedom over the frozen mountains. This graceful, long-necked, shy animal was never domesticated. Indeed, within minutes of its birth it can scamper away with its mother and outrun a man. They have always been hunted for their fine wool, which is even finer than cashmere. The Inca rulers who brought centralised rule to the entire Andean region organised great hunts involving 100,000 peasants, in which thousands of animals were rounded up, channelled into corrals, shorn and then set free to graze unmolested for four years until their wool was replenished.

The people the Cork priests dealt with, either in their natural setting in the mountains or in the coastal slums to which they migrated, were the descendants of the great people who had achieved so much so long ago. It was of this people that one of Peru's great intellectuals, Luis Alberto Sánchez, wrote in poetic terms. For anyone anxious to penetrate the Peruvian mind this tiny part of his work makes useful reading:

> The mountain zone is the richest and most beautiful in Peru. Everything that endures in Peru resides in the mountains or originates there, the lasting heritages like

the two Imperial cities: Cuzco and Cajamarca, the megalithic Machu Picchu. In Peru, as in Mexico and Quito, the mountain chain was both the trampoline to fame and the last refuge of the conquered race: its fortress and its palace during the glories of Empire ...

Implacably falls the rain. Sometimes the water turns to hail and snow. Hailstones pelt the roof tiles. And in the midst of all the desolation the Indian maintains his diaphanous serenity. Like the stones of Cuzco, he is statuesque, a part of the architecture like a cornice or a column. (Luis Alberto Sanchez, *La Literatura Peruana,* Ascuncion del Paraguay, Editorial Guarania, 1950/5. My translation)

The Coast of Peru

The appointments of the Cork priests who first joined the Society of St James were decisive in determining the location of the subsequent Cork and Ross mission. All three were appointed to Peru, with two going to the Andes and one to the Pacific coast. Had it happened that they were sent to some other South American country – the St James mission operated in Bolivia, Ecuador and Peru – things might have turned out quite differently. Had they not had the advantage of getting to know the mountains and the coast, the decision on where to locate the Peruvian mission might also have been quite different.

The men working in the high Andes quickly became aware of the health hazards of living at high altitude. They also saw that the sparse distribution of the native population over great distances and difficult terrain would have made it impossible for a tightly-bound group like the Cork priests and nuns to work effectively as a team. The coast, on the other hand, presented a highly concentrated population in a climate reasonably suitable to Irish people.

The immediate appointment of Michael Crowley to a coastal parish provided the group with first-hand knowledge of the conditions in that region, as well as an idea of the problems faced by the local population. The first parish in which Michael Crowley worked was Monsefú, located five hundred miles north of Lima, where an irrigated river valley was cultivated for the production of sugarcane for one of the largest *haciendas* in the world: the plantation of Cayalti.

His first journey by road from Lima to Monsefú introduced him to the blue-grey coastal desert of Peru that runs from Ecuador in the north to Chile in the south. Turning off the Pan-American Highway, the little town of Monsefú is reached by straight flat roads bordered on both sides by vast fields of sugarcane, the cultivation of which is made possible by the waters of the river Zana, flowing from the melting glaciers high up in the Andes to the sea at Eten. The residents of all this area were employees of the *hacienda*, providing the great labour force necessary for the harvesting of sugarcane by hand.

Those first months living in Monsefú made such a lasting impact on Michael Crowley that forty years later, as a retired priest in Ireland, he was still making reference in his sermons to the social injustice he had seen there. Coming from a comfortable farming background in Ireland, followed by boarding school, college, New York presbyteries and suburban houses in Cork city, it was no surprise that he described the Monsefú presbytery as the most primitive house he had ever lived in.

Monsefú, a town of 13,000 people, had no water supply, no sanitation and no electricity. Its unpaved streets were lined with mud-walled huts occupied by large families living in sub-human conditions. The primitive infrastructure and physical deprivation were matched by intellectual starvation. The school-going children attending overcrowded and insanitary schools were barely literate, and not much better than their totally illiterate parents. All the men were employed by the sugar *hacienda* either as harvesters of sugarcane, cut by hand with machetes, or factory workers in the sugar refinery or rum distillery. The *hacienda* owned all the village houses and the shops were also part of that vast property.

The men wore raggedy shirts over baggy trousers tied up with string, a battered straw hat, no socks and their footwear comprised home-made sandals of old rubber truck tyres strapped on with twine. All were Catholics in name, possibly baptised, but in the majority of cases without First Holy Communion or any further sacraments. Of the first group of six couples that Michael Crowley prepared for marriage five had not received their First Communion. What religious practice existed was left entirely to the women and children; men and teenage boys took no part. The little churches that each village boasted were for the most part locked up throughout the year, except during a festival when a priest from Chiclayo was brought to supply Mass and walk in the procession of the local Saint's statue. Michael Crowley wrote home that the people were friendly and respectful, but added some shrewd observations regarding their illiteracy.

The climate was good except for the dust which was ever present, in manageable quantities for most of the year, except in the spring and autumn afternoons when the stiffer breezes from the Pacific blew it up into yellow sandstorms that stung eyes and faces and ears and penetrated every dwelling, no matter how tightly shuttered. When the breezes died down and the sun shone, swarms of flies replaced the dust in a relentless campaign of human annoyance.

In those early months, Michael Crowley formed a vivid picture of the serious social problems that bedevilled Peru. Here was a community fully employed producing a product for a worldwide market, yet existing in sub-human conditions. The question was: why should this be so? It could not be blamed on idleness as the men were constantly employed in back-breaking work. The low income could not be attributed to lack of education as the manual work of cutting cane called for no level of literacy or numeracy. The poverty could not be explained by profligacy, idleness or extravagance as the workers' whole lives consisted of little else but work and sleep. In the old saying of investigative journalists: to find the explanation you follow the money trail.

The money trail from the sugar plantations of Monsefú led to a golden circle that included thirty families whose vast wealth beggared belief. The money trail led to gilded urban palaces in Lima, to the Hippodrome in Monterrico, yachts in the bay of Ancon, ocean-front villas on the Costa Verde. The tentacles of this oligarchy reached into newspapers, breweries, banks, merchant shipping, cotton fields, rice paddies, sugar *haciendas* and mines.

The more Michael Crowley studied the role of the thirty families in the management of the country's economy, government and military power, the more he realised that Peru was a country of extremes: extreme heat on the coast; extreme cold on the high Andean plateau; drought in the desert; humidity in the Amazonian jungle; extreme wealth among the few; extreme poverty among the many.

The rise of these wealthy families went back to the Industrial Revolution of the previous century in the developed world when Peru found a new and enormous market for its products, such as cotton, sugar, guano and metals. But while this new wealth enriched a very small number of families, it was never used to industrialise Peru itself, thus dooming the country to a century of poverty.

The thirty families took their origins from the Spanish colonial settlers, or from immigrants from other countries who 'made good'. Within two generations, in the early 1900s, the families were so closely interwoven by marriages that their fortunes were consolidated in the hands of what became known as 'the Oligarchy', a group of rich men who met in the private Club Nacional, whose shy classical facade on the Plaza San Martin in Lima belied the political and financial power wielded by its members. For most of a century, the Oligarchy openly controlled the country through its members, who were elected to the presidency and government, or covertly through the military dictators whose good will they purchased with money and patronage.

Up to 1919, the presidency and congress were completely in the hands of the Oligarchy. Sixteen of the thirty families were represented in congress, often by more than one member. The nucleus of the governing elite formed an informal group known as 'the twenty-four friends', who met nightly in the Club Nacional to discuss public affairs. This small group of rich *hacienda* owners, bankers and businessmen included two who occupied the presidency for a total of twenty-four years, at least eight ministers of State, five of them ministers for finance, three presidents of the senate and the directors of the two principal newspapers, *La Prensa* and *El Comercio*.

As the twentieth century advanced, the Oligarchy worked in a more covert way to maintain their political hold on the country by courting the favour of new presidents. An example of this was the case of the president elected in 1932. He was of humble origin of *mestizo* blood, yet they introduced him into the Club Nacional and invited him to the urban palaces in which they lived. The Aspillaga family, who owned the vast sugar plantation of Cayalti, where Michael Crowley later worked, patronised the new president. A son of the family wrote to his brother: 'I see that the President has become a frequent visitor to the family mansion in La Punta and is having long chats with Papa who can give him good advice from his experience. It is good to see that the President has tendencies to be with good people, with those who have helped him so much.'

When a reforming government in the 1940s considered the claims of labour, the Oligarchy put up the money to buy some army generals to instigate a *coup d'état*, which installed a dictator/president who immediately appointed one of the Oligarchy as head of the Central Bank and another president of the Chamber of Deputies. In this way, the Oligarchy guaranteed itself the economic conditions it always needed to consolidate its wealth: total control of the labour force in an export-orientated economy.

Nowhere was this accumulation of personal wealth at the expense of the labour force more evident than in the sugar plantation surrounding Monsefú, the *hacienda* of Cayalti run by the Aspillaga family. When the family purchased the plantation in 1870 it included 7,000 acres, but this expanded later to 15,000 acres. Machinery for the production of sugar was imported from England and a labour force of 'coolies' was imported from China. With backing from the English commercial house of Henry Kendall and Son, they constructed thirty kilometres of railroad to the port of Eten, from where they exported their product economically.

The Chinese workers were cruelly exploited. Paid very little, they were subjected to a system of private justice involving floggings and imprisonment in a private jail in the *hacienda*. When the importation of the Chinese was finally prohibited, the *hacienda* owners looked to the mountains for a replacement labour force, and by the year 1900 the 1,000 workers were predominantly Peruvian. In return for money advanced to them, these worked for a fixed number of months, but many opted to remain on the coast where they were joined by their families. Their working conditions, though better than those of the Chinese, still allowed for a more subtle and paternalistic method of control. The right to imprison was lost. However, the Aspillaga family resisted all attempts to unionise the workers and in this they were supported by the government, of which they themselves were either members or 'king makers', as in the case of the 1930s dictatorship.

Again, the Aspillagas were involved in bringing a dictator to power in 1948 and it was during this presidency in the 1950s that the most tragic chapter in the story of Cayalti was written in blood. In that year, wages had been increased by the government to compensate for the rise in the cost of living. The Aspillagas, however, neutralised the increase by raising prices in the company store, where all the workers had to buy food to feed their families. The strike that followed involved public protests, which were suppressed by the police with a severity that left one worker dead and many more arrested. The strikers were on the point of surrender when another incident, much more serious, took place. This time the police opened fire on a meeting of workers outside the police station and pursued them through the town, shooting savagely at the escaping men. At least 120 died. Numerous workers fled to their homes in the mountains after setting the cane fields on fire. 'That night', said one worker, 'they killed hundreds. Then they gathered up the dead and transported them in the company trucks to a hill in the desert where they buried them in a communal trench. I was the driver of the truck and I was sick at what I saw. I will never forget it to the day I die.'

The massacre of 1950 changed forever the relationship between the Aspillagas and their workforce. At the end of the decade, a trade union was finally formed. By then the family's political power had waned and they waited in vain for another right-wing dictator.

Just two years later Michael Crowley came to the parish of Monsefú in the heart of the plantation of Cayalti. His letters to Bishop Lucey remarked on the tendencies towards communism so widespread in the community of sugarcane workers – understandable in the light of the history of the *hacienda*. He saw the uphill fight that faced priests who would try to counteract the extreme left-wing views with the Church's social teaching.

The hundred-year dominance of the thirty families over the whole Peruvian nation was then coming to an end and leaving behind a legacy of poverty, illiteracy, human degradation and social injustice on a monumental scale. The post-World War II economic recovery would pass Peru by, thanks to the total absence of a middle-class and the social cohesion that such a social class brings to every developed country. Fifty years later, in the new twenty-first century, Peru would still lag far behind other nations in a state of poverty perpetuated by the long-term effects of economic exploitation.

Cork Chooses a Mission on the Coast

In the spring of 1965, Bishop Lucey finally made his decision to embark on a missionary endeavour, which was unique in the history of the involvement of the Irish Church in the foreign missions. The Bishop of Cork and Ross took, by agreement with a South American bishop, an area of a South American diocese as an extension of his own Irish Diocese, assuming total responsibility for the staffing of the area and financing of all its needs, including church building, convent construction and the provision of educational and medical services.

It is probable that the ideas expressed by the late Archdeacon Duggan in a letter home just after his arrival in Peru and just before his unexpected death there influenced Bishop Lucey in his choice of missionary structure. Writing to Bishop Lucey, he said:

> As to work, obviously the Columbans are helping the urban proletariat: they have three contiguous parishes (which form a deanery). Where they are, there was literally nothing and (how they did it the Lord knows) now they have a church, rectory and schools in every parish.
>
> The St James Society has an HQ in Lima and in addition one parish. But their concentration – or rather dispersion – is on the mountains of Peru pushing north into Ecuador and east into Bolivia. The Maryknolls follow the St James pattern but their strength is in Bolivia.

55

> The whole campaign – and the components are all good men – could do with some central organisation. What they could use would be a sort of super-Nuncio.
>
> I'd imagine an Irish team would best work on its own. Boston would help in the capital expenses, churches, rectories and schools. Thus equipped they could really get going.
>
> In my opinion, after a five-year stint everyone should go home, their contract fulfilled. Then, if a man were a conspicuous success, he could be allowed back – having rehabilitated himself in the routine work of an Irish parish for a year …
>
> With love and affection,
> Tom Duggan.

Archdeacon Duggan's thinking was obviously influenced by his military background: mention of a campaign and a HQ recalls the language of the regiment, while the ideas themselves – such as forming a type of Irish Brigade – come straight from the British Army, which always favoured regiments composed of men from the same place of birth, whether they be Munster Fusiliers or Gurkhas. For a man just arrived in Peru he showed a remarkable talent for planning and, indeed, some of his ideas were adapted to the new Cork mission, such as limiting the term of missionary duty to six years for older men and three years for the newly ordained, as well as concentrating men from Ireland in one tightly-knit geographical region.

In the summer of 1964, Michael Crowley and Michael Murphy returned to Ireland and took up appointments in Bandon and North Cathedral respectively, but they knew that these were to be short-term assignments because the bishop was in continuous contact with them planning and discussing the venture upon which they would embark in the new year.

A year earlier, Michael Crowley, at the suggestion of Bishop Lucey, had asked Cardinal Cushing to let the men from Cork organise the mission along the lines of the Newfoundland mission in Monsefú, but the cardinal did not warm to the suggestion, as he wanted to bear the whole financial burden of the St James Society and therefore have control over it.

In 1965, Bishop Lucey decided to 'go it alone' and sent out Fathers Murphy and Crowley with *carte blanche* to choose the place of the apostolate. Their most important local contact was Mike Crowley's friend in Monsefú: Fr Charlie Conway of Newfoundland. The latter hoped they would take over the parish of Chepén, a town with a population of 25,000, with another 10,000 living in the sugar plantations nearby. The parish priest was an energetic Peruvian priest of the Diocese of Trujillo, who felt that he lacked the manpower and funding to develop the Church presence in his huge parish. Chepén was something of a commercial centre with both water and electricity. This would make it a fairly safe environment for Irish people who might be a little short on acquired immunity to disease. Since this parish belonged to the Archdiocese of Trujillo, Bishop Lucey first called on the archbishop of that city on his journey northwards after his arrival in Lima on 8 March. The vicar general brought his visitors on a short tour of the shantytowns cropping up in the desert around the old city of Trujillo, where they saw first hand the unbelievable poverty and depravation of a community living in straw huts without power, water or sanitation. What he saw on that afternoon remained in Bishop Lucey's mind and, even though he travelled on to Chepén, his final decision was to base his mission in the shantytowns of Trujillo, where 40,000 people existed in the poorest conditions without schools, churches or medical centres. Fr Conroy, writing in a diary that was published later, gave a first-hand account of his meeting with the Cork delegation in Chepén:

> When I went to Chepén this afternoon I found Bishop Lucey surrounded by four Cork men. In deference to the tropical heat he was wearing a sports shirt and made an undistinguished figure, until one looked into the eyes, which, under heavy brows, are smiling, shrewd and

alert. I was present at the conference that followed but did not take part, except to point out that proximity to us in Monsefú would be an advantage to both.

The matter has not definitely been decided yet, but the bishop feels that Chepén is already on its way to salvation and does not need Irish priests. Moreover, he feels that people back in Ireland who are supporting them would find it hard to understand why an established parish, which is well served by two native priests, should be taken when the need elsewhere is so much greater.

By 17 March, St Patrick's Day, the new Missionary Society of Santo Toribio was established and the agreement between the Diocese of Cork and Ross on the one hand, and the Archdiocese of Trujillo on the other, was signed in the presence of the Cardinal Archbishop of Lima and the Papal Nuncio, Archbishop Carboni. The mission to Peru was then founded, a mission that would later expand to Ecuador and last until its closure in the next century in the year 2004.

Trujillo: A Spanish Colonial City

The choice of the city of Trujillo as the venue for the Cork and Ross mission had one immediate negative aspect: it was a name difficult for English speakers to pronounce correctly. Francisco Pizarro, who had discovered and conquered Peru for the Spanish Crown, had been born in the city of the same name in Extremadura, a barren region of western Spain. When he founded what was to become the second city of Peru in importance, he named it after his own birthplace. Many Corkmen and women, as they tried to pronounce the name correctly giving the double 'L' the necessary 'Y' sound in Spanish, regretted that Pizarro had not been born in a more pronounceable place like Madrid or Toledo. Apart from the name difficulty, Trujillo was a most fortunate choice thanks to its temperate climate – the Peruvians call it 'the capital of springtime' – and its rich heritage of Spanish culture.

The best way to travel from Lima to Trujillo, though not the most comfortable, is by road, as the passage through three hundred miles of desert increases the expectation with every weary mile that a white city in a green oasis will make the journey worthwhile. The journey by road from Lima to Trujillo introduces the visitor to the blue-grey coastal desert of Peru that runs from Ecuador to Chile in a succession of sandy wastes that arouse feelings of tedium and melancholy. Cooled by the Humboldt Current that washes the coast with waves still chilled from the Antarctic icecap, the coastal climate is one of almost permanent autumn, in spite of its location in the tropics. The long stretches of desolate desert are relieved every so often by the valleys watered by mountain rivers flowing from the snow-line, 20,000 feet up in the Andes.

In the valleys, dusty little towns of adobe walls and balconies of moth-eaten pine house the workers who harvest the sugarcane of the great plantations and mill the product to be refined into sugar and distilled into rum. This is a rainless region without change of season, where a placid ocean never rages with storms or batters the low-lying cliffs with angry waves. The only sound by the seashore is the monotonous sigh of waves rolling on sand and the whistle of wind through sand dune grasses. For eight hours the driver presses on along the paved Pan-American Highway, which is said to run from Alaska to the southern tip of Chile. Its only variety is the quality of the surface, which ranges from a generally poor standard to practically impassable where seasonal floods have washed away whole sections of road embankment, forcing the motorist and trucker to drive down a ramp of firmed sand to the desert floor, crawl carefully for perhaps a hundred yards and climb a similar ramp to regain the highway once more.

Between the fertile irrigated valleys, the desert presents a panorama of sand dunes blown into surreal shapes and rippled by the wind in the way retreating tides mark the beach. The only vegetation visible is the lonely outline of solitary algarrobo trees, native to this part of the world and fully adapted to a rainless environment. The Pan-American Highway is set back some miles from the coast so that even the placid ocean vista is hidden from the traveller's eyes.

Approaching the valley in which Trujillo is built from the south, the desert gives way to a green cultivated expanse stretching for miles between the foothills of the Andes and the Pacific Ocean, a great oasis which has been home to several civilisations over the centuries. The Spanish were not the first to build a city in this fertile valley, where a mountain river cuts across a plane to the sea. One thousand years earlier, a great civilisation known as the Mochica flourished in this irrigated oasis. Remarkable for sculptured pottery portraying scenes from daily life with incredible realism, the Mochicas left a legacy of priceless craftsmanship that can be viewed in museums throughout the world.

Trujillo: A Spanish Colonial City

Within a few minutes' walk of the modern city there still stands the largest pyramid in South America, a vast structure built by the Mochicas of mud brick that has survived earthquakes, freak rains, floods and the ingenuity of gold-hungry Spanish conquistadors, who diverted the river onto the site in an attempt to flush out the treasure buried with mummified kings.

Archaeologists speculate that the sudden collapse of the Mochica civilisation in the tenth century was due to a climatic change that brought tropical rains that destroyed not only the crops on which the community depended, but even the irrigation system which made cultivation possible in a desert region. It is probable, too, that the same natural disaster which would have been more devastating in the equatorial region of the continent caused the migration of another tribe, the Chimu, who arrived about this time in the valley of Trujillo.

On the ruins of the Mochica civilisation, the new arrivals developed a culture that rivalled the achievement of any prehistoric people in economic organisation, urban planning and magnificent craftsmanship in gold and silver. The ruins of the Chimu city Chan Chan cover an area of four square miles between Trujillo and the sea. Once the home of 100,000 people, graced with luxurious palaces, adorned with massive temples, refreshed by pleasure gardens and an underground water supply, today Chan Chan is an awesome moonscape where blown sand finely dusts its crumbling roofless walls. The Royal Road that leads northwards in a straight line from the ancient city is barely discernable beneath the drifting sand. Clearly visible is the defensive wall that ran a distance of eight miles across the valley's northern approach, bearing silent testimony in its conception and physical structure to the engineering genius of the Chimu Indians. The Chimu were conquered by the Incas shortly before the arrival of the Spanish in America. Francisco Pizarro, when he arrived for the foundation of Trujillo on the 5 March 1535, found Chan Chan in much the same state of desolation and ruin that greets the tourist today. But if time has wrought havoc with the Indian city of Chan Chan, it has kindly stood still for the city the Spanish built. A film producer in search of a location for a colonial period drama could use the centre of Trujillo for his work without making any alteration to the buildings. Even the overhead electric wires have been buried underground by an enlightened city council. Preservation rather than restoration is the task those interested in the city's past have undertaken, and now the whole city possesses an authenticity that restored historical monuments sometimes lack. An example of this authenticity is the plaza, which still serves as the nucleus of city life, just as Pizarro intended.

The plaza is large and very beautiful. Tall palm trees and flowering shrubs shade its marble seats where old men read newspapers and students chat between lectures in the old university whose library opens on to the square. The elegant facades of the buildings flanking the plaza are ornamented with baroque mouldings and cornices that cast contrasting patterns of light and shadow on white and magenta walls. Glimpses of inner-pillared patios are caught through the open doorways of colonial mansions. Window grills wrought in lacy swirls of iron and crowned with plaster canopies hang like giant lanterns from latticed balconies made of aged wood. The white cathedral dominates the square, its twin towers leading the eye gently upwards to belfries that frame the sky. The same authenticity is found throughout the old city that was once enclosed by defensive walls, sections of which stand as reminders of a time when pirates threatened the tranquillity of Pacific coastal cities. Ancient convent walls still enclose cloistered nuns. The noise of school children at play comes from the patio of a school that was founded in the year 1625. The great town houses of the aristocracy, who once controlled the economy of the region, accommodate today their successors, the bankers, whose computers chatter deep within ochre walls ventilated by lace-like iron windows.

The architecture can be accurately described as 'Spanish American': Spanish in the rococo plasterwork, wrought iron and arabesque decoration in encaustic tiles; American in the exuberant use of space. Not for the American town planner were the narrow streets of medieval Spain. In a new continent of unlimited territory, the planners laid out wide streets in logical gridiron formation, allowing open spaces for intimate parks as well as the great central plaza. Even to accommodate the traffic of a busy modern city, the generous width of the streets and their logical layout has made it unnecessary to demolish a single building. It is a city in which traffic jams are unknown.

The sumptuous decoration of the great urban mansions of Trujillo and the disproportionately large number of churches and convents bear testimony to the prosperity and political stability of the city over the centuries since its foundation. The vast agricultural hinterland in the mountain valleys, as well as the coastal sugar plantations, guaranteed the economic prosperity of the city and made possible the leisure for a cultured life second only to that of Lima, the nation's capital.

The colonial town house is a prized example of the cultural heritage of Trujillo. Apart from the finer *casonas*, as the town houses are called, which in recent years have been carefully restored with the assistance of the banks and students of the Cultural Institute, the city abounds in others neglected over the centuries, in varying stages of decay now awaiting restoration. The town houses of the Spanish colonists and their descendants were designed in the same spirit of urbanity as the city itself. Turning its back on the surrounding countryside, the Spanish city, following the old Roman tradition, looked inwards on the gardens of its plaza. In the same way, the *casona* looked inwards on its patio or courtyard. It presented to the outside world a shy facade of window grills, shuttered balconies and heavy brass-mounted entrance doors wide enough and high enough to admit a horse-drawn carriage. Immediately inside the great doors lay a paved patio ornamented with balustrades, classically framed windows and plastered doorways, all shaded by a classical colonnade. Blue porcelain tiling added colour, as did oriental *jardinières* cascading blooms. Further in, through high-ceilinged reception rooms, lay a private patio used only by the family and intimate guests, with its marble fountain and pots of flowers. Through more rooms, the final patio was reached: a simple cobbled area where servants worked and horses were stabled. The uniformity of the basic plan of the town house allowed for a diversity of decoration, with window grills of different design, colonnades and balustrades varied by the Greek orders and tiling of different colour and pattern, so that in a city of many, no two town houses looked alike. A well-represented feature of the Trujillo *casona* is the balcony, ingeniously designed to maintain a link between the social life of the house and the passing scene on the street below without any loss of privacy. Carved in dark wood like a piece of fine furniture, the balcony shaded the ground floor windows from the vertical tropical sun, while admitting the summer breeze to first-floor rooms.

The Spanish culture, at once Catholic and urban, transformed a desert into an oasis of civilisation, where the aristocratic owners of the sugar plantations and mountain *haciendas*, missionary friars, cloistered nuns, administrators of the civil powers and the great mixture of soldiers and adventurers that made up the colony could live in an environment which was both Catholic and European. Trujillo developed a civilisation eminently religious, so that today, the city's skyline presents a silhouette of church towers, cupolas, domes and belfries free of the harsh outlines of modern high-rise buildings. Located within two blocks of the central plaza are the colonial churches of Belen, the Merced, Santo Domingo, San Augustine, Santa Clara, San Francisco, Santa Ana and Carmen, as well as the cathedral, which has been designated a minor basilica.

The religious life of Trujillo began on the day of its foundation with the celebration of Mass and the marking out of the site of the Franciscan monastery. Within ten years, the Dominicans and Mercedarians had added their churches and monasteries to the infant city. All these friars set to work immediately at preaching Christianity to the Indians as well as supporting the faith of their Spanish countrymen.

The Jesuits built their church on a corner of the plaza. As their congregation no longer works in the city, their old church now forms part of the university. The Convent of Santa Clara was founded in 1587, soon to be followed by the Convent of Carmen, which still houses the enclosed Carmelite Sisters. The religious history of Trujillo records the visits of two saints. Santo Toribio, Archbishop of Lima, passed through the city on two occasions during his pastoral

Trujillo: A Spanish Colonial City

tours of the vast territory that then comprised his archdiocese. In 1618, San Francisco Solano preached in the church of San Francisco from the gilded pulpit that is still preserved in that beautiful church.

Religious devotion from the earliest days seems to have centred on the Blessed Sacrament and the Mother of God. Records that go back as far as 1656 show that the Confraternity of the Most Blessed Sacrament was holding devotions on the feast of Corpus Christi, with the city fathers taking part. As early as 1681, the procession of Our Lady of Help was taking place in the nearby fishing village of Huanchaco.

It is surprising that the colonial churches survived in an earthquake zone when one considers the humble materials – mud-brick and bamboo – with which they were built. To ride out the frequent earth tremors, the adobe walls were supported by massive buttresses tapering towards the dome and barrel-vaulted roof. The roof itself, made of bamboo smeared with mud, was ideally suited to the desert climate, but hopelessly inadequate to cope with the periodic rains that devastate the area once or twice each century. The basic building material of adobe and bamboo was ingeniously concealed by superb plasterwork both inside and out. The facade and towers transformed structures of simple materials into elegant places of worship while giving visual expression to the spiritual aspirations of man.

The glory of the churches of Trujillo and the city's unique artistic achievement are the rococo *retablos* or giltwood altar backdrops, each a symphony of swirling pillars heavily encrusted with carved fruit and leaf motifs, shell-shaped niches framing antique images of forgotten saints, intricate arabesques superbly carved and overlaid with gold leaf that glints in the light of votive candles or shafts of sunlight that enter through tiny windows. Not only do the innumerable elements in each backdrop harmonise perfectly with one another, but the whole artistic conception also blends with the other giltwood side altars that line the church's nave.

It was with justifiable pride that the Catholic Church in Trujillo could take stock of its achievements during the National Eucharistic Congress held in the city in October 1943. Records of the congress, which was certainly the biggest religious event in the city's history up to the Pope's visit, show that the Church was moving with the times in its concern for religious education for adults as well as children, especially in the field of social justice, as outlined in the great papal social encyclicals. The numbers who received the Blessed Sacrament during the congress indicated a living active Church, while the degree of lay participation anticipated the changes brought about by the Second Vatican Council some twenty years later.

By the 1940s, Trujillo was no longer contained within the original defensive walls. New avenues encircling the inner city opened up perspectives in the manner of nineteenth century French urbanisation. Old aristocratic families left their elegant city centre *casonas* to live along the new avenues in modern houses that looked onto open gardens. The expanding city sent out tentacles to the seafront where the wealthy would soon build North American-style homes within sight of the sea and within easy reach of the golf and country club. Within another decade the lifestyle of the United States would challenge the long-cherished Spanish culture. Then the unexpected happened. A great movement of population began as the mountain dwellers left the interior of the country and came to live on the outskirts of the coastal cities. In ten years the population of Trujillo doubled; its territorial extent quadrupled. Neither Church nor State were prepared for this unforeseen development. The city's normal development was changed profoundly and the concept of the Catholic Church as a devotional service for a middle-class city population was destroyed forever.

The Mission Begins

With Bishop Lucey seen off on the flight for Miami on his return to Ireland and Kevin O'Callaghan and Michael Riordan enrolled in the language school run by the St James Society in Cieneguilla outside Lima, Michael Murphy and Michael Crowley drove in their newly acquired VW Beetle northwards to Trujillo to embark on the task of establishing the Cork and Ross mission in Peru. There they spent some days with the Marionist Brothers until they rented a two-storey terraced house in the Palermo district of the city. Later they would purchase this house for their use until the first presbytery in the *barrio* was completed. Then the Irish Mercy Sisters lived there until their convent was built, as did the Bon Secours Sisters in their turn. When the last of the Sisters were permanently housed, the Palermo house was sold off for approximately the same price for which it had been purchased initially.

Setting up house took a few days and the first attempt to engage a housekeeper failed – she left after one day – but they subsequently succeeded when a daily help came from the El Porvenir district where they were about to set up their first parish. The practicalities of setting up house and locating the boundaries of their new mission territory must have been quite daunting in a strange city with practically no local contacts, no parish base from which to work and no decent church in which to celebrate Mass. During the weeks of the bishop's visit, the exhilaration of participating in and shaping historical events had raised the spirits of all just a little above reality. Unceasing discussion on the ultimate location of the mission left little or no time for consideration of the mundane details of the day-to-day running of the operation, such as transferring money across time zones and three currencies – sterling, dollars and soles – negotiating the purchase of land, engaging building contractors, securing state funding for schools and all the other practicalities of surviving as an alien in a foreign country.

The men on site, however, enjoyed two great advantages over many other South American missionaries: proficiency in the language and guaranteed funding from home. They had a wide knowledge of the Peruvian people and landscape – one from his experience in the high Andes; the other from his work on the Pacific coastal sugar plantations. In spite of this, however, they still had much to learn about working among the displaced people of the mountains, who found themselves adapting to city life in horrific poverty. The mission's desert allotment, though little more than five minutes' drive from their middle-class house in Palermo, was decades behind in development and living standards. In one there was light, water and paved streets; in the other there was no power, no sanitation, unpaved sandy streets and no employment.

To visit their newly acquired area of responsibility, the priests drove inland past the last of the city houses, through fertile irrigated market gardens until the road ended abruptly on the bank of a narrow canal of dark water known as 'The Mochica', named after the Moche river from which its waters were diverted. Beyond that point the terrain rose steeply to levels that prohibited further canalisation from the river. This canal was the point of demarcation between, on the one bank, the irrigated Moche Valley with its fertile farmland, Spanish city, ruined city of Chan Chan and earlier settlement of Moche Indians whose thousand-year-old pyramids crumbled among the fields of pineapple, yuca and asparagus, and, on the other bank, the *barrio* where the mission would operate.

Standing on the bank of the Mochica with one's back to the city, one looked up at the first foothill of the Andes, the Cerro de Cabra, meaning 'the hill of the goats'. The hill is of bare, black, cone-shaped rock with its lower folds wrapped in a robe of desolate sand blown up by the winds of centuries, which in sunshine resembled a glinting glacier. In foggy conditions, which pertained for most of the year, it

The Mission Begins

looked like a flow of volcanic lava, grey rather than black, spreading down the valley until the Mochica abruptly halted its flow. On this windswept dreary slope, which extended some three miles around the foot of the hill, no plant grew and no life moved, except for the occasional dark vultures noisily squabbling over some animal corpse. A depression in the landscape to the east marked the Rio Seco, the dried-up river that only flooded once or twice a century when freak rains poured through the Quebrada de Leon, 'the gap of the lion', in the blue Andes in the distance.

Over the centuries, there had never been a human settlement on this arid slope; the Spanish in 1600, the Chimu Indians in AD 1000 and the Mochican Indians in AD 200, all favoured the fertile valley below the Mochica canal as their dwelling. However, in the 1950s when the invasions from the mountains began, the impoverished settlers had nowhere else to go. Housing in the city was beyond their slender means; the cultivated irrigated land surrounding the city was untouchable because it was food-producing terrain. The only option for them was the inhospitable desert slope above the canal. Here they 'pitched their tents': shacks of straw matting and rags knocked together on the banks of the fetid canal. Thus, the first *barrios* of Trujillo began life, unmapped, unsupervised by the city council, unlicensed by the Ministry for Housing. Over fifty years, the sandy hillside grew, year after year, invasion after invasion, into a huge suburb greater in extent and greater in population than the original city which it surrounded. It is on this vast habitation of 200,000 people that the imprint of the Cork and Ross mission will remain forever. Just as the colonial churches of the old city will commemorate forever the work of the Jesuits, the Carmelites, the Franciscans and the Dominicans, so the churches that the Irish built – San Patricio, El Buen Pastor, Sanctissiomo Sacramento, La Sagrada Familia – will perpetuate the memory of that enriching encounter between Cork and Trujillo.

All of that was far in the future and beyond the imagination of the two Cork priests who stood looking at their parish on 4 April 1965. Where to begin was the question uppermost in their minds. They would begin by meeting their predecessor who had worked in the *'pueblo joven'*, 'the young town', for some years before them. This man was a Spanish priest: Fr Jaime Pons. He was a colourful character not untypical of many of the foreign priests who worked all over South America at that time. Many of these were men of rather vague provenance: some were diocesan priests from North America or Spain, connected loosely perhaps with some religious order though not belonging to it, full of enthusiasm for mission work but lacking any reliable funding from home, yet managing to source funds on foot of their personal talents for publicity. An Irishman of this vintage once ran advertisements in an Irish Sunday newspaper seeking help for a pig farm he was establishing for some impoverished community. As this appeal touched the hearts of Irish pig farmers, who were many at the time, his efforts funded a huge development among the poor of his parish.

Pons was a native of the island of Mallorca, not from any of the coastal hotspots like Santa Ponsa or Magaluff, but rather from the rural interior somewhere near Petra, the birthplace of Junipera Serra, the founder of the California missions. In appearance he suggested a man from a farming background: broad shouldered, large, expansive, observant. The fact that he was supplanted rather abruptly by the Irishmen never bothered him in the least. Perhaps he knew that his talent lay with peasants in their natural habitat, for it was to such a setting that he moved up north near the Ecuadorian border where he evolved many schemes for the betterment of the rural poor, like making jam from freshly-picked wild fruit. This product he packed into a VW and drove to the markets in Lima, 1,000 kilometres away. On these marathon trips he always overnighted with the Irish priests in Trujillo, even twenty years afterwards.

The work done in the *barrios* of Trujillo before the Irish mission came into being had a decisive influence on the shaping of that great enterprise. This was in the area of education. Coming from a background of the St James Society, which had never been involved in school-building, the two founding Irish priests had no intention of changing that pattern. But when they encountered Jaime Pons' network of primary schools educating about five hundred children,

The Mission Begins

they realised that the most direct route to winning acceptance by the adult population was through the school children. In a community where Mass-going had never been a tradition, how else could contact be made between priests and people? Both Fathers Murphy and Crowley became converted to the idea of schools and for the following thirty years education became a major weapon in their arsenal.

The formal arrangements for the handing over of the *barrios* to the Corkmen took place in the archbishop's office with the vicar general in attendance. Fr Pons outlined the existing facilities: two Mass centres, one an old church attached to a convent school run by Dominican nuns, the other an old shed that had once been used by a rifle club, which had a shooting range in the desert before the 'invasions' dislodged them. The Catholic schools that he had set up had an enrolment of five hundred children. It had been possible for him to build and run these schools because the Ministry of Education, while running its own State schools, also aided private schools with grants. The grants, however, were always slow in coming and when they did it was in instalments, so that private schools always found themselves in debt awaiting the arrival of the State grants. Because of such delays, the schools in the parish were in debt. Without hesitation or waiting for clearance from the bishop in Ireland, the Corkmen accepted the debt and took over the whole operation in the expectation that Bishop Lucey would approve, which in the event he did whole-heartedly, making the point that it was best to begin entirely on their own without any further involvement with Fr Pons.

When Fr Pons departed for the north of Peru, a certain amount of continuity was maintained by a group of volunteer, middle-class ladies from the city, who had been working in the *barrios* with the priest in a form of lay Catholic action among the poor. One of these ladies came from a prominent legal and political family, the Santa Marias. Her brother, Lucho, a lawyer who later became mayor of the city, turned out to be one of the mission's most loyal and useful friends, helping each succeeding superior of the mission in handling the labyrinthine intricacies of property and employment law. Among these volunteers there were also teachers, some of whom actually came to work later in the mission schools giving the rest of their teaching lives to this great work, becoming at the same time the closest and most trusted friends of the priests and nuns.

Michael Murphy began immediately to set about a building programme, which continued for his remaining three years in Peru and was in itself a massive achievement. He contacted a builder, Nyra Bisso, to discuss plans for a new church, a large priests' house, a convent and medical clinic, as well as classrooms for the existing schools.

On the first Sunday, 4 April 1965, the Cork priests began their mission with a morning and evening Mass in the 'Glorieta' – the disused shed – and an evening Mass in the old church attached to the Dominican convent. The nuns had happily handed over the key of the church to the priests and wished them luck with their enterprise. In the Glorieta, about two hundred people attended Mass. In the other church there was a full attendance, but with a congregation made up almost entirely of children. A little crestfallen, Michael Murphy wrote home that much needed to be done if this situation was ever to improve and as a practical step he mentioned that a decent principal in one of the State schools had offered to lend the school building for Sunday Mass in the Florencia area, where no Mass was being said at all. It was to these State schools that his colleague, Michael Crowley, turned his attention and unbounded enthusiasm. Morning after morning he plodded through the sandy streets to these forbidding buildings of concrete block and asbestos roofs, where outnumbered teachers tried to maintain order and teach without the help of books or pens, often in classrooms that did not even have enough desks for the pupils. Without the least inhibition he would sail into each classroom, shout greetings to the children, shake hands with the teacher, write his name on the blackboard, if he could find enough chalk, and tell them who he was, what the Irish priests were doing here and invite them all to Mass on Sunday. Then, as the class relapsed into its habitual pandemonium, he would assure the teacher of every support in the fine work they were doing and promise to help the school with the First Communion Fiesta, which was an integral part of the school year. Finally, with loud shouts of *'Chau, Padre Miguel'*, he would move on to the next room where the pantomime would be played out again.

By August, Kevin O'Callaghan and Michael Riordan had completed their course in the language school in Lima and had joined the others in Trujillo. In the mornings they visited schools and in the afternoons they visited the homes of the parish, trying their best to develop fluency in their newly acquired language. In their letters home they remarked on how slowly fluency came.

Breaking the News in Cork

Shortly after the completion of the formalities of setting up the new mission, which took place in the Nunciature in Lima, Bishop Lucey departed Peru on the 7,000-mile flight to Ireland, which was broken briefly by flight changes in Miami and Boston and ended with his arrival in Shannon. The long-held dream of establishing his own mission had finally become a reality. The first attempt at such an undertaking in the Diocese of Savannah, Georgia, where Cork priests on loan would work side by side with Cork nuns ruled by their superiors in the Cork mother houses, had of its very nature failed to leave the Bishop of Cork in full control – that would be the role of the Bishop of Savannah. The only involvement of the Bishop of Cork would be in the loaning and recalling of the Cork priests. The new arrangement with the Archbishop of Trujillo meant that Bishop Lucey would be in full control of every facet of religious activity in his new territory: he would have personal responsibility for the welfare of the priests and Mercy nuns (though not of the Bon Secours Sisters, who belonged to a congregation which was independent of the bishop), as well as the overall obligation of funding both themselves and their projects, like the construction of churches, convents, clinics and schools.

The long sixteen-hour flight, made on his own, afforded plenty of time for reflection on the varied implications of what he had undertaken. His personal background had in no way prepared him for the role of superior of a foreign mission. His academic background as Professor of Ethics in Maynooth College meant that he had no pastoral experience apart from his two years as parish priest of Bantry, while as coadjutor bishop he awaited the demise of his predecessor, Bishop Daniel Cohalan. His two-year stay in Innsbruck, Germany, as a post-graduate student was his only experience of life abroad. He claimed afterwards that he then found himself the only English speaker in a totally German environment, and that this total immersion gave him proficiency in the German language without any formal classes. It was this personal theory of language-learning that influenced the despatch of a series of Cork clerical students to Spanish seminaries, each to a different city, for one or two years to acquire Spanish for possible use later in Peru. He also sent the first Bantry Mercy Sisters to separate Spanish convents prior to their departure for Peru. He was convinced that the new language would come effortlessly in such isolation from fellow Irish people, forgetting that he himself was an academic of first rank, while few of the priests and nuns he sent to Spain would have the same aptitude for acquiring the complicated grammatical structure and vocabulary of a foreign language.

On that long flight he would also have planned his public launch of the new mission. As an astute realist he well appreciated the enormous risk of presiding over a failure, which could result from the lack of further volunteers or a break-up of the founding staff through disagreement or the tensions of living in such close proximity. If his major decisions on recruitment of volunteers had gone seriously wrong, his innocent enthusiasm would not save him from the 'I told you so' comments of the long-established missionary congregations, nor from the angry disappointment of Corkmen everywhere, who took any failure of a local enterprise, be it sporting or religious, as a blot on the city and county's reputation for success. Indeed, it was this unique Cork pride in imaginative projects that Bishop Lucey would encourage in much of his publicity campaign.

In undertaking a foreign mission on his own, Bishop Lucey had gone on that much used and much admired Cork sporting strategy: the 'solo run'. The price of this, however, could be the alienation of old and useful friends. It meant that the connection with Savannah would have to come to an end, which indeed it did the following year when the last 'loaned' priests came home, never to be replaced.

Relations with the Cardinal Archbishop of Boston were more delicate, considering his extraordinary generosity to the Cork Church Building Fund. During his brief stopover at Logan airport, Boston, the Bishop phoned the hospital where the Cardinal lay ill and left a message of greeting. He was concerned that the Cardinal would react negatively to Cork's going it alone after already participating in the missionary work of the St James Society. Later in the summer, these fears were somewhat allayed when Cushing came to Ireland for the opening of Galway Cathedral, visited Cork, lauded the new mission and promised financial help. There was some talk about Boston's funding of a Children's Hospital in Trujillo to be run by nursing Sisters from Cork, but that came to nothing, as did the promise of further financial help.

Finally arriving at Shannon, Bishop Lucey was interviewed by a reporter from Irish television, who later did a feature from the Bishop's House in Cork. Even though the publicity campaign for the mission had not yet been launched, news of the undertaking was getting about and subscriptions were already coming in. Within days of the bishop's return, a man he knew who had never before made a large contribution to any of the diocesan projects came up with £7,000 (almost €300,000 today).

He planned to use the Confirmation ceremonies, then about to begin, as platforms for the announcement of the project. In the 1960s, the Confirmation round was of greater impact than it is today. At each parish Confirmation – it was then possible for the bishop to do them all himself, as the attendance of the laity was much smaller and the churches could easily accommodate all the attendance at one ceremony, unlike today – the bishop made a major address on topics more related to national and political matters than to the sacrament itself, and the script was carried in full in the *Cork Examiner* of the following day and sometimes even by the national daily papers when the content was of a more controversial nature.

After each Confirmation, the bishop met the priests of the parish and the neighbouring parishes for dinner in the parochial house. That spring in 1965 he used these social gatherings to expound on the mission to Peru. Here he encountered complete support, which

Breaking the News in Cork

was not really surprising at a time when dissent was neither known nor tolerated by any bishop in the days before priests' councils, finance councils and all the other consultative processes introduced by the new Code of Canon Law, which was not to appear until some twenty years after the Second Vatican Council.

In his original vision of the mission, Bishop Lucey saw it as an all Ireland venture, with priests from other Irish dioceses volunteering to work with it. At the June meeting of the Irish bishops in Maynooth, he canvassed support for this idea and seems to have met with an encouraging response, but in the event only two other dioceses ever participated: Kerry sent a total of five men over a period of twenty years and Cloyne sent one. Looking back now from a new century, when the number of clergy in Irish parishes has declined so spectacularly that there is no curate in rural parishes and full-time chaplains to Religious Orders have practically disappeared, one can only regret that the Irish bishops of the time were so insular in their thinking. In the mid-1960s, most Irish dioceses had around thirty priests in the twenty-five to thirty-five age group occupying appointments as chaplains to religious communities requiring little more than a daily Mass and benediction on feast days, or else as curates in the remotest and least populated rural districts with little else to do other than offer daily Mass for three or four people, attend the occasional funeral and baptise six or seven children per year. The brighter young priests spent their first ten years teaching languages, history or mathematics in minor seminaries, which duties could have been better carried out by lay men endowed with a teaching vocation which, for the young priest, may never have been his choice of occupation in life. One can speculate how much more fulfilling life on the missions would have been for these men and how much more useful their contribution to the universal Church would have been also. Of course, it must be said in fairness to the other Irish bishops that Bishop Lucey never reduced the number of these chaplaincies, rural curacies or teaching positions to free up men for missionary work; he staffed the mission from the surplus of vocations that Cork and Ross enjoyed at that time.

The immediate focus on the publicity campaign of the spring of 1965 was on the church door collection planned for the end of May. The results of this collection were extraordinary in the amount of money contributed and in the enthusiasm for the bold undertaking by the bishop. On that Sunday over £26,000 was donated with the town of Dunmanway taking the lead with a figure of £1,450, followed by the smaller parish of Rosscarbery returning £1,400. As well as the £26,000 given at the church doors, about half as much again was sent to the bishop personally. In addition to this, about £16,000 had been given to the bishop in the proceeding weeks. The total made up about £60,000 (approximately €2.5 million today).

Buoyed up with the success of his appeal, Bishop Lucey urged the priests in Peru to spend, spend quickly and spend freely, provided they got value for money in what they purchased and built. He encouraged them to build, and build spaciously, and ensure that the presbytery and convents would be comfortable and that the churches would be large. The experience of that first fund raising effort convinced him that money would never be a problem for the mission and events of the next thirty-nine years proved him correct.

Opposition from Evangelists

Any expectation of an unopposed welcome for Catholic priests in the new parishes was dashed within a matter of weeks by the discovery that they were not the first missionary groups to compete for the souls of the migrants from the Andes. The long years of spiritual neglect in the mountains and the virtual absence of any Catholic parochial services or organisations in the mushrooming communities on the coast had left the stage clear for the Protestant sects. Loosely connected with the fundamentalist sects in the United States, these groupings, collectively known as the Evangelists, including Seventh Day Adventists, Baptists, Mormons and Salvation Army, operated from tiny adobe churches or halls scattered among the *barrios* where recruitment was easy because of the absence of resident Catholic clergy and a general ignorance of the teachings of the faith. Indeed, one of the main messages of these sects that was expounded between revivalist hymn-singing and hand-clapping was a horror of the 'superstitious' practices of Catholic sacramental liturgy.

The Evangelist pastors were drawn from the communities themselves. They were generally uneducated men enticed into the ministry by some financial incentives from abroad and schooled in hatred of the Catholic Church. Their followers seemed to assume a somewhat superior attitude to Catholics with a hint of class snobbery that set them above the 'ignorant peasants' who were Catholic, and this found expression in the way members of the sects reacted to a meeting with a priest. When greeted by the priest on home visitation, they never looked him in the eye, but with eyes cast down, and a knowing smile of superiority informed him that they belonged to 'the religion'. Their children playing outside on the street were less devious in expressing their hatred of Catholics; they broke into a type of diabolical laughter and put their index fingers to their foreheads in the form of horns, suggesting that the priest was the devil.

The appearance of the Cork priests visiting the houses in the *barrios* quickly alerted the Evangelist pastors to a new challenge to the free run they had enjoyed up to then in the districts of El Porvenir and Florencia de Mora. When word got out in June that an area of land had been granted to the Catholics by the housing authority for the building of a parish centre, the Evangelists set to work to block the development of a rival mission to their own proselytising activities. It became obvious that they were behind a move to have the square of land (desert in reality) turned into a public park. The response of the mission on local advice was to put up a hoarding stating that it was Church property given by 'resolution number so and so' by the local authority. This was true, as the relevant documents giving legal ownership were already deposited in the archbishop's office in the city. The priests hoped to build a temporary church as soon as possible to publicly establish the ownership, which was already enshrined in law. The long-term plan was to build a permanent church and presbytery.

No sooner was the sign erected on the site than a group, at the instigation of the Protestants, built a monument to the Peruvian poet, Cesar Vallejo, in the centre of the square of sand, thus staking a claim to the land. The monument itself was no more than some mud bricks finished with plaster, humble enough as a memorial to the poet, but sufficient to make its removal without any undue fuss a major challenge because of the extent to which this Peruvian poet was revered. The unfortunate advice to put up the sign to protect the site had, in fact, the opposite effect and now the situation under Peruvian law was unclear.

A month later, the so called monument still stood in the middle of the lot and the housing department showed no enthusiasm to become involved in a land dispute between a group of foreigners as

Opposition from Evangelists

yet unknown in the community. There seemed to be no alternative to purchasing another site in the area, one which had already been identified and found to be at once larger and more central. Even though this new piece of terrain was in private ownership, demands were being made by locals to have it designated a football pitch. In case the term 'football pitch' calls to mind a green field with goal posts, terraces and stands, it should be explained that football was played in the *barrios* on sand so fine that the runners threw up a wake of fine dust not unlike the wake of a speed boat on a lake. As well as being demanded as a pitch, the site was already being 'invaded' by new arrivals who were putting up their shacks during the night, while the forces of law and order provided no protection for the legal owner or defence of his property. The vicar general of the diocese knew all about this but did nothing, so the Corkmen felt badly let down. The outlook for their mission in Florencia looked gloomy indeed.

Bishop Lucey's advice from home was to proceed with the purchase of the land anyway and begin the building of a school, which would have more appeal in the estimation of the residents than football grounds. He also suggested that the area should be enclosed with a wall as soon as possible. This intelligent advice was acted upon as a gamble that might pay off and by October the encircling wall was being erected and the vicar general's brother, who was both a priest and civil lawyer, was helping with the legalities of the purchase. Soon the crisis was over and the development of a church, presbytery, school, clinic and convent was going ahead on the alternative site.

The incident of the public park/monument is instructive in the insight it provides into the patriotism of Peruvians at all levels of society. In Peru, the mild cynicism that sometimes dilutes patriotism in Europe is unknown. Self-consciousness of nationhood was born with the liberation from Spanish rule achieved in the early nineteenth century by Simon Boliver in Columbia, Eucador, Peru and Bolivia, as well as the Irishman, Bernardo O'Higgins, in Chile and San Martin in Argentina, men who were eponymous to countries, cities, streets, squares and urbanisations all over the continent. Though liberated originally by the same band of patriots under the influence of the French and North American revolutions, each new country quickly developed its own identity, boasting a separate governmental administration, national flag and national anthem, known in almost religious terms as the 'Hymno National'.

The Liberators themselves were either native Europeans, the descendants of immigrants or *mestizos* (men of mixed blood); none were 100 per cent indigenous. Because of that, one would not expect that patriotic sentiment would impinge much on the imagination of the poorest classes (those of pure Peruvian blood, without education, property and with little hope of ever rising in society). Nothing could be further from the truth. For all classes in Peru the most deeply felt awareness of identity is that of being Peruvian. This awareness finds expression in the singing of the national anthem every morning in school assembly, hand on heart, beneath a fluttering tricolour (the red/white/red national flag), the Sunday morning hoisting of the flag in every city central square with the participation of marching columns of schoolboys and girls and goose-stepping army units to the martial music of an army band.

The inauguration of any public work, no matter how humble, features similar patriotic embellishments such as the flying of the flag and the singing of the national anthem, while the *padrinos* (important personages who act as godparents of the new development) hold ribbons in the national colours. This civic ceremony would invariably be preceded by a blessing of the new work by the parish priest. As the *barrios* developed over the years and a network of sewer pipes were laid beneath the sandy streets, the priests frequently attended such ceremonies, the centre piece being an open manhole surmounted by three broom handles forming a tripod from which hung a bottle of 'champagne' (the cheapest gassy wine) adorned with the red and white ribbons held by the *padrinos*. Long speeches would be made by local politicians and all would be assured that the miserable shanty community would one day develop into a great urbanisation.

New arrivals on the mission experienced their first taste of Peruvian nationalism when they visited the immigration

Opposition from Evangelists

department in central Lima, appropriately located on a street known as '28 July', which is the national holiday celebrating national independence, like 4 July in the United States. It was not unreasonable that the Irish priests and nuns coming to Peru dedicated to the improvement of the health, education and spiritual life of the people would expect a warm welcome from both the population and the officials of the nation itself. A visit to the *extranjeria*, or immigration office, quickly disabused them of such expectations.

All immigrants, be they missionaries or otherwise, were subjected to the same immigration process, which included the filling out of endless official forms and the submission to medical testing for Tuberculosis and V.D. The bureaucratic procedures ranged from logging the names of all brothers and sisters at home in Ireland to giving blood tests. Only after all the relevant forms were filled, finger prints taken and mugshots stamped could permission to remain in the country be granted.

The atmosphere of suspicion which prevailed in this office was well captured in the book published in the early 1950s by the Norwegian explorer, Thor Heyerdahl, who in 1949 sailed a balsa raft, the Kon-Tiki, from Lima to Polynesia. His crew was joined in Lima by a Swedish scientist who had canoed up the Amazon from Brazil and finally arrived in Lima. This man was Spanish speaking and so was able to conduct his business personally at the immigration office where he had to fill out the necessary papers to leave the country. The conversation went like this:

> 'What is your name?' asked a ceremonious clerk looking suspiciously over his glasses at the Swede's huge beard.
> 'Bengt Danielsson,' Bengt answered respectfully.
> The man put a long form into his typewriter and began to type Bengt's answers.
> 'By what boat did you come to Peru?'
> 'I didn't come by boat, I came by canoe.'
> The man looked at Bengt dumb with astonishment and tapped out 'canoe' in an open space on the form.

> 'And by what boat are you leaving Peru?'
> 'Well,' said Bengt politely, 'I'm not leaving Peru by boat, I'm leaving by raft.'
> 'So likely, so likely!' the clerk cried angrily, and tore the paper out of the machine, 'Will you please answer my questions properly?'
> (Thor Heyerdahl, *The Kon-Tiki Expedition*, London: The Book Club, 1954, p.71)

Not only did every foreigner have to go through immigration to enter Peru but, like Bengt, they also had to get permission to leave the country, a procedure equally complicated, if not more so, owing to the necessity for a tax clearance, which was difficult to obtain for missionaries, who never earned anything while in the country. It was against this background of endless and pointless bureaucracy that one of the Kerry priest's last comments before coming home for good was: 'This was a hard country to get into and a hard country to get out of, and in between things were not too easy either.'

Arrival of the Irish Nuns

When Bishop Lucey focused on the needs of the poor in his newly acquired mission territory in Peru, it was to be expected that he would envisage a mission that would be staffed not only by priests, but also by nuns from Cork and Ross. It was a most propitious time to invite the convents to spread their wings and make new foundations abroad. Many of the convents, especially those of the Mercy Order in west Cork, had recently celebrated the centenary of their foundation made in the mid-nineteenth century, an event which could be marked appropriately by establishing a new foundation elsewhere. Coincidentally, the numbers of Sisters in these communities had reached an all time high since their foundation. The Convent of Mercy in Clonakilty, for instance, which had been founded in 1855 by four Sisters from Kinsale, had grown to a total of seventy in 1965 and there was as yet no indication that the trend would not continue into the immediate future.

Indeed, many of the religious communities had already made foundations in the United States: Skibbereen in Boca Raton and Clonakilty in Jacksonville, both in the State of Florida. In the United States the post-war drift to suburbia had created an urgent need for new Catholic parishes and they looked to their native land for Sisters to meet this urgent need.

However, the foundation of a new community of Sisters in Peru was, in a qualitative sense, in a different league from those made in the United States because of the challenge of operating in a new language, Spanish, and in a culture derived from Spain rather than from Ireland or England. The language requirement would call for a proficiency way beyond that of honours Leaving Certificate standard, which would have been the level attained by the Irish Sisters in a modern European language, usually French rather than Spanish.

The first convent to which the bishop looked for volunteers for Peru was the Convent of Mercy in the town of Bantry, where he had served as parish priest while he waited to succeed Daniel Cohalan as Bishop of Cork. Immediately on his return from Peru in the spring of 1965, he visited this convent and presented the Sisters with a first-hand account of the poverty in Peru and the tough nature of the living conditions volunteer Sisters could expect there. His presentation of the hardships of the assignment seemed only to whet their appetite for the challenge. Far from seeing the new missionary Sisters as some kind of adjunct to the priests, the bishop regarded them as an essential and integral part of the undertaking. In this, time would prove him correct – years after the priests had left for good the Cork convents would still continue the work of evangelisation firmly based on the native vocations that the early Irish nuns had recruited. From the start he showed great solicitude for the welfare of the sisters, giving detailed specifications regarding their comfortable accommodation in the new convents he was building and the day-to-day requirements of working in the desolate environment of the desert. Even before their departure for Peru he asked the priest in charge, Michael Murphy, to model the first convent on the plans of a convent at Monsefú, some miles up the coast, where a community of nuns from Newfoundland had set up some years before, as well as requesting pictures and patterns of their habit so that the Bantry nuns would arrive suitably attired for the tropics.

The priests already laying the foundations for the new mission hoped that some of the nuns would be teachers rather than nurses so that they could work in the public schools where religion was theoretically part of the curriculum, but was in fact woefully neglected through the inability of the teachers to teach a subject about which they knew very little themselves. In a letter to the Bantry nuns before their departure, the bishop encouraged them to spend a lot of time studying Spanish so that they would be confident and effective religious guides to both teachers and pupils in the schools.

The language problem was addressed in an unusual way and in a manner that was never repeated. The pioneering Sisters from Bantry, Sisters Aloysius Kerr, Gabriel O'Donnell and Columba Barrett, were sent off to different convents in Spain for a period of three months to learn the language. Whether this system worked or not for the Bantry nuns we do not know. We do know, however, that all the Sisters who subsequently went to Peru took formal classes in Spanish in Lima.

The Bantry nuns remained in Spain from September until Christmas. The arrangements for their passage to Peru, which occupied the first weeks of 1966, were even more bizarre than those made for their language course. It was decided, by whom it is not known, that they should travel to Peru by sea, not on a passenger liner but on a cargo ship, the 'SS Flamenco', bound from Liverpool to Salaverry, the small sea port a few miles from their ultimate destination, Trujillo. The thinking behind this strange choice was influenced by the amount of luggage they wished to take, which would be impossible by air with the weight restrictions and which, if sent by ship unaccompanied, might never arrive. Michael Murphy, who had travelled to New York in the 1940s pre-jet age, had some idea of the hardship the long voyage would entail and proposed that the nuns fly to New York, collect the luggage there and sail on down through the Panama Canal to their destination. This would at least spare the travellers the hazards of a trans-Atlantic crossing in mid-winter. He also pointed out that the customs procedures had been tightened up at the Peru end of the voyage and advised that the Sisters be selective in what they would pack. He was also confident that the new convent would be ready for them on arrival. In this, however, he was overly optimistic, as in the event they were only able to move into it some months later.

Bishop Lucey was fortunate in having the support of a prominent Cork businessman and director of Irish shipping, Liam St John Devlin, in making the arrangements for both the twenty-five boxes and trunks of goods as well as for the nuns themselves. The SS Flamenco was a cargo ship with a small complement of passengers and the journey would take about three weeks. The ship would put in at San Juan, Puerto Rico, in the Caribbean, and continue through the Panama Canal to the Peruvian coastline. At Puerto Rico the captain would be able to say if he would put in at Salaverry, Trujillo, or else continue on to Callao, the Port of Lima. The nuns would send a message from Puerto Rico to Trujillo indicating both the time and place of their disembarkation so that the priests could be on hand to shepherd them and their extensive cargo through customs. The priests in Peru were asked to send home a list of the things they urgently required. Their agreed list of requirements included light Mass vestments, chalices, ciboria, monstrances, tabernacles, Holy Oil stocks, a sixteen millimetre sound projector, black and white copes and rolls of film, also black and white. The Pacific Steamship Navigation Company had offices in Callao, which could be contacted for news of the arrival of the Flamenco. As well as personal possessions, the sisters would fill their twenty-five boxes and trunks with medicines, medical instruments, typewriters and books. Should the ship continue to Callao, the luggage could be left in bond and trans-shipped by coastal steamer to Salaverry where it could be put through customs. News from the Columban Fathers in Lima was not encouraging about getting the goods through customs in Lima.

On 17 February 1966, the three Sisters of Mercy set out on their 7,000-mile journey, leaving Cork by train for Dun Laoghaire from where they would sail to Liverpool. The night before they left Ireland, word came through that the Flamenco would not sail for another week. Both the bishop and Liam Devlin thought it best for the nuns to depart immediately and wait in Liverpool. However, while there, Sr Gabriel got the flu and ran a high temperature and arrangements had to be considered for leaving her behind to fly out later. However, when the ship finally sailed she was well enough to travel so they and the luggage were eventually on their way.

The image of a trans-Atlantic crossing that one has in the twenty-first century is that of a luxury liner complete with swimming pool, gourmet restaurants, deck games and endless promenade decks as

Arrival of the Irish Nuns

long as Croke Park. The reality of a cargo ship was as different as a five star hotel from a run down B&B. Because the cargo occupied most of the ship, passenger movement was confined to a restricted area near the stern. This confined living area, combined with the slow progress of the vessel and the typical February weather with its cloudy skies and rolling seas, must have made the first days of the voyage a test of endurance coupled with sea sickness and the natural home sickness that accompany one's abrupt separation from community and family. An engine breakdown held the ship up at sea for some days while repairs were carried out.

While the Sisters were at sea and out of communication with the rest of the world the bishop at home was sending out detailed instructions about their standing in canon law when they would arrive to form a new community. As the Bishop of Cork was their major religious superior at home, he now delegated that position to Michael Murphy and whoever should succeed him as superior of the mission. Arrangements would have to be made to appoint a confessor for the new community. With regard to the practicalities of establishing a new convent, the arrangement was that the mission fund would build their convent and the clinic in which they would work. Also, a Volkswagen would be purchased for their use (Michael Murphy hoped one of them could drive). Their day-to-day maintenance would be the responsibility of their mother house at home in Bantry.

What some might have taken as a bad omen for the Sisters' enterprise also came while they were at sea. The Sisters of Mercy from Newfoundland, who were based in Monsefú, were involved in a disastrous road accident. These nuns were to be the nearest support for the Irish women, because they were English-speaking and they had come to know Michael Crowley well when he spent six months after his arrival in Peru helping their parish priest, Fr Charlie Conroy.

On the last day of February 1966, Charlie Conroy stayed with the Cork priests in Trujillo. Next day, driving the minibus owned by the Sisters, he set out on the three-hour drive northwards on the Pan-American Highway with four of the Sisters who worked in Monsefú

89

and two Sisters of an American order, who were serving in the mountain parish of Santa Cruz and were on a visit to the Mercy Sisters. The Cork priests asked them all to wait for supper, but the Sisters were anxious to get home.

A light truck was speeding southwards along the highway. This truck had been stolen some days before from its owners in Chimbote, a city south of Trujillo. It had been recovered by the police and the owner and his brother had gone northwards to Chiclayo, a city near Monsefú, to bring it back. As these men were speeding home, a small car was proceeding sedately southwards in front of them. Rapidly, the men in the truck overtook the car, speeding up more as they swung out suddenly to pass it and at once crashed head-on with the minibus in which the priest and the nuns were travelling. The two occupants of the truck received only minor injuries, but the lighter minibus was practically demolished. One of the nuns died instantly, another lingered unconscious for nearly two weeks before succumbing to her injuries. Fr Conroy died without regaining consciousness as he was being carried into the hospital in Chiclayo.

Fortunately, the Cork nuns were on the high seas when this terrible accident occurred and knew nothing of it until they arrived. The good news of their final arrival in Lima was sent on by Tim O'Sullivan on 13 April, almost eight weeks after they had left Cork. Tim had gone to Lima from Chimbote, where he still worked with the St James Society, in order to meet them and help them get through customs. Through some friends of his he managed to get the president's secretary on his side and after that there were no difficulties. Some days later they made their way to Trujillo none the worse for wear after their long, drawn-out ocean saga.

Michael Murphy wrote to Bishop Lucey in Cork and his words, normally so controlled and reticent, exuded the excitement of opening the trunks and boxes: 'Everything arrived safely and we are doing nothing but opening up the "treasure chests". It is wonderful to find so many things we needed badly. It will take a week to sort everything out but it is a very pleasant task.'

The nuns were lodged in the house in Palermo where the priests had lived until their presbytery in El Porvenir was built. Their own convent would not be ready until October. The Mercy Sisters were now safely installed in Trujillo and had begun work in their clinic and visiting the homes of their new charges. But for Michael Murphy there was no rest from the logistical challenge of moving nuns from Ireland to Trujillo. Within a month arrangements had begun for the arrival of a new religious order: the Bon Secours from College Road in Cork.

The Bon Secours differed from the Mercy Sisters in that they were a congregation independent of the bishop of the diocese in which they worked, whereas the bishop was the major religious superior of the Mercy nuns (a responsibility delegated to the superior of the Cork mission for those in Peru), the Bon Secours had a mother general in Paris who was their major superior. They were coming to Peru as associates of the Cork mission, but not legally as part of it. Apart from getting permission from the Archbishop of Trujillo to make a 'foundation', they would carry on their work in close cooperation with the Cork priests and with ongoing social contact with the Mercy Sisters.

In October, Sister Rose Anne, the mother general of the Bon Secours in Cork, and Sister de Sales flew to Peru to inspect the mission area with a view to building a convent. Up to now the mission had included two parishes, El Porvenir and Florencia de Mora. An option had been take on a third area, La Esperanza (the Hope), located on the desert flanking both sides of the Pan-American Highway to the north of Florencia. This area had been recently 'invaded' by more arrivals from the mountains and the desert sands were being rapidly appropriated for their makeshift shacks. The Irish priests had succeeded in getting a promise of a large area across the highway from their own little church and future parish centre. The delegation of Bon Secours Sisters asked the priests to act for them in the purchase of it and proceed to build a clinic and convent as soon as possible. Meanwhile the Sisters would live in Palermo when the Mercy nuns had moved to their new convent.

Sister Maria de Sales Humphries would head up the new foundation and her three companions, Feilim Duignan, Joseph

Finbar O'Sullivan and Columba Byrne, would fly to New York from Shannon and travel on by sea on the Grace Line, which would dock at Salaverry, Trujillo. They finally arrived in March to work in the mission after their travels and their language course in Lima and went to live in Palermo. One of the main differences between the two orders was that the Bon Secours was a nursing order while the Mercy worked in schools as well as in hospitals at home. Now the nurses from both orders were staffing medical clinics and though fully qualified to work as nurses in Ireland, they had to have their professional qualifications recognised by the medical authorities in Peru. Like all the bureaucratic processes in Peru, from getting a resident's permit to getting a driving license, this would involve the long, drawn-out filling of forms and presentation of documents from their nursing colleges in Ireland. Meantime they were dangerously exposed to compensation claims in their nursing work. If any patient died or suffered, allegedly as a result of the treatment they proffered, they would be in the worst possible difficulty and would have no defence. The fact that they were providing free treatment for the poor would not help much. As for the compensation the sky would be the limit. Peruvian medical staff could get away with anything while a foreigner would be fair game if they made the slightest slip. The bishop sent out instructions that a Peruvian doctor should be employed for eighteen hours a week to supervise the prescription of medicines and the treatment of patients, thus providing cover for the Irish nurses.

There were now three parishes to be serviced and only two communities of nuns, so the bishop invited the community of St Mary's of the Isle in Cork City to help in the third parish. Volunteers came forward and in the autumn of 1967 the new Sisters of Mercy arrived and set up the third convent in El Porvenir. Writing in November of that year, the bishop said that their arrival would give the mission 'a finished look'.

The Mission Gets a 'Finished Look'

What Bishop Lucey described as 'a finished look' to the Cork and Ross South American mission in 1967 could more accurately be expressed in Churchillian terms as 'the end of the beginning'. Looking back at the story of the development of the project there is a temptation to divide it into identifiable periods such as the first years, middle years and so on. This would be possible and desirably neat if the mission experienced complete changes in personnel every five years, as governments do after defeat in general elections. In a missionary endeavour, continuity could only be maintained by staggering the changes instead of making total replacement of the missionaries at the one time. In June of 1968, however, a major break was made with the past when the time to return home was coming for the founding fathers and their replacements were arriving to begin language studies in preparation for the changeover the following year, when as many as five men would return home. Taking June 1968, then, as an imaginary pause in the continuous flow of the stream of history, one can take stock of what had been achieved in the space of three years and three months, from the signing of the agreement to the beginning of the end of the missionary sojourn of the founding priests. During that short time, thirteen priests had worked on the mission as well as sixteen nuns. One church, three convents, three presbyteries, four medical clinics, two schools and seven school extensions had been completed.

The thirteen priests were as diverse a group as one could get from the point of view of age, experience, talents and personalities. Nowhere was this diversity more evident than in the case of the two founders, the two Michaels: Murphy and Crowley. The elder by four years, Michael Murphy was the silent type whose impulses were strictly controlled, while Michael Crowley was the outgoing type, entertaining in conversation, full of humorous anecdotes and colourful expressions. In the words of his friend Charlie Conway: 'He sings Handel and old Gaelic songs, has a great sense of humour and a deep simple charity. He is a born debater, but he doesn't at all mind having an opponent who takes up little if any of the talking time. I very much enjoy and profit by his lectures, especially on pastoral theology and psychology, Gaelic literature and song, European economics, agriculture, bee culture and human life in all its aspects. He is an extraordinary person.'

Kevin O'Callaghan and Michael Riordan were the younger members of the four-man team that first worked in Trujillo. Classmates and friends from Farranferris and Maynooth colleges, they were ordained in 1959, after which they went to Africa as volunteers with the Kiltegan missionaries of St Patrick. It was this recent experience of missionary life that obviously recommended them as founder members of the new mission. After completing their first six-year stint in Peru, both would return later in life to work there for a further six years.

The first priest from the Diocese of Kerry to work with the Corkmen was Sean O'Leary. Sean already had a connection with South America through his brother who worked as a Columban in Chile. His sincerity and strength of personality so impressed his colleagues that they spoke for years of a man who was larger than life, a rock-like Kerryman whose personality was well symbolised by the huge stone altar quarried in the Andes that he chose for the first church built by the mission in El Porvenir and dedicated to *El Buen Pastor* (The Good Shepherd). Yet in spite of his apparent rugged health, Sean was a very sick man for much of his time on the mission. He was forced to return to Ireland to enter the Bon Secours Hospital in Cork where he underwent surgery on two occasions, and only for an emergency blood transfusion he would have lost his life. Always indomitable, Sean O'Leary returned to Peru and completed his contract with the Cork and Ross mission.

The Mission Gets a 'Finished Look'

Two Cork priests, Denis O'Donoghue and Tim O'Sullivan, joined the mission when their contracted time with the Society of St James was completed. Denis had worked with that Society for three years in La Paz, Bolivia. A most gregarious and sociable priest, he brought a light-hearted dimension to the small group of Irish priests working in Trujillo, and his ingenuity in the use of the Spanish language provided many comical moments that gave heart to new arrivals who were taking the learning of Spanish too seriously. Denis saw communication as a total body-personality exercise that transcended grammatical rules and communicated feeling and emotion to others much more directly than grammar and syntax. Though a big man he too suffered ill health, which necessitated rest time at home in Ireland.

Tim O'Sullivan, after a short stint in the mountains, moved to a parish run by the St James Society in Chimbote, a neighbouring coastal city to the south of Trujillo. Tim had a talent for photography and leaflet production in general and his work in such publication added greatly to the teaching resources of his colleagues, as well as to the publicity campaign back in Cork, which produced continuous financial support for the mission. His perseverance in overcoming bureaucratic hurdles, whether in securing teaching posts for the mission schools or helping new arrivals from Ireland through immigration procedures, became legendary.

Sean McGann, newly ordained, arrived in August 1966, the youngest priest to appear so far. Blond, athletic and fluent in Spanish from a final seminary year spent in Spain, he fascinated the young people of the parish where his blond hair stood out in a world where every head of hair was jet black. Sean brought a sense of youth and the irreverence towards established institutions that goes with it, which gave a fresh rounded finish to a missionary group that could easily have become conservatively cautious and perhaps even boring. Michael Murphy, the superior of the mission, was always a man who placed his trust in youth rather than age and he took to the new arrival with alacrity. The fact that McGann was an accomplished golfer may have helped the friendship that developed between the older superior and the Benjamin of the group.

Another newly ordained priest, Fr Charlie Nyhan, arrived the following year. His seminary background included five years in the Irish College in Rome, followed by a final year in Spain leading up to ordination. It never seems to have occurred to Bishop Lucey that sending a man proficient in Italian to add Spanish to his portfolio of languages would be a huge imposition. Yet Charlie, who had been one of the most intellectually gifted of his generation at Farranferris college, accepted the challenge without hesitation.

In 1967, the Diocese of Kerry sent another volunteer to the Cork and Ross mission: John B. O'Sullivan. John B., as he was always known, took a special interest in catechetics. He worked with other priests of the Diocese of Trujillo in preparing up-to-date religious programmes for both Catholic and State schools. This experience stood to him when he returned much later to teach ecclesiastical history in the major seminary located outside Trujillo. John was a man of great intelligence and application to study, a man who gave total commitment to his priesthood, a man of great devotion mixed with a surprising sense of irreverent humour. While parish priest of Killorglin and canon of the Diocese of Kerry he suffered from cancer, which led to his death in his sixties. On the Sunday before he died, he wrote a thank you note to his parishioners in the parish newsletter, leaving an inspiring legacy of faith and courage to the sick and the old of his parish.

Two other Cork priests arrived in Trujillo in 1967 to begin their six-year service. Michael Crowley, known as 'small Mike' because of the presence of his namesake who was taller, worked in the newly acquired area of La Esperanza, taking a special interest in the Legion of Mary, which still survives in that parish over forty years later. Pat O'Brien, who was slightly older than Michael, joined him in La Esperanza about a year later. During his six years he lived in all three parishes for varying periods. Later in life he went to Peru again to work from 1978 to 1982, and finally he spent the last years of his life on the mission, only returning to Ireland in August of 1995, dying of cancer in December of that year.

The three mission parishes so deprived of parish infrastructure when the Irish arrived in 1965 had been spectacularly developed by

The Mission Gets a 'Finished Look'

1968. El Porvenir had its large parish church completed and blessed in June 1967. A tall modern structure, the church of the Good Shepherd towered over the surrounding neighbourhood sending out a message of hope to a deprived population and reminding them of their Catholic heritage of four centuries, which they had already cherished when they lived in the Andes. Now 'exiles' on the coast, they were reminded by the building that the Catholic Church had not abandoned them but still travelled with them on their journey into an unknown future. Already the promise of hope was being fulfilled in the other parish buildings that had by then been constructed: the school rooms built in three sectors of the parish; the parish meeting rooms; the medical clinic where the Mercy Sisters worked and the convent where they lived. Mass was being said every Sunday in three centres, strategically located in the parish, and a complete liturgical and sacramental service was being provided.

In the second parish, Florencia, two priests lived in a new parish house, the Mercy Sisters occupied a newly built convent and staffed their medical clinic nearby. A completely new parochial school was completed in one centre while another new school already had an extension. Masses were still being said in school buildings until the planned churches would be completed.

In La Esperanza parish two centres were flourishing with schools that were being extended almost annually to accommodate the huge enrolment and two medical clinics staffed by the Bon Secours Sisters whose new convent was completed in December 1967. Also in that year, the parish house had been completed beside the small parish church that had been inherited from the Carmelite priests who had taken care of the parish since its foundation in 1957.

All this development had been completed and paid for in the short space of three years and three months. When the bishop spoke of a 'finished look' he probably thought that would be the final shape of the mission: a spread of territory that could be improved with some new churches to accommodate the growing numbers attending Mass and more school extensions to cater for the huge population of young children. He could not have known that the desert surrounding the present mission would within the coming decades be populated with wave after wave of migrants from the mountains who would have nowhere to turn for help, spiritual and material, except to the Irish priests.

Life in a Shanty Town: Housing

Perhaps the most reliable indication of the economic situation of a family is the condition of the house in which they live. This is equally true of any human settlement. Whether it be in the developed or the Third World, the whole townscape comprising streets, footpaths, houses and public buildings taken together gives a true picture of the wealth or poverty of a community.

A drive through the *barrios* of Trujillo, as well as visits to individual houses, told a tragic story of economic deprivation unlike anything to be found in even the poorest sectors of cities in the developed world. While it is true that the streets in the *barrios* of Trujillo were wide and straight, laid out with true Peruvian optimism for the day when the area would become a large prosperous suburb, the general appearance of the houses lining the streets was a far cry from the planner's vision of the future. In fact, instead of being lined with houses, the streets appeared to be bordered with brown, mud-brick walls, ten feet high, into which houses had been inserted at irregular intervals. The reason for this was that the plot of land assigned to each resident had a longer street frontage than the family could afford to develop, so they contented themselves for the present with a small hut, the door and window of which were set into the adobe wall surrounding the family plot.

The surface of the street consisted of gravelly sand scarred by furrows and potholes, in which a car was liable to sink. Laid along the centre of the streets were piles of household rubbish or smouldering bonfires where someone with a semblance of civic duty had tried to burn the trash. The stretches of adobe walls were often daubed with election slogans somewhat faded with the passage of time. Here and there someone had begun plastering and whitewashing the walls, but these ambitious projects had petered out leaving the unfinished paint work as unsightly blotches on the otherwise monochrome adobe. The houses were constructed entirely of adobe bricks, except for a concrete lintel over both the door and the window opening, which was bricked up indefinitely awaiting the day when the family could afford a glazed window frame.

Stepping into a house from the bright midday sunshine one found oneself in unexpected darkness, caused by the absence of a glass window. Only when one's eyes became accustomed to the internal gloom, or when the hostess removed a brick from the window space to admit light, could the interior be seen at all. The floor was firmed sand, the walls unplastered adobe and the roof comprised heavy eucalyptus logs covered with straw matting smeared with mud. The real shock on seeing the family living room was its total emptiness except for a stool by the wall and, perhaps, a rough hewn table. No pictures on the walls, no decorations, neither delft nor crockery – nothing. A scuttling form beneath the stool betrayed the presence of some guinea pigs being fattened for the family stew pot. Here the family lived, ate, possibly slept, and the children did homework seated on the floor. A rear door led out to the back yard or corral, as it was called, a large area enclosed by adobe walls with a tree or two growing in the centre. Here the family cooking was done in a large pot placed on stones above a bonfire of broken timber boxes, salvaged from some dump.

By day the family lived mainly in the corral. Here too one found members of the family who seldom emerged from the house: a grandmother, perhaps, sitting on a broken log dressed entirely in black, shrivelled with age, speaking, through gapped teeth, a language which was a mixture of Quechua and Spanish, quite unintelligible to a stranger, her leathery face lit by dark alert eyes, her once black plaits now silver. These *ancianas* (ancient women) were always surrounded by children and were treated with love and devotion as the centre of the whole extended family.

Life in a Shanty Town: Housing

In these houses one noticed the look of hunger, especially in the children, whose limbs were underdeveloped and their skin pimpled. All had the habit of rubbing their eyes as though they were infected with some kind of irritation, which in all probability was linked to malnutrition. This was ironic in a country like Peru where the best of fresh food was in abundance right through the year not only in the city's huge central market, but also in the smaller ones that operated in the *barrios*. The products on sale included potatoes of many varieties, probably the finest in the world, corn on the cob, sweet potatoes, freshly caught fish, vegetables of all descriptions, herbs in abundance and fruit like pineapples and mangoes – the list was endless. The prices were extremely low by international standards, but for people without money these products were beyond their reach. Few in the *barrios* had enough money to purchase any of these wonderful foodstuffs. Only the least expensive foods found their way to the stew pot in the corral, and even those in the most limited amounts. Pasta, rice, beans and weak vegetable soup comprised the main diet of the poor. Every afternoon a barrow man passed through the streets calling out that he had bread rolls for sale. Few emerged from the houses to buy.

The type of homestead just described corresponded to the majority of dwellings in the *barrios* in the second half of the last century. Strangely enough, this low standard of existence was compensated for by the friendly courtesy shown by the dignified people who lived in such subhuman conditions. Every visitor was greeted with a handshake and, if well known, a warm embrace. They were always offered a seat, even if there was only a box to sit on. Occasionally a homemade sugar chair was found and placed outside for the guest to sit on. This courteous gesture often proved embarrassing when the four legs of the chair began to sink into the soft sand. Some type of refreshment was always offered, even if it was no more than water enlivened with a squeeze of lemon or lime juice.

Before any serious discussion about health, education or religion took place, polite small talk was obligatory. The Irish priest or nun was asked about their families at home: whether their mother was living and if they were lonely to be so far away from home. The visitor was brought out to the corral and introduced to the grandmother, who responded with incomprehensible chatter. An old man, perhaps a grandfather, stood up, shook hands and nodded silently at the visitor. Women seemed to be the ones in this particular society who spoke the most.

This kind of household was the average type in the *barrios*. More recent arrivals lived in conditions far inferior in the scale of development. To reach such deprived homes one left the car and, proceeding on foot through the soft sand, climbed higher up the desert to those more rudimentary settlements. Here again the streets were laid out wide and straight, but as yet there were no adobe perimeter walls; the plots were simply marked out with string. The building of some houses had already begun. This began with the manufacture of the adobe bricks made from clay delivered from a truck, some straw and water that were mixed together, shovelled into timber moulds and left to dry in the sun, often in the middle of the street. Development was piecemeal as some families, unable to purchase the load of earth for the manufacture of the bricks, still lived in huts made of straw matting tied around a wooden framework. This accommodation was the most primitive of all and during the winter months, when a cold damp mist blew in from the sea, posed a terrible danger to health. Here there was no water and no sanitation – a situation for some unfortunate families that continued for years.

At the other end of the economic scale, however, things seemed to improve. After five or ten years the average type of house already described received an upgrade with the construction of four reinforced concrete pillars at the corners and even a flat concrete roof, which gave some hope of safety if an earthquake struck. The hope of building a second storey some day was signalled by short lengths of reinforcing steel rods projecting from the tops of the concrete columns. However, such improvement was never guaranteed in a country whose economy was so fragile that five years of progress was often followed by a decade of recession. At family level, economic advancement was often set back by sickness.

In Peru there was no State help for the sick, apart from a free bed in hospital. All medicines and medical attention had to be paid for by the relatives of the sick person. When a father or mother developed TB or cancer, everything the family possessed went towards the purchase of medication. A family with a small corner shop, for instance, would see their shelf stock run down week-by-week, unable to replenish it as all the money had gone to the pharmacy. When all the stock was gone the shop would close and, if the sick person lingered longer, even the house itself was sold and the family headed back up the desert hillside of the *barrio* to construct a basic shelter and begin the long cycle again from a straw hut to some kind of solid habitation. To add to their grief the patient would in all probability have died by then.

Life in a Shanty Town: Surviving

The greatest mystery to newcomers visiting the *barrios* of Trujillo was the question as to how the people lived at all without any visible source of financial income. In any normal society the family income is explained by the presence of a local factory or farmland, or some other commercial operation located in the area. Here there was no such source of income. As the Irish priests and nuns came to know their community intimately it became clear to them that survival for each family depended on its ingenuity in finding some source of income, either within the *barrio* itself or in the nearby city. While most adults went outside the settlement to earn some small income in the most menial forms of employment, there grew up within the community itself a type of basic commercial life whereby the people lived off one another. In a way that is mysterious to everyone except economists, trading within a community seems to generate wealth. In the *barrio* this commercial life was at its most rudimentary. An example of this economic interdependence would be the process whereby a woman would buy a sack of green grass from a truck arriving with products from the mountains. This she would retail to her neighbours to feed their guinea pigs. With the proceeds of her sale she would buy some vegetables from another lady at a stall in the local street market who, in turn, would buy a fish from another trader. In this way money circulated and seemed to provide a living (or, more accurately, a means of survival) for all those involved.

For most, however, the only hope of making a living was by going elsewhere to work. At dawn every morning there was a general movement of men heading on foot towards the old city in search of work. They usually headed for the central market where the trucks of supplies from the mountains unloaded their cargo for distribution to the stallholders. This called for strong bag carriers and the men were willing to loft huge sacks for little more than a tip. Perhaps they felt a link with their mountain origins in unloading the products that they had once grown in a previous life. In the afternoon they would head home with the few coins they had earned, which would be used immediately to purchase food for the family.

Women also went out to work, often with a child bundled in a shawl on their back. Those who were least acquainted with modern living, those whose previous life was spent completely in remote parts of the mountains, had to look for the lowest type of employment, for example, picking crops by hand in the irrigated market gardens surrounding Trujillo. Women more familiar with the modern manners of the coast secured employment as housemaids in the houses of the middle class at the other side of the city, out towards the sea where teachers, lawyers and policemen lived. Some such women also got casual employment for their husbands as gardeners in the same house. As daughters grew up they became employed as housemaids if they were prepared to work almost as slaves in the houses of the well off.

All of this employment was casual and miserably paid. The women had to pay a bus fare to their place of employment each day. At the end of the week there was no certainty that the lady of the house where she worked would pay her at all. Instead she might tell her to wait another week for her pay and if the housemaid complained she might lose the job. In this situation women often turned to the Irish sisters to give them the bus fare so that they could keep their jobs. Families lived from day to day. Earnings were used to buy food. When there were no earnings the family went without decent nutrition.

Proper permanent employment was scarce because the whole country – indeed, the whole continent – was in economic recession from which regular loans from the World Bank failed to rescue it. For what skilled or semi-skilled work was available in industries like construction and transport, the men, newly arrived from a different culture in the mountains, had neither the skills nor confidence to avail of it.

In the struggle to fend for their family and educate their children, some women went to heroic lengths to maintain the necessary family income. One woman, who succeeded in bringing her daughters through high school to university where they trained as nurses and teachers, ran a 'restaurant' in the major market in the city centre. The term 'restaurant' is rather an exaggeration, as her food outlet consisted of no more than a stool, a low table and a little charcoal fire that kept a stew pot warm. Each morning, this lady rose at some unearthly hour, took a bus into the market to buy fish and vegetables. She then returned home with her purchases, prepared the ingredients and boiled a fish and vegetable stew. Carrying the large pot of fish stew, she returned again by bus to the market, collected her chair, table, spoons and bowls from a friendly stallholder who stored them (for a fee), lit her tray of charcoal and began business at about 7 a.m., serving her regular customers, who were either stallholders or porters unloading the trucks. By noon she would have emptied her stew pot, stowed her equipment and returned home to run her house and feed her family. This wonderfully brave woman became one of the parish leaders of prayer groups and helped the priests and nuns in their parish work.

Some men showed imagination in trying to earn something to feed their families. One man had a simple business idea – which did not seem to work out for him as he soon abandoned it – involving a bathroom scales that he must have scavenged in a dump, which he carried into the city centre, placed on a sidewalk and allowed passers-by to weigh themselves on it for a small fee. Men who had some education and a typewriter set up business with a chair and table outside banks and government offices filling out forms for a charge that was negotiable. The Cork priests frequently availed themselves of this service as they went from office to office, filling out applications for driving licences, certificates of residence for foreigners, social security forms for domestic employees, and all the vast range of documentation required for even the simplest transaction.

Life in a Shanty Town: Surviving

Dressmaking was another cottage industry that in some instances called for high levels of skill, as in the case of one woman who made up the ceremonial capes worn by bullfighters as they paraded into the arena. Scrap pieces of building steel were welded together to form a stretcher mounted on legs to hold the cape during the embroidering process. The stitching needle could be inserted from above with one hand and returned from beneath with the other. Gorgeous coloured thread, some of it gold, was used in the ornamentation. The design usually featured the image of a saint at the centre, with embroidered swirls radiating from the image and finishing at the cape's hem in an ornamental border heavily encrusted with cloth of gold and tiny sequins. All the stitching was executed by hand and took many weeks to complete. It was hard to believe that the processional cape glinting in the sunlight of the bullring could have come from a workshop as humble as an adobe family living room in the *barrio*.

In the struggle to survive in extreme poverty and barely human accommodation, the ingenuity of people was exemplified in endless ways. The fundamental economics of supply and demand apply in the near starvation of the new towns just as in the world's most developed economies. It was not unusual to encounter 'factories' mass-producing some product in the corral to the rear of a dwelling house. One such factory produced brooms for the Lima market. The brooms used for sweeping the streets of Lima were replicas of the traditional witch's broom, nowadays only used in Ireland for the decoration of shop windows for Halloween. In Peru they were still functional and in good demand. In their production the entrepreneur employed a workforce of three or four. The broom was made from straw-like reeds attached by wire to a wooden handle. The reeds arrived by lorry from the north and were dropped by the side of the Pan-American Highway, where they were carried in huge bundles to the factory. Limbs of trees, still bearing their bark, arrived in a similar way. The wire used in tying the bristles to the handle would probably have been the most expensive raw material had it been purchased in a hardware shop. It was, however, sourced free of charge in the following manner: old truck tyres were picked out from a nearby dump, rolled down to the house and set on fire in the middle of the street. When the black smoke had cleared and the hot ashes cooled the wire that reinforced the rubber was salvaged from the embers for use in the factory. The timber handles were peeled of their bark and whittled smooth with machetes and cut to size. The bristles were tied to the handle with the salvaged wire and trimmed with a homemade guillotine: a sharp machete blade welded to scrap metal levers hinged to a timber chopping block. The resulting off-cut of the reeds contained seeds which were then fed to fowl in the corral, yielding up a by-product of eggs and meat. When a consignment was ready for shipment, the brooms were carried in huge bundles back up to the highway, loaded on top of the freight in a passing truck and sent on their way to the markets in Lima.

At another home a 'factory' produced sweets, which were sold either wholesale to little market stalls or retailed by 'walking traders' at football matches, bullfights or street corners. The equipment of this factory and the environment in which it operated were as basic as you could get. In the corral of a dwelling a bonfire was lit beneath a recycled forty gallon petrol drum, in which a mixture of sugar, water and colouring was boiled down to form solid candy, stirred all the while with a 2" x 2" timber spar. The molten mix was then poured into small lozenge-shaped plastic moulds and left to cool and solidify in the sun. It did not seem to matter that flies landed in swarms on the drying sweets nor that wind-blown sand passed over them. When ready, the sweets were counted into small plastic bags and packed in cardboard boxes for sale wherever crowds gathered.

As well as this, wherever there is industrial production there is advertising, and the new towns were no different. Here a white flag flying from the roof of a house did not indicate some form of surrender, but rather that the premises was open as a *shebeen*, where homemade beer could be purchased. From time to time a household produced a quantity of alcoholic beverages to celebrate a wedding, christening, anniversary, birthday or simply the arrival of cousins on a visit from the mountains. The beer was produced according to an inherited formula going back long before the Inca Empire. Yucca, a tuberous plant, was mixed with water. The fermentation process was initiated by women who chewed the root and spat it into the mix. As it was made in copious quantities at a time, there was always some left over after the celebration. This was sold to neighbours and passers-by, who spotted the square white flag flying from the roof advertising the product. Because of its method of production, *chi cha*, as it was called, was unappealing to foreigners, though, according to reports, it was most effective in producing a state of intoxication, which was evidenced firstly by rhythmic clapping and singing coming from the impromptu *shebeen*, and later by the sleeping bodies recumbent on the sand the next day.

Life in a Shanty Town: Sickness

Because the health of a community depends on its standard of housing and diet, it is not surprising that the community in the *barrios* suffered from a variety of diseases directly related to the shortcomings in both these fields. The houses were both crowded and insanitary. Hence the proliferation of infectious and contagious diseases bedevilled so many families, while the diet, which was directly related to the earning capacity of the family, provided little nutritional value as a defence against infection. In the Peruvian family the first call on earnings was for food. Over the centuries the people had developed a cuisine peculiar to the country. Before the arrival of the Spanish seasonings, salt and ground pepper were never used, instead flavour was provided by *ahi*, a small, red chilli widely available and considered indispensable to every prepared dish. Garlic, peppers and onions were also used generously. Thanks to these powerful and pungent seasonings even the least expensive food was made palatable. Vegetable soup diluted heavily with water to meet the needs of a large family was still made attractive with the addition of these flavours.

Homemade soup was a stable ingredient of the family diet, even though its nutritional value varied with the amount and type of ingredients used in its preparation. Among the very poor, what passed for chicken soup meant little more than a large pot of water with the cheapest vegetables added, lots of spices and the claw of a chicken, which was not only boiled but also served with the soup to be chewed by whoever was lucky enough to get it in their portion. If the family could afford it, the soup was enriched with maize and

Life in a Shanty Town: Sickness

thickened with flour. For the main meal of the day rice was provided, sweet potatoes, yucca (a tuberous parsnip-like vegetable) and corn on the cob. Meat was rare because of the cost while bread rolls were a treat for Sundays. A type of homemade pancake was prepared if funds were available for the purchase of flour and cooking oil.

As in Mediterranean cooking, the use of cooking oil was fundamental to the preparation of Peruvian dishes of quality. Good olive oil was quite out of reach for the poor, who had to manage with a kind of lard, which explains why relief food from the United States with its high-quality olive oil was welcomed when distributed by the mission. Without oil or lard the meals were nothing more than insipid tasteless stews. The drink of preference with the meals of the poor was a homemade 'lemonade', produced by the addition of a squeeze of lemon and a little sugar to a jug of water. Fresh milk was unavailable and tea was rarely used, except for a sort of herbal tea prepared from green herbs on sale in bulk in the market.

In short, for the poorest families the nutritional value of this diet was negligible. Watery soup, rice in small portions, water to drink and a little pan-fried bread lacked the essentials for growing children and many showed the symptoms typical of the malnourished: bloated stomachs and shrivelled, underdeveloped limbs. While hunger was assuaged by the volume of the food provided, its nutritional value counted for little. The result of this daily diet was stunted physical development matched with a disposition to other diseases, which the crowded insanitary living conditions produced, such as cholera and tuberculosis, which were endemic. This was the situation that the Irish Sisters faced when they opened their first clinics on arrival in Trujillo. The Mercy Sisters set up in two of the parishes and the Bon Secours Sisters in the third.

The clinics were staffed by Irish nursing Sisters, some Peruvian nurses and attendants, and supervised by a Peruvian doctor employed by the mission. Different days were set aside for the various conditions and illnesses, such as maternity, tuberculosis, children's ailments and general debility. The clinics were well built and spotless, featuring rooms for the different services as well as a small pharmacy where the medicines were sold and distributed through a hatch, either at no charge to those unable to pay or at a much-reduced cost. This small charge did little to defray expenses but did a lot to maintain the dignity of the sick, who felt independent when they paid a nominal sum for their medication. Equipment for x-rays and laboratory work was either purchased in Peru or else brought out from Ireland when difficult to obtain locally.

TB was perhaps the most prevalent disease and, unfortunately, it carried a stigma that added to the patients' distress. Diagnosis was made with both the laboratory equipment and the x-rays. The treatment took a three-pronged approach: injections, tablets and a food programme supplied from Caritas, the United States surplus food aid programme. Particularly effective in treatment was the Irish powdered milk, purchased in Ireland and shipped out to Lima. One particular group that participated in the TB programme recalled poignant memories of Ireland of the 1940s: the Peruvian teenagers stricken with the dreaded disease. Listlessness and coughing were the first indication of the onset of the illness. During treatment, the young people remained at home from school and rested. Perhaps because of their youth these young boys and girls responded to the three-way treatment, resumed their education and some even continued on to university, so that today there are many men and women bringing up their own families and living normal lives thanks to the funding provided at home in Ireland by people whom they never met, but whose generosity saved their lives.

Sometimes, especially in the case of old men and women, treatment came too late in life or when the disease had advanced too far. The Sisters visiting the sick in their homes in order to administer medication came face-to-face with the misery of the poor in all its stark horror. The patient, by then coughing blood, lay on straw matting on the sandy floor, covered by little more than rags. They knelt on the filthy floor to nurse these poor sick people, sometimes with success, but more generally with little hope. Soon they passed away with a terminal haemorrhage that endangered the health of everyone else in the crowded home. The rest of the family would be encouraged to come to the clinic for tests where they frequently tested positive and had to be added to the already overstrained resources of the TB programme.

One may gather from the description of the health situation that there was no adequate public health service in the sense that it is understood in Ireland. The State did provide a free bed in hospital, but after that everything else had to be paid for by the patient. When a patient needed surgery or when a mother was about to enter hospital for the birth of her baby, the inadequacy of the health service was highlighted by the list of requirements that patients had to bring with them before they were admitted to the hospital. The sick person first called to the hospital where they were given a full list of requirements that included whatever medicine they would need before and after surgery: surgical gauze, syringes, bandages, catgut, bed sheets, blankets and, if a blood transfusion was anticipated, some relative or friend who would donate the required amount of blood. Armed with this extensive and costly shopping list and without any money to pay the pharmacy, they turned to the Irish Sisters' clinic and obtained all the supplies from the stock in the clinic, or they were purchased in a pharmacy by one of the Sisters. The patient then returned to the hospital and was admitted to a bed. However, a member of the family had to remain at all times by the bedside to attend to the patient, help feed them and also protect the supply of medicine and surgical equipment stored in the bedside locker in case it might be stolen while the patient slept.

The skill of the surgeons was quite extraordinary. From time to time Irish medical students visited Trujillo under the Surgeon Noonan Scheme, and while they were incredulous of the infrastructure in the hospitals, they were fascinated by the professionalism and expertise of the surgeons they saw operate. Because of the excellence of the surgical teams there was little danger to life during surgery, this arose from the inadequate aftercare and the danger of infection. The Sisters did all they could to support their patients by visiting them in hospital and ensuring that they lacked nothing by way of medication and other personal requirements.

'Invasion' from the Andes

In the summer of 1966, Michael Murphy took a vacation in Ireland, during which he had long discussions with Bishop Lucey about the future of the mission. He had a most encouraging report to make to his bishop: seven building projects were completed, fourteen more had already begun and would be completed in the following year, the Sisters had begun working on the mission and the Bon Secours Sisters were due to arrive in a mater of weeks. The takeover of the shantytowns of Trujillo was completed and, divided into three parishes, the people were receiving full pastoral care. The task before the mission was enormous in view of the poverty of the people and the size of the population, which would obviously grow as young people married and set up families of their own. It was assumed that this natural development would be the only source of population growth in the years to come. This rather complacent outlook was suddenly shattered by a letter received in August from Michael Crowley, who was in charge in the absence of Michael Murphy. In it he wrote: 'We had a very extraordinary invasion of Esperanza the night before last when over six hundred families moved in. They occupied all the free ground at the seaside of the Pan-American Highway about five hundred yards north of our parish centre. It was like a town on the move. It was a new experience for me. They came in organised groups mostly from the mountains.'

This was a new experience for the Cork priests, because when they had arrived in the *barrios* of Trujillo little over a year earlier, the new families were already settled in and there was a semblance

'Invasion' from the Andes

of an established community in El Porvenir, Florencia and Esperanza. All their planning for construction of schools, churches and clinics was based on the size of the population already living there. It does not seem to have dawned on them that this was only the beginning of further 'invasions' from the Andes.

Already in their work in Ireland, the priests had seen suburbs expand with the building of new housing estates in Blackrock, Ballinlough and Bishopstown, but the pattern of development in Cork was one of organic growth that was spread over a generation. Even later, when villages like Ballincollig and Carrigaline grew into communities of up to 20,000 people, it took a generation for this to happen. The original residents of these parishes had adequate warning as land was purchased for development, planning was sought, machinery moved in and new housing estates were occupied. The expansion of the Cork parishes was totally different to that in Peru, which happened practically over night. On the morning after that night time invasion of 1966, as Michael Crowley concluded his morning Mass in the old chapel he was using until the permanent church would be constructed, one of the congregation rushed in and told him to come quickly, that there had been an invasion during the night. They immediately climbed into the Volkswagen and drove up the Pan-American Highway a few hundred yards to what had been up to then the limit of the *barrio*. The day before there was nothing beyond that limit but flat sand. Now hundreds of families were busily marking out squares and streets and corrals in which each family would establish its new home. The transformation reminded him of the coming of the circus to a west Cork town in the 1940s. One day a little field on the outskirts of the town was home to a lone donkey munching thistles; the next morning it sported tents, caravans, flags, exotic animals and men sledging tent poles into the ground. Here, however, the extent of the operation resembled more the establishment of a mediaeval army camp than a village circus.

Towering trucks from the mountains were pulled in at the side of the highway from which poured forth droves of men, women and children, as well as sheep and goats, rushing around to stake their claim on a newly marked out corral in the desert. They were dressed in the coloured ponchos of the Sierra, wearing broad-brimmed straw hats and bearing bundles of their possessions on bent shoulders. Sweet smelling wood smoke rose from the camp fires where women bent over cooking pots, their babies slung over their shoulders in coloured shawls. The men who seemed to be in charge carefully lined up the streets with the existing streets of Esperanza so that in the future when proper streets would be developed and perhaps paved, no houses would have to be disturbed. Children played and screamed with excitement, some of them pulling a sheep or a goat by a rope as they tethered the animal in their new corral, guaranteeing a few meals for the family in the days to come. Men hammered wooden posts into the sand to mark off their claim, as well as longer poles to support the straw matting that would provide a roof over their heads on the first night.

Long eucalyptus poles from which fluttered the national flag were raised in every block of corrals. This, they believed, gave a semblance of legality to the claim they had staked. A jeep full of police looked on helplessly at the invasion of State-owned land, as is all unoccupied land in Peru, too outnumbered to enforce the law of the land.

In his report to Ireland, Michael Crowley stated: 'I moved among the people assuring them that they were welcome to the parish, and offering all the help at our disposal. It seems to be an ideal time to contact them.' In this astute observation events proved him correct. Twenty years later, when that invasion had developed into a parish of 40,000 people with its own churches, many of the parishioners still recalled with great gratitude the welcome they had received from Padre Miguel on that historic morning when they took their first step into a better future. It is hard to over-emphasise the historical importance of that defining moment in their lives. Few of them would ever have come down from the Andes before or even seen the Pacific Ocean, which now sparkled in the distance. Their previous contact with a priest would have been both superficial and transient, when an unknown priest from some distant city would have appeared for a *fiesta* and departed as suddenly as he had come. Here for the first time they found a priest walking among them,

'Invasion' from the Andes

welcoming them and giving them their first experience of belonging in their new and alien environment.

Michael also sounded an ominous note in his letter when he wrote: 'It is a sobering thought to think that there are seven million more Indians up there looking towards the coast. Let's hope they don't all decide to come down at once.' The sudden arrival of the people from the Andes had already rendered obsolete the tidy plans for the Cork mission, which had been developed during the previous months. Projections of church and school requirements had suddenly become outdated. The mission funds and number of vocations were obviously limited by the resources at home. Now they would have to be spread a little thinner on the ground.

It was understandable that the Peruvians would in the twentieth century drift away from the Andes and head for the coast in search of a better life. In the middle of the century, there was a growing awareness that life on the coast offered an alternative to the primitive life of hardship that the mountains offered. Always challenged by the terrain that they farmed for a modest existence, remote from proper schooling and medical care, they came to know more about the coast through improved travel, the cinema and radio. Faced with the choice of living the primitive life of their ancestors or reaping the benefits of the modern world for their children, they opted in their thousands for the latter and began a major migration in the 1950s.

The movement of people from the mountains to the coast was not like the Irish emigration to England or the United States, which involved young, single adults, instead it meant the movement of whole extended families, including aged grannies as well as newly born children. Such migrations always cause hardship, both emotional and physical, even when the destination enjoys employment opportunities and a reasonable standard of living. Coastal Peru offered neither. Impoverished by a stagnant economy the country lacked the infrastructure, such as sanitation and housing, for much of its settled population, let alone for penniless migrants.

The 'invasions' such as the 1966 one of La Esperanza were well planned beforehand in the mountains. The planning had to be done in the greatest secrecy and the chosen destination had to be occupied by surprise, as the civic authorities in the coastal cities would have resisted with force if they had adequate warning of hundreds of families coming to live on their doorstep. These cities, proud of their colonial elegance and fearful of any upset to their delicately balanced economies, did not welcome the construction of shantytowns around their productive irrigated market gardens. Hence the imperative of secrecy in the planning of the movement.

Based on knowledge of the Peruvian way of doing things, one can speculate about the initial planning of the invasions. Some native of a mountain village who had lived on the coast for some years would assume the role of organiser. Returning home he would sign up the families willing to travel and collect the truck fare from them in advance, furnishing a formally worded, written agreement as a receipt for their money. Preparations for the great move would then take place over a period of weeks: the few animals they possessed would be sold; their cabin doors made secure; the legal papers entitling them to ownership of their little patch of land in the mountains carefully stowed away by the women; provisions like rice and potatoes, guinea pigs and, perhaps, a goat were prepared for the journey and loaded onto the truck. Depending on the remoteness of the village in the Andes, the journey to the coast might take up to sixteen hours.

The piece of desert earmarked for the new settlement would already have been spied out. All would be set for a dawn 'invasion', as these migrations came to be known. The initial weeks of life on the coast would test to the limit the Peruvian quality of stoic endurance of hardship. As soon as the food supplies brought from the mountains and the derisory financial reserves put together were used up, hunger threatened. It was to invasions such as this that a gracious Cork Columban, Fr Michael Fitzgerald, brought visitors like Archdeacon Duggan and Bishop Lucey when they visited Lima. The impression made on both visitors was lasting and decisive: Duggan resolved to resign his Cork parish and go to Peru; Lucey decided to found a Cork mission to Peru. The migration from the Andes to the coast set off a debate among foreign missionaries as to the merits of working in the mountains or on the coast. Some felt that the most useful work was to deepen the faith in the hills, so that they would have something solid to take with them to the new environment on the coast; others held that the missionary could be of greater use on the coast where they would stand with the poor in their hour of crisis. The St James Society and Maryknoll for the most part opted for the mountains; the Columbans stayed for decades on the coast near Lima. When Cork decided to go it alone the coast was chosen as the mission location.

Correspondence

The years between 1965 and 1969 were the most decisive and formative years of the mission. The decisions that were taken in those years set out a pattern of development that was followed for the remaining thirty-five years in Peru and profoundly influenced the expansion to Ecuador. The main protagonists in those dramatic years were Cornelius Lucey, Bishop of Cork and Ross, and Michael Murphy, superior of the mission and Bishop Lucey's immediate successor as bishop. Because Michael Murphy's holidays in Ireland were rare and brief and the bishop's visits to Peru were equally rare, practically all discourse between the two men is well documented in the correspondence that flowed between Ireland and Peru during those four years. The fortnightly letters they exchanged both discussed possibilities and recorded decisions taken, and all of these decisions are extant in the almost two hundred letters that remain in the Cork diocesan archive.

This correspondence amounts to an indispensable treasure trove for future historians of the establishment of this unique Irish undertaking in the twentieth century. The lucky survival of the bishop's letters was not at all certain, on the one hand because of the conditions obtaining them regarding their destination, where the recipient moved house three times during those years and house moving is, perhaps, the greatest threat to the survival of archives, and on the other hand because of the fragile notepaper which the bishop used. Possibly in order to economise on postage stamps, the bishop eschewed the use of the more formal envelope and airmail notepaper in favour of what were known as 'air-letters'. These were made of green ultra-light tissue paper, gummed at the edges, which folded in on themselves to constitute an envelope, requiring because of its lightness the minimum of stamps, costing ten pence (or thirteen cent in euro). On this ephemeral stationery the bishop wrote in blue biro. Michael Murphy typed his replies on printed airmail notepaper, which he mailed in a traditional stamped envelope. Perhaps there was unconscious wisdom in the bishop's use of air letters, since any prospective thief along the hazardous journey from Redemption Road in Cork to the post office of Trujillo would know at a glance that they did not contain any enclosure such as cheques or bank notes. The bishop filled all available space on the air letters, which were written fluently, formally and always to the point. Michael Murphy's letters, on the other hand, gave the appearance of careful preparation. The absence of the use of correcting fluid showed that they were carefully typed from an existing corrected and polished draft. Men who shared accommodation with him in those years still recall the afternoons he could be seen pacing up and down the garden composing these letters reporting on the progress of the mission. Both the bishop and mission superior were men who came from the period when English composition was taught in secondary school with emphasis on clarity of language and accuracy of grammar. Sentences had to be complete and clear, while paragraphs were confined to one theme only. 'Buzz words' and current fashionable expressions that characterise so much of modern communication were invariably avoided. What was remarkable about the correspondence was its formality. The bishop was always addressed as 'My Lord' and Michael was addressed as 'My Dear Fr Murphy'. The few lapses in the bishop's formality are significant: each came after a personal encounter either in Peru during the bishop's visit, or in Ireland during the priest's visit home, when he became only 'My Dear Michael'.

The subject matter of the letters to and fro varied little. The bishop allowed himself a sentence or two of gossip, which might refer to clerical changes at home or the result of an All Ireland or Cork County hurling final, or during exceptional weather conditions one sentence might refer to that. Michael Murphy's letters from Peru rarely included gossip, being confined instead to matters strictly of a business nature. No mention was ever made of colleagues on the mission unless they were sick or making travel arrangements for a holiday at home. The correspondence discussed money, building and the logistics of personnel movements to and from Ireland.

In the 1960s Irish money was tied to sterling – the punt and the euro were still far in the future. This meant that any fluctuation in the value of sterling automatically affected Irish money. Right through the first and second years of the mission, the bishop mentioned the possibility of devaluation of sterling. Aware of the danger of devaluation of the funds he had raised at home he constantly urged rapid investment in buildings, which accounted to a great extent for the enormous building programme undertaken in those first years. Not until December of 1967 were his fears realised and the devaluation of sterling took place. It was a tribute to his financial astuteness that anticipating this event some weeks earlier he had procured quite a lot of US dollars and Swiss franks at the old rate and sent $30,000 on to the Lima bank.

The transfer of funds from Ireland to Trujillo was a constant challenge and occupied much of the correspondence. Money was transferred from the Munster and Leinster Bank on the South Mall in Cork to the Banco de Londres in Lima, Peru, and from there to the mission account, which was held in another bank in Trujillo. Invariably there was an unexpected delay in the arrival of the money in the bank in Trujillo. These delays caused Michael Murphy much grief in a country where there was no such thing as a bank overdraft and where builders and suppliers had to be paid immediately. In his letters home there are constant requests for funds, sometimes £10,000 or £15,000, accompanied by almost apologetic explanations of why the money was needed and needed so urgently. The replies were always reassuring that the more spent the better, as it indicated that the buildings were progressing. He was reminded not to spare on anything provided he got good value for money. Sometimes these reassurances arrived much faster by air letter than the actual money arrived into the account and were of little comfort to a superior with suppliers calling for payment. The bishop continuously emphasised the fact that money was no problem; plenty was coming in and reserves were strong.

While the bishop was always optimistic about funding, Michael Murphy seemed to be obsessed by gloom and foreboding that they were taking on too much expansion and too much expenditure. He frequently mentioned the increased price of cement and the frequent strikes that delayed its delivery, which resulted in further price increases. He wondered if state grants to Catholic schools would come through in time, if at all, and counselled caution on further expansion, wondering if the mission had gone too far too soon and too fast. These gloomy prognostications never seemed to be commented on in the letters of reply from the bishop, whose theme remained unchanged: spend, spend, spend.

Building was the second major theme of the trans-continental letters. The bishop's positive attitude concurred with his attitude towards spending and sometimes expressed a gentle impatience with the slow progress of starting up new builds. Having made his appeal for funds so effectively and productively at home, he felt that results were needed rapidly to show the many donors that their generosity was having an immediate effect on poverty in his newly adopted territory. Pictures of newly built churches were requested even before their completion. Michael Murphy's letters were perhaps more realistic, describing delays in getting final drawings from architects, getting approval from State authorities, legal delays in getting title to land purchased, all of which built up a picture of a man exasperated with his position between the local delays and the pressure from home to get on with the job.

In spite of the vast distance that separated the areas of the world for which he was spiritually responsible – Cork and Trujillo were 7,000 miles apart – Bishop Lucey was very conscious of keeping control over everything that was being undertaken in that far off land. Michael Murphy obviously acquiesced in this. He never undertook any building project without requesting formal permission to go ahead and this permission was given with brief formality in the recurrent letters. While this consultation was understandable in regard to the broad outlines of the building projects, the detailed involvement of the bishop in the plans was surprising. In the case of churches, convents and presbyteries, though not in school extensions, Bishop Lucey requested to see the architect's plans, studied them carefully and wrote back detailed commentaries on them. Regarding the positioning of the tabernacle in the church of El Buen Pastor in El Porvenir, he specified that the tabernacle be located eighteen inches higher than the altar table so that when you knelt in the body of the church you could see the tabernacle clearly. In the case of the presbytery in the same parish, he queried the location of the door leading from the kitchen into the dining area.

The overall impression given by the letters is that the bishop approved every detail before the buildings were put up. This belied the general assumption among the priests at home in Cork that the men in Peru could do what they liked, while those at home had to clear everything with the bishop. However, absence and distance gave Michael Murphy one advantage over the parish priests at home: his work could not be inspected as frequently. This advantage he utilised when building the presbyteries.

Coming from a background of elegant clerical living in Washington DC on the one hand, and spartan living in the Andes with the St James Society on the other, Michael had made up his mind that each bedroom should be en suite. He had no intention of condemning men who lived four to a house lining up for the bathroom in the mornings. However, he also knew that it was most unlikely that a mid-century Irish bishop would approve such plans for the missions. The plans for the presbytery were sent home showing a bedroom and study for each priest, but with the drawing of the bathroom omitted from each bedroom outline. With a hawk eye for detail, the bishop wrote back suggesting that the bedrooms were too large in proportion to the study. Michael replied that in a hot climate airy bedrooms were essential. This was perhaps the only occasion in four years of correspondence where his candour with the bishop had been somewhat deficient.

The planned visit by the bishop some months later was awaited with a certain modicum of trepidation, which proved to be justified when he saw the en suite arrangements and pouted more than attacked passing remarks that suggested 'washing was not an Irish thing'. In due course, during his visit he was, like so many tourists in the tropics, afflicted with a stomach upset, which confined him to his room for some days. After that there was no further opposition to the inclusion of in-apartment facilities!

Apart from this mild cultural clash between the 100 per cent Irish bishop and the semi-Americanised priest, there was never a suggestion that the presbyteries or convents should lack amenities. On the contrary, the bishop showed an extraordinary solicitude for all the personnel in Peru. He always insisted that they build well and roomily. He inquired if the priests were taking time off every week and taking leave periodically. He even hinted that going away was as important for the house-mates as it was for the man going away: 'They got a rest from each other.' Not for nothing had he been a professor of psychology!

Holidays in Ireland were also encouraged. Michael Murphy, who had lost his parents in childhood, did not have the same motivation for coming home to Ireland as the other men of his age group who normally had parents living. Often, the bishop encouraged him to come home for a holiday or at least take a break with the Columban or St James priests in Lima. While other Corkmen took time to visit Chile or Argentina, Michael dismissed such trips away from Peru as 'seeing more of the same'. The only recreation available in Trujillo was a weekly visit to the beach to 'puck around' a hurling ball. This must have amused any Peruvians who passed by, as they never visited the beach outside the three months of summer, the only period when the sun shone through the chilly fog.

Once the first priests were settled in, the bishop's main concern was focused on the nuns who arrived in dribs and drabs over a period of two years. Their accommodation and distribution among the parishes occupied much of the correspondence between the bishop and Michael Murphy.

Coming up to Christmas 1967, a most important decision was made in regard to the amount of time one could remain on the mission. According to the regulations laid down, both Michael

Murphy and Michael Crowley, who had already served some years with the Boston missionaries, would have the maximum number of years served and should return the following March. Already, however, they had received an extension until September of 1968. Bishop Lucey was already writing that he would probably visit Peru at Easter time to make arrangements about the appointment of the next superior. Assuming that Michael Murphy's tenure of office was about to come to an end within months, he uncharacteristically permitted himself a sentence or two of praise for the work achieved: 'What you have done in the two and a half years is beyond my wildest expectations. I would not have thought we would have got as far in ten years.' Writing in reply, Michael mentioned the possibility of remaining for another full year from the coming March, quoting in full a resolution drafted at a meeting of the priests: 'In view of the pastoral position here at the moment we appreciate your willingness to extend the stay of Michael Murphy and Michael Crowley until September. However, we would be grateful if a further extension could be given them provided this would be in conformity with your plans and regulations.' He added that he would be willing to stay another year.

Bishop Lucey replied: 'The extension does not accord with my plans and regulations. But in view of the wishes of the men I am prepared to go against the rules and grant it. So you can stay until March 1969.' He added that he would not now go on a visit until the spring of that year. In subsequent letters he encouraged Michael Murphy to take a holiday in Ireland in the coming year, even if for a short time, pointing out that there was an inexpensive three-week trans-Atlantic fare that might appeal to him. In fact, this excursion fare was availed of in March 1968, leaving him one complete year to finish up his work in Peru.

The decision to remain on for that extra year had in the event long-lasting repercussions. Had he returned home in March of 1968 he would not have been appointed to Farranferris, as there was then no vacancy at the time. Instead, he would have re-entered the home diocese as a curate and have little hope of ever becoming bishop. As things turned out, a vacancy had arisen in 1969 which he filled, and the position of president of the diocesan seminary set him on the road that led to his appointment as coadjutor bishop a mere five years later.

The last year in Peru was not without its particular problems for Michael Murphy. At home in Ireland his brother's wife was dying of cancer and about to leave a family of boys still in their teens. In the event, the two boys, in spite of the loss of their mother, applied themselves to their studies and qualified, one as a medical doctor and the other as a dentist, the doctor eventually achieving high office in his profession as president of University College, Cork.

There were also health problems with the men on the mission. One of the priests, Sean O'Leary of the Diocese of Kerry, was in hospital in Ireland and close to death with a bleeding ulcer, which he developed in Peru. Denis O'Donoghue was threatened with a heart attack and yet refused to return home. It was not until later in the winter when his mother was dying that he agreed to go and subsequently accepted a curacy in Ss. Peter and Paul's church in Cork city centre.

Then a dramatic family tragedy afflicted a housemate of Michael: Fr Charlie Nyhan. Charlie was a newly ordained priest who had studied in Rome and Spain and had joined the mission the same summer. In March of 1968 an aeroplane crashed off the Tusker Rock in the south east of Ireland, with the loss of all passengers. Charlie's brother was among the casualties. His body was never recovered. It is an indication of the primitive state of communications in those days that most of a week had passed before word of the tragedy reached Trujillo. Were such a family bereavement to occur these days a flight home would immediately be arranged. In fact, Charlie did not visit home until his holidays the following December.

Even though still in the midst of an ongoing building programme, Michael Murphy could look during that final year on his many achievements: the completion of two churches, three convents, three presbyteries with parish offices, four clinics and new schools and school extensions too numerous to mention. Three more churches were in the process of construction. This achievement would be immense in the developed world; in third world conditions it was quite extraordinary. Side by side with all that building, he had built, in another sense, good relations with the wider community in the city of Trujillo. With an eye for good public relations he had always kept in touch with the civic authorities in the city. The mayor and the leading political figures were always invited to the inauguration of the new churches. Even the leading representative of the founding colonial families, the Orbegosos, with a lineage of four centuries, was always invited and attended. Such diplomatic gestures ensured that the Irish priests gained the respect of the city's long-established ascendency classes, as well as the affection of the poorest of the poor in the *barrios*. No longer was the missionary organisation seen as a fly-by-night phenomenon, but rather as a serious force dedicated with complete unselfishness to the betterment of the poorest community in the city. It was no surprise that in his last few months Michael Murphy was given a civic reception by the mayor and city council and was presented with an address of gratitude to be sent on to the Bishop of Cork and Ross.

Even though the mission was established a mere three years, visitors were already coming from Ireland to admire the work being done. Cardinal Conway visited and found to his amazement that the small mission station that he expected was in fact a complex of three parishes, providing full parochial and social services for over 100,000 people. A former Lord Mayor of Cork, Gus Healy, also visited and gave an enthusiastic interview to the *Cork Examiner* newspaper on his return.

In March 1969, the bishop came on visitation to make arrangements for a new superior to be appointed to replace Michael Murphy. He stayed in the presbytery in Florencia and visited the other convents and houses in turn. Returning with Michael from one such late evening visit, he asked him (Michael) to stop the car so that they could take some air. They were just outside the house in Florencia on the banks of the Mochica canal, its almost stagnant muddy water reflecting the Easter moon then waxing in the southern sky, when the following historic exchange took place:

Correspondence

Bishop: 'I have been thinking of what you will do when you go back home. I will make you president of Farranferris.'

Michael: 'But I will have to do the Higher Diploma in Education if I am to be recognised as a paid teacher.'

Bishop: 'Yes, you will. I will have you enrolled when I go home.'

Michael: 'If I fail the Dip. I will be ruined.'

Bishop (with a smile): 'We'll all be ruined.'

They stepped inside the house to join the others. The conversation had changed Michael's life forever, as well as the history of the Diocese of Cork and Ross.

Michael Murphy, Defender of the Poor

The relationship between Bishop Lucey and Michael Murphy had been creative in the sense that it produced something new for two Catholic communities: one in Ireland and the other in Peru. Michael later described it as a business-like relationship in which he felt free to differ from the bishop and tell him that he did not always agree with him. While there is no evidence in their correspondence that they argued about anything, some differences of attitude do appear in the letters. The bishop constantly urged expansion at a rapid rate; the superior of the mission always expressed caution in the fear that such speed might leave them over-exposed to financial embarrassment or a shortage of personnel. While the bishop frequently stated that his priests in Peru were the men on site and therefore in the best position to make decisions, in the same breath he would look for details of what was being done and look for the plans of buildings, information that was immediately forthcoming in the fortnightly exchange of letters.

The almost frenzied construction programme, always motivated more by the needs of the poor people in the *barrios* of Trujillo than by the need to make a good impression on the laity at home who were funding everything, revealed a deep-rooted sympathy with the poor, the oppressed and the underdog. Whenever the argument was put to Michael Murphy that the main function of a mission was the preaching of the Word of God and the administering of the sacraments, to the exclusion of any kind of social work, such as building schools and clinics, convents and churches, he was quite clear in his mind and expressed his opinion with passion – that you cannot preach the Word of God to starving people, to uneducated people, to oppressed people, without doing something to better their situation. For him, the whole field of education and preventive medicine was nothing more or less than the continuation of the daily work of Jesus during his three years of ministry of teaching and healing. While some would deny that the attitudes of most adults are the unconscious product of experiences in childhood, Michael made no secret of the fact that he had learned the importance of liberty from the deprivations of his own childhood. Reflecting on those traumatic years, he had developed the view that God always brought forth good out of evil and misfortune. As he put it, he was never angry with God in spite of the heavy hand that was laid upon him personally as a child. On the contrary, his faith assured him that God can bring good out of any misfortune that might befall human beings.

Michael Murphy had been born into a comfortable farming family in Ireland, but, unfortunately, his father had just died before his birth. Then when he was just seven years old his mother took ill. He remembered clearly the telegram boy arriving on a bicycle with the sad news that she had died and remembered being at Mass when the priest called out her name and asked for prayers for the repose of her soul. It was decided by relatives that the children would be divided out among them and not sent to orphanages, that the farm would be rented to provide for their upkeep and that all the contents of the home would be sold. Among the bitterest memories of childhood was the day the auctioneer arrived to conduct the sale. Everything was put up for auction: the pony and trap, the furniture, even the knives and forks were tied with string, numbered and laid out on the table for sale. In the evening his uncle came from the town in a car to take him away. Though his relatives were good to him he always felt there was no substitute for a normal home. The brutal scars left on his psyche by the sudden collapse of his childhood world remained with him all his life and gave him a sympathy for those who suffer, which, perhaps, could never be appreciated by those who had had a normal upbringing.

As a school principal, and later as a bishop, Michael Murphy was remembered for his spirit of tolerance of human weakness and of the shortcomings of others, but he was very short of tolerance for injustice and oppression. Within months of his ordination to the priesthood he came face to face with social injustice and the denial of civil rights to the black community in Washington DC, where he began his work as a priest in the autumn of 1949, well before the civil rights movement had begun in the United States. When he arrived for his first weekend in his first parish, his pastor advised him to take things easy for a start, told him not to preach on the first Sunday and limit his sermon to a few words of introduction and the reading of the weekly announcements. When he looked over the Mass notices, he was flabbergasted by what he read: 'Next Sunday will be the Communion day for the Negro Children of Mary; Wednesday is the day for the monthly meeting of the White Sodality.' It was a mixed parish of black and white people. During the Mass when he looked down at the congregation he saw that all the white people were at the front and the black people at the back. His reaction was one of anger and he discussed the situation with white parishioners, as he could not see how Christianity could be reconciled with such segregation. Naturally they gently pointed out that this was his first day in town, that the parish lay on the Mason-Dixon Line where the Ku Klux Klan were still active, and that if they integrated the parish the church would be burned down and then they would have nowhere to say Mass. The horror of poverty in America, which he naively thought of as a land of full and plenty, was brought home to him when he visited the homes of the black community. They lived in shacks in the woods, made of weather-beaten timber and rusty, tin roofs. Over forty years later, speaking on an hour-long interview on a radio programme, he still showed emotion recalling how a white mother called her children in from the street where they were playing with black children.

In setting up the mission in Trujillo, Michael Murphy always put the needs of the poorest and most deprived as a priority. Next in order of importance he placed the Irish priests and nuns whose health and safety influenced all his decisions, from the standard of food to the psychological needs of people living far from home. On his return to Ireland to a teaching position, he probably believed that a page had been turned on the missionary epoch of his life. Little did he know that just a decade later he would be in full charge of the mission as Bishop of Cork and Ross, and that the mission he had helped to found and build up in its formative years would rely on his judgement in its hour of greatest peril, when many of the priests and nuns had their names on a list of those to be murdered by the communist guerrillas. In that dangerous moment his calm judgement and diplomatic approach ensured that no lives were lost.

Building in an Earthquake Zone

In setting up the Cork and Ross mission the founding fathers got to work in a methodical way driven by a sense of urgency flowing from the realisation that, in the case of those who had already served with the St James Society, their period on the mission would not exceed four years. Whatever contribution they had to make would have to be completed within that timeframe. The building programme of the first two years speaks eloquently of both their personal commitment to hard work and the financial support forthcoming from the people of Cork.

The initial building programme saw the completion of two presbyteries, four schools, or school extensions, two parish offices, one medical centre and one church. In the three years that followed, up to the end of 1970, five churches were built, another presbytery and parish office, eight school extensions, three medical centres and three convents. In all, over thirty building projects were completed in the first five years of the mission's existence.

The buildings were constructed of what was known in Spanish as 'noble material': fired brick and reinforced concrete, as opposed to 'adobe' or sundried mud brick. This standard of quality was dictated by the ever-present threat of earthquake in that part of the world. While no one can predict the time an earthquake will strike, everyone knows for certain that an earthquake will, sooner or later, test the quality of the materials and workmanship employed in every structure, be it a building, bridge or road.

In Peru, the dwellings of the poor are always at the greatest risk from natural disasters because of the inferior materials used in their building. These dwelling houses are built of adobe brick without the reinforced concrete columns at the four corners necessary to hold a shaking building together. Such walls collapse immediately when shaken by an earthquake of even moderate severity. When the walls collapse, the large roof beams of rough-hewn eucalyptus baulks fall on the residents, crushing them at once or trapping them in a cloud of dust and debris. It is significant that the first thing that a family will invest in if they manage to get some money together is the strengthening of their house with concrete columns and lintels capable of protecting them from the sudden collapse of the roof. However, for the majority of families in the *barrios* such enhancement of the house remained a dream, even after twenty years.

While the collapse of a family home did not always involve loss of life – residents usually made it onto the street at the first tremor or the underground rumble of the earthquake – the collapse of a public building such as a church or school crowded with people was usually catastrophic, hence the necessity of constructing public buildings to a high standard.

In 1970, just five years after construction began, the mission buildings were tested to the limit by an earthquake that shook Peru, the epicentre being a mere fifty miles from the mission, with an intensity measuring 7.8 on the Mercalli scale. Measured in loss of life, the Peru earthquake of 31 May 1970 ranks as one of the greatest disasters in human history, accounting for 70,000 deaths (compared with 600 in the great San Francisco earthquake of 1906). It was the most catastrophic quake in the western hemisphere in recorded history.

What pushed the casualties to such phenomenal numbers was what happened at the highest point in the Peruvian Andes. Along the topmost ridge of these great mountains stands the snow-covered Huascarán at 22,205 feet. At the peak's feet on a level plain lay Youngay, a town of 25,000 people. That Sunday afternoon the quake reduced the town to ruins, but the damage was not complete until a further disaster followed within a few minutes, when the movement of the ground caused a great chunk of the glacier to break off the top of the mountain, bringing with it a mix of mud and giant boulders estimated at two billion cubic feet of rock and ice, tumbling at a velocity of three hundred miles per hour. In its path lay the collapsed city with its survivors lost in the murky dust of broken bricks. In an instant the town was covered forever by the great blob of muck, which came to rest on the valley floor where the town once stood. One man who survived told his story fifteen years later to a newspaper:

> When the earthquake began my wife was in my house, so I went out of the shop and ran in that direction. While I was running, people were on their knees, crying and saying that it was the end of the world. I reached my house and found my wife inside, knocking at the door, which had jammed. I began to push and just as the door gave, I saw a part of the Huascarán break off. We began to run but not very quickly because the debris of the quake blocked our way. Suddenly we saw the mud that was coming, making a terrible noise, covering everything and throwing rocks in all directions. It seemed like a huge black cloud. We went on a few steps and then the mud swept us. When I opened my eyes I was buried up to the waist. The mud had swept me along about eighty metres. I pulled myself out of it and someone gave me a poncho because the mud had left me naked. I never saw my wife again.

On a hillside beyond the town some children were attending a circus. The mud settled before it reached the hill. Helplessly, they wailed for their parents who never came. Crying in the cold on the hillside these mountain children, disorientated and terrified, experienced further horror when the army helicopters – machines they had never seen in their lives – thrashed in the air above their heads with swirling propellers, engines roaring, search lights raking the ground like the eyes of flying monsters.

Today, only the ruined cupola of Youngay's church and the tops of four palm trees mark the place where the town once stood, now doomed to remain forever a *campo santo* or cemetery, the Huascarán towering serenely above, the dark cleft in its summit not yet covered with glacial ice.

The mission building programme was, of necessity, at its most intensive during the first years after the arrival of the Cork priests in Trujillo. They probably thought at the time that it would tail off once the presbyteries, convents, churches and schools were in place, leaving the priests and nuns free to concentrate on pastoral work. Such was not to be. As the 'invasions' from the mountains continued and the natural growth of the established communities demanded more housing for new families, acres of sand were populated with new communities in need of healthcare, education and religious services. Consequently, the building programme continued throughout the whole history of the mission in Peru and Ecuador.

Michael Murphy had seen during his years in the mountains with the St James Society the dangers to health for men from the developed world living in less developed communities, where clean water, mosquitoes and the unhygienic handling of food threatened the health, if not the very lives of missionaries. Fresh from that experience, he had an obsession with standards of hygiene that profoundly influenced his planning of presbyteries and convents. He always insisted on the highest standards in the preparation of food, the storage of water and the exclusion of flies and mosquitoes by fitting all doors and windows with insect-proof screens.

He rejected the theory that missionaries should live under the same conditions as the native people on the logical grounds that foreigners lacked the degree of immunity to disease that life-long exposure to inferior conditions had given the native-born. For the foreigner, lacking such immunity meant even one unlucky exposure to contamination could result in the contraction of hepatitis, malaria or typhoid, leading to the loss of mission personnel through illness, disability or even death. The wisdom of building houses and convents to the highest standards was borne by the results: no Irish priest or nun ever died on the Cork and Ross mission.

It is difficult to measure the success or failure of a mission, as the passage of time and the mortality of those who were touched by its work tend to erase its memory from the collective psyche of a community. Even the greatest cultures and civilisations pass away with time, their sole legacy often being only the ruins of their buildings. People, cultures, even languages disappear; only stone, bricks and mortar remain. The Cork and Ross mission will not be remembered for any particular architectural style because its buildings varied according to the taste of the missionaries on site at the time of construction. Personnel changed every six years. Consequently, some churches were built in the modern style of the 1960s; others were strictly functional constructions incorporating two stories of meeting rooms, function rooms and chapel. A few were replicas of the traditional Spanish colonial churches, without the excesses of rococo ornamentation. A case study of one of these, El Milagro, might illustrate the story of the whole building programme, since it exemplifies the basic methods of construction, the manner in which projects were managed, the materials used and the personal involvement of the priests, all of which were more or less similar over the life of the mission. For the most part, the priests on site were given the freedom to choose designs, the only regulation insisted upon by the bishop at home in Ireland being the rule that the superior of the mission visit the building site every day to ensure that the architect's design was being followed exactly, and that proper materials were delivered and were not being stolen.

Most of the churches were built on sand. Readers of the New Testament might raise an eyebrow at this information and wonder at the durability of any structure so sited. However, when one took into account the amount of steel used to reinforce the columns and roof, fears for its stability disappeared. Furthermore, before laying the foundations steps were taken to pack the sand in a dense mass by soaking it with water drawn by tankers and allowing the wet sand to compress before digging out the holes and trenches, into which the concrete footings and foundations would be poured. This was not necessary in El Milagro because the terrain there was stony rather than pure sand.

In those days, El Milagro was a godforsaken settlement, located about a mile outside the boundaries of La Esperanza where the mission was already established. It grew up at either side of the Pan-American Highway and then extended downwards into the endless desert that stretched some miles to the Pacific Ocean. Here, no plant grew; no animal lived; only vultures floated in the misty air. Someone, perhaps an engineer or a politician, had marked out a huge square, which some day in the future might become the town's central square or plaza. On a side street off this plaza the mission had built a simple Mass house/meeting room with no more than an asbestos roof, cement floor and plain windows. The area had neither electric power nor piped water. Each day a tanker called with water for sale for the use of the householders. A large county prison was planned for the place and Trujillo's licensed brothel operated about half a mile away. Life in El Milagro was more miserable than in any other shantytown in the environs of the city.

One Sunday morning after Mass in the little chapel, a delegation from the village's local council met the priest and accompanied him to the stony space designated for the plaza, where they offered a site for a church on the western perimeter. The month was July, mid-winter in the southern hemisphere, and a cold, damp, salty wind blew across the bleak sands from the sea. The men of the delegation were dressed not in their 'Sunday best', but in the only clothes they possessed: worn shirt, baggy trousers and patched sandals over bare feet.

There was much formal greeting with introductions and handshakes. The priest assured them that a church would be built on the site to the design of a 'cathedral'. Pessimistically they shook their heads like men who had often heard promises from politicians that had never been kept. All they hoped for, they said, was a simple chapel. In due course the legalities were completed for the acquisition of the site. All that remained to be done was get the approval of Bishop Murphy during his forthcoming Christmas visit.

During his visit, the bishop was taken to El Milagro to inspect the village and the newly acquired site for the church, and to talk to the residents who were already involved in the mission's prayer groups and catechetical programmes, all of whom spoke longingly of the day when there would be a proper church for their deprived community. The bishop was a shrewd judge of some of his missionaries' impetuosity and overzealousness in seeking funding for their own favourite sectors. On this occasion he heard everyone out, but gave no immediate approval for the project. After shaking hands all around and getting into the pick-up truck again, he was driven a mile or two northwards along the Pan-American Highway to the point where a newly made tarmac road joined the country's main highway. This new road was a bypass of the city of Trujillo. El Milagro lay in the triangular area where the two highways joined. The bishop, from his long experience of South America, knew that huge development was inevitable in such a well-serviced location. The go-ahead was given – El Milagro was to have its church built to a neo-colonial design. It would be the only church the mission built on an urban plaza.

In the early years of the mission, the building of churches was given to a contractor. By the time El Milagro came to be built the priests had enough experience of construction and of the unreliability of contractors, who delayed or even failed to complete the jobs, to organise the project themselves. The priest in charge engaged an architect, an engineer and a foreman and, working with them, delivered the project on time and at less cost. The architect chosen for this particular undertaking was a lady of Japanese extraction, Nelly Amemiya Hoshi, and an engineer with a native Peruvian name, Juan Juamanchumo.

The site was marked out and the foundations for the principal supporting columns were dug by hand, the labourers working like gravediggers, chest deep with pick and shovel. Meanwhile, others worked on the reinforcing steel rods, making them up to their ultimate shape, twisting the wire by hand and snipping it with pincers. The steel frames they assembled were stood into the deep foundations, tied to an embedded steel frame and then the hand-mixed concrete was poured into the foundations from recycled tin boxes that previously held cooking oil. No machine was used on site. Everything was done by hand: the fabrication of the timber shuttering for the columns, the mixing and pouring of the concrete, the heavy lifting.

Building in an Earthquake Zone

The huge pitched roof of reinforced concrete was also all done by hand with the most primitive equipment. Working with a transparent hosepipe filled with water to mark out levels, the unlettered workmen produced a building with levels, verticals and roof angles of an exactitude comparable to anything achieved with present day theodolites and infrared levelling equipment. The steel of the roof beams was securely fastened to the rods protruding from the tops of the columns. The massive timber shuttering for the concrete roof was propped with rough-hewn eucalyptus poles at intervals of one metre, so that during construction the interior of the church resembled a forest of bare trees. Viewed from above the shuttering, the cavity into which the concrete would be poured looked like a cat's cradle of steel wire and honeycombed terracotta bricks. The whole steel frame of the church from the roof to the foundations was designed to hold the church together, so that it could ride out the seismic waves of an earthquake like a steel-hulled ship riding out a storm at sea.

When all of this was meticulously prepared and checked by the engineer, final arrangements were made for the great day of pouring the roof. A team of specialists was employed for the day: blockey men, small of stature, hard as nails. It was said that they all came from the same place high up in the Andes. Crates of beer had to be on hand to maintain their energy during the operation. All were dressed alike in football shorts, singlets and sandals. They wore paper hats, which kept the dust from their hair and absorbed the perspiration. Each carried a five-gallon square tin box with the top cut out, which had begun life as a cooking oil container. Tipper lorries had delivered sand and gravel, which was piled around the two ancient cement mixers towed to the site for the day. A tanker of water stood by. A timber gangway sloped up one side of the building to the roof and descended from the opposite side.

At first light of dawn the operation began. Teams of men shovelled sand, gravel and cement into the mixers. While one machine was mixing the concrete, the other poured out its prepared contents into the tin cans of the waiting roofers. As each can was filled and hoisted up on the shoulder of one man, the next man was ready with his can for filling. The men trotted up one gangway, the box of concrete on their shoulders, tipped its contents onto the roof, trotted down the other gangway and refilled. Like ants swarming in single file up and down the gangways, these men kept pace with the mixers without a halt. Only men reared in the rarefied air of high altitude, accustomed to climbing steep peaks carrying the produce of their agriculture in huge sacks, could produce the energy to accomplish the task they were set without complaint or collapse. Far from complaining, they kept up their spirits by shouting encouragement and banter as though they were high on something. By afternoon the whole roof was poured in one piece, the mixers were towed away and the team of roofers went home to rest before another day would find them on some other roof in some other town.

Once the roof was poured, the ordinary workers returned to continue their work without the help of any machinery whatsoever. All the delicate finishing of the exterior of the neo-colonial church with its mouldings, cupolas, crosses and recesses for statues remained to be completed. The twin cupolas called for perfect workmanship, as they would be the most prominent and obvious feature of the whole building. The proportions had already been perfected on paper by the architect; it only remained for the foreman to reproduce those drawings in brick and plaster.

On the church's cement floor, which was not yet tiled, the foreman drew out with compass line and chalk the cupola to full size, fitting a piece of wire over the curve to form a template for the final finish of the cupola. He supervised the building of an internal dome with adobe bricks, which would act as a support for the real reinforced concrete structure until it had set and then could be removed to reveal the interior hollow of the dome. Over this temporary dome he fitted the wire mesh reinforcing, covered it with cement and, swinging the wire template from an axis on the top of the dome, got a perfectly smooth finish that matched the architect's drawing perfectly. This final effect was achieved by shaving off the surplus in places and buttering on more plaster where the finish was slack.

Once the twin cupolas were firmly set, two domed pinnacles were constructed on top of each cupola and the beautiful topping-off was

Building in an Earthquake Zone

completed. The final touch to the facade was the finishing off of the mouldings. Already bricks were left overhanging the wall as a basis for the mouldings. Again, a template corresponding to the architect's drawing was made from scrap tin cut to shape and nailed to a timber frame, which was dragged along the fresh cement moulding, shaving here, buttering there, until a perfectly shaped dado or ogee moulding ran the length of the wall or swung over the windows and doorways in perfect geometric proportions and distances.

On the day of the official opening of the gleaming white building, no one could guess that apart from the motorised cement mixers used for the roof concrete, no other machine was used: the whole creation was handmade. Today the Irish priests are gone, but the gleaming white church of El Milagro still presides over a gracious plaza, now built up with commercial buildings.

Baptism: Revered but Postponed

In each parish in the mission Baptisms took place every week, normally on a Saturday afternoon, the numbers of children varying from five to ten, with a special surge around the great feast days and the national holiday on 27 July, celebrating the liberation of the country from Spanish rule. 'Doing the Baptisms', as the priests described the duty, might seem a simple enough procedure, but then, in Peru, nothing was really straightforward – everything brought with it its own complicated bureaucracy.

The bishops of Peru insisted, as indeed did all the South American bishops, on a course of preparation of parents and godparents before the celebration of the sacrament. A fixed number of 'talks', usually three, were given to the main participants over a period of two or three weeks, outlining the essentials of the Catholic faith and the new religious obligations of parenthood and godparenthood, the latter office carrying obligations of a familial nature quite unknown in Ireland. To ensure that this regulation was complied with, a bureaucratic procedure was followed. First, the mother came to the parish office to sign the child up for Baptism, where she received a card bearing the names of the parents and godparents, which had to be date stamped opposite to each name after each of the 'talks' and, thus completed, presented on the day of the Baptism as proof that each person had attended. Otherwise, Baptism would be refused. Therefore, in theory, the pre-Baptismal programme was simple in the extreme: four people would attend the talks on matters of faith. Central Catholic offices in Lima circulated simple catechetical programmes suitable for use in these talks, covering those areas of dogmatic and moral theology that were appropriate to the occasion, together with some practical hints on passing on the faith to growing children.

The first crack in this admirable structure appeared, usually on the opening night of the talks, when it became apparent that the father of the child would not be attending due to work commitments ('He works far away in the jungle') or because he had deserted the family ('He has another *compromiso*', meaning that he lives with another woman). At other times the father had *enganared* the mother, meaning he had tricked her – he had fathered the child on a promise of marriage, which the mother believed, but the father had no intention of fulfilling. So, after lengthy explanations of one of the above unfortunate situations, or even of all three, it became clear to the priest that the most he could hope for was an attendance of three people: the mother and the two godparents.

The next absentee was usually the godfather. In Latin America, the godfather holds a particularly privileged, honoured and responsible position in the life of his godchild and of the whole family, which he has joined because of his newly acquired spiritual relationship. The godfather, called the *padrino*, is usually selected from a higher social class in the hope that he would be in a position to help the child materially in the years to come, even to the extent of adopting the child in the event of the death of the parents. The godparent system was brought by the conquistadors from mediaeval Europe and still survives in Latin America, even though it now plays a much-diminished role in modern Europe. The search for a suitable *padrino* is often a protracted affair, especially in the case of the poor in the *barrios*, who had little if any connections with the wealthier population. Due to this, the Baptism could be deferred indefinitely until, perhaps, the child was almost of school-going age when an official document such as a Baptismal certificate would come in useful. The long delay in having the child baptised did not worry the parents at all, because it was possible that the child had already received an emergency Baptism at birth. Indeed, the practice of a form of emergency Baptism appeared to have been widespread in the mountains, where priests only visited once a year and child mortality was so high. Priests often heard mention of the *'agua de socorro'* or 'water of help', which was poured on newly born children. No one was sure if this was a valid infant Baptism or not, as the descriptions of the ceremony were so vague. In fact, a native-born Peruvian archbishop once said at a clergy conference that he had never heard of it until he left Lima to take up the position of archbishop in the provinces.

Eventually a *padrino* would be found through complicated connections of employment or domestic service or some blood relationship impenetrable to foreigners. His higher social status would be indicated by the wearing of a tailored suit and arrival at the church in a taxi, inevitably half an hour late. He would be introduced to the priest as 'Doctor', a title given to lawyers as well as medics, even though he might be no more than some form of legal clerk or city official. The title 'Doctor' would also come in useful when the family might not be too sure of his name – on many occasions the formal introduction would run like so: 'Reverend Parish Priest, permit me to present to you my *compadre* and great friend ah … ah … what's-his-name.' It was, of course, assumed by all that the *padrino*, because of his position in society, his learning and 'profound catholicity' had no need of the talks on the faith, which in any case, because of his extensive civic duties, he would be unable to attend, while his good wife, who would normally act as godmother, known for her charitable work as a confraternity member, would obviously be excused as well. So, after all that, the only person left to attend the talks was the mother.

So the mother would come along for the talks carrying on her back her youngest child, who would not necessarily be the child that was to be baptised, and take her place among the twenty or so others who had come for the same reason. She would gaze impassively at the Irish priest, perhaps understanding the words he spoke in his strange accent, but definitely not comprehending the ideas he expounded while she nursed her child noisily. Quite often both mother and child slept quietly throughout. The few men present gazed at the ground, stoically, acceptingly nodding heads, perhaps in agreement or in fighting off sleep. When Peruvians set their hearts on getting something they tolerate every obstacle placed in their way with grim passivity. Eventually the priest concluded, the cards were date stamped and everyone shook hands and trudged off into the night.

On the Saturday afternoon the priest crossed to the church to begin arrangements for the Baptismal ceremony. The building usually resembled a children's playground more than a church, with children of all ages running over benches, shouting happily to one another or wailing loudly when they fell over a kneeler and ran to their mother for comforting kisses and hugs. The candidates for Baptism varied in age from one year to five, and in dress style according to the wealth of the *padrino*. Little boys of five were dressed in newly tailored white suits with matching shirt and tie – the long wait for a wealthy *padrino* showed – and tiny girls were dressed in white like little dolls.

The problem for the priest was to assemble each family party of parents, godparents and child in one place. This was an almost impossible undertaking as half the party would not have arrived on time at all, while the child would have gone missing, playing somewhere in the area of the church grounds. The photographer played a very active part in the whole proceedings, taking shots of the different ceremonies as well as family groups. Posing for the pictures, neither men nor women ever smiled for the camera, yet they ordered many prints. Central to every group was the *criatura*, the newly baptised child.

When all was over, no one left without shaking hands with the priest and bidding him goodbye before heading homewards for the party, which would also be financed by the *padrino*. As each family group left the church, they were harried by children calling for the boon, their insistence rewarded by a fistful of almost valueless coins thrown to them on the sandy street to be fought over with enthusiasm.

My College and My Professor

Wherever in the world you find a Catholic church you are highly likely to see a school nearby. Far from being a modern phenomenon, this close linkage between religion and education goes back to the first European universities, to the mediaeval monasteries and to the earliest residences of clergy.

When Jesus commanded his Apostles to teach all nations, he neither set a limit to the number of nations to be taught, nor to the subjects in which they should be instructed. Not even the bitterest critics of the Catholic Church could ever suggest that instruction in Catholic schools was limited to religious knowledge alone: the widest range of subjects possible was always provided. The Cork and Ross mission to Peru enthusiastically embraced the immemorial Catholic tradition of founding and administering centres of education. As Irish men and women who were themselves the product of Catholic education, they realised that the only sure exit from poverty was through the doors opened by a proper comprehensive education.

When the Mission was founded in 1965, one small school already existed under the guidance of the Mallorcan missionary, Fr Jaime Pons. This was immediately expanded while two new schools were built from scratch.

While Peru did have a system of free primary education, the delivery of this service everywhere was hampered by the extent of the country, its geographical complications and the sudden movement of whole sectors of population from the mountains to the coast. Even where the State succeeded in building a school, it

My College and My Professor

lacked the funds to equip it and pay a sufficient number of teachers. It was a familiar sight to see a little girl carrying her own homemade stool to school each morning so that she would not have to sit on the floor all day. The State did provide one great service that enabled the mission to run its own schools: it paid the teachers' salaries once the school had satisfied the required standard of qualification in its staff. With the pay taken care of, the mission could invest confidently in the building, furnishing, equipment and maintenance of the schools.

The first schools began as a few classrooms built on a site provided by the State. Then, as the enrolment grew, more classrooms were built, sometimes reaching as many as twelve in all. In Peru, all school children wore identical uniforms to a design laid down by the Department of Education: white shirt or blouse, navy pants or skirt and black shoes. Each child took enormous pride in their school – 'My college and my professor', as they put it with a certain pride of ownership. In an otherwise drab existence lived in an adobe house on a sandy street, school became an uplifting experience. Great care was taken of the uniform: each evening the white top was washed and hung out to dry and worn again the next day, gleaming white; rips and tears were swiftly repaired and the shoes were removed immediately on returning home.

Some parishes helped out in the provision of uniforms by purchasing the materials in bulk and selling the dress and suit lengths on to the parents as required. With inflation running at huge percentages per annum, selling the material at cost price amounted to making a gift to the parents. Such help programmes were not limited to the pupils of parochial schools only, but extended to all children who wished to avail of the service. The State schools were also linked closely with the mission. Priests and nuns were always welcome to speak to the children in class, while all schools liaised with the parishes on the occasion of First Holy Communion. For that great traditional event food for a party was provided by the mission, which the teachers then prepared and served in the schools. Dressing the girls in white was an unbreakable Peruvian tradition, regardless of the poverty of the community.

The teachers in the mission schools became the loyal friends of the priests and nuns. These women came from the educated middle class, married to bank clerks, lawyers, politicians or other more well-off professionals. They lived in the elegant suburbs of the city, distant in every respect from the *barrios* where they worked. With their education and social contacts they could easily have left the mission schools to work in more elegant surroundings with more well-off children, but they chose to dedicate their professional lives to the mission's commitment to the poor and the marginalised. For them their profession was elevated to the level of a vocation.

The teachers treated the children with love and respect and, even fifty years ago, never used any form of corporal punishment. For the children, the teacher who they referred to as *'mi profesora'* was close to a surrogate mother. The parents were also treated with the greatest respect and became involved in the life of the school at every level.

The Irish priests and nuns found in the teachers invaluable associates in the work of the mission, helping in the drafting of official letters, ensuring that the standard of Spanish language used would impress whatever government official or legal representative it was for – something practically impossible for people writing in a foreign language. Their social contacts in the city were equally useful in speeding requests through the official channels in a country where bureaucracy was endemic. In return, the mission staff placed great confidence in the teachers and frequently socialised with them, especially during visits by Bishop Murphy who, of course, had been a former colleague of many of the more senior staff.

The mission never entered the field of secondary education. Instead, youth groups and Confirmation classes were organised to maintain contact with young people already known from primary school. Later in the life of the mission, family catechesis was developed, especially in Ecuador where the mission never established a system of parochial schools.

By the 1980s the mission moved away from building parochial schools because by then the State was providing more extensive education. However, help to the public schools was given by the construction of new classrooms as extensions to State schools using funding from German missionary agencies such as Adveniat and Misereor. This was possible because of the peculiar arrangement in Germany whereby the Churches received funding from government taxation. All German taxpayers are asked to nominate the Church of their choice on their tax returns. If, for example, the taxpayer entered 'Protestant' or 'Catholic' on the form, then a percentage of the tax paid was given directly to the religion nominated. If they did not nominate a specific religion then the same percentage was deducted and divided equally among the Churches. The result of this system was that the German Catholic bishops found themselves with surplus funds, which could be applied to missionary development overseas.

The drawing down of these funds placed a considerable burden on the priest who undertook to organise the building of a school extension. He had to engage a design team and foreman, purchase materials, supervise construction and forward receipts and a photographic record of the project to Germany. In this way the poor village of El Milagro, for instance, had a fine State school built for its children by the efforts of the mission priests.

This brief description of the involvement of the Cork and Ross mission in education does little justice to the personal commitment of the priests who masterminded the system. The key to the whole operation lay in securing approval from the State for the teaching posts so that the government rather than the mission paid the teachers' salaries. Until such approval was forthcoming, the mission had to bear the cost of salaries.

In search of approval for the teaching positions, priests spent tedious days away from their mission in Lima filling out application forms, lobbying officials, going from one department to the other, sometimes with success, frequently with disappointment. What motivated these men was the belief that a mission could have no more effective arm in its overall work than a Catholic parochial school. Their tenacity was fully vindicated by the long-term success of the schools, which are still functioning half a century later and which still receive financial support from Cork and Ross mission funds.

Marriage or Living Together

In the middle years of the mission when the optimism of first fervour had waned a little, the men, then on site, tended to question the whole purpose of the undertaking. Those who had once hoped naively to establish a 'little Ireland' in Peru where everyone went to Mass, married in the church, baptised their children in the first few weeks of life and through good education bettered themselves, found instead that Peruvians went about their lives in much the same way as their parents and grandparents had done, so often taking whatever pleasures life offered and leaving tomorrow to take care of itself.

There were, however, occasions when all the investment of money, manpower and energy proved to be worthwhile. One such occasion would be the wedding ceremony of some young person – usually a girl – whose parents had been helped by the mission on arrival from the mountains, who spent her early years in a mission school, her teens in a parish youth club, was helped financially as a university student and now, established as a nurse or teacher, was being married in her parish church by her Irish pastor. For such a wedding the church would be transformed with flowers and candles and paper bows and ribbons. The wedding march would be played over the tannoy. The best man, in the Spanish tradition, would be the girl's father and the bridesmaid would be the groom's mother. As the couple walked down the aisle to the strains of 'The Blue Danube' they would be showered with rice (which the little children of the neighbourhood would later sweep up to bring home for their dinner). These weddings were moments of fulfilment for the priest,

Marriage or Living Together

who knew well that but for the presence of the mission the bride might still be eating the sweepings of a church floor.

Such weddings were all too rare because so many of the young people who had been educated by the mission, integrated into parish life and on terms of personal friendship with the Irish priests and nuns, distanced themselves from the Church in their late teens, dropped out of school and, unqualified and jobless, set up home with a partner in a shack on the sandy edge of the *barrio*, just as their parents had done, without blessing of Church or State. This drift from the Church always saddened the priests, just as, ironically, the same tendency would sadden them again back home in Ireland some twenty years later.

In the last century, the practice of unmarried couples living together was unknown in Ireland until perhaps the final decade before the new millennium. Thirty years earlier, Irish priests would never have come across such a situation. Hence their difficulty in understanding and coming to terms with it. Only after some research into native traditions could the Irish priest see the point of view of couples who lived all their adult lives together without ever having either a civil or religious marriage.

For the Peruvian coming from the Indian tradition, 'living together' is a form of marriage authenticated by immemorial tradition. In places distant from priest or judge it was the only form available. Communities visited by a priest once every two or three years could hardly be expected to time their marriages for the date of his arrival, which was, in any case, surrounded by the uncertainties of weather as well as the possible unavailability of a priest at all. This justification possibly explained the couple's unawareness of any guilt about their situation. As well as the uncertainty about the availability of a priest to solemnise marriages, there was another strong influence on marriage patterns exercised by a tradition of Andean marriage older than the Spanish and Inca civilisations.

In order to contrast the Indian and European marriage traditions it is necessary to analyse the various stages in both. The European couple traditionally began their courtship with a pattern of dating that increased in frequency as formal engagement approached. Marked by the presentation of a diamond ring as a promise of permanent commitment, the engagement ushered in a stage of serious preparation for the wedding and the provision of a home. The relationship, however, could still be terminated by either partner. The crucial point in the process was the marriage ceremony itself, which permitted the couple to live together as man and wife in a permanent union. The Andean marriage process also had three stages: initial courtship, formal engagement and marriage, but the major difference was that the couple, on becoming officially engaged, immediately began their married life together. The church ceremony, which gave absolute permanence to the union, only came later after a delay of two or three years, if, indeed, it came at all.

The engagement stage, or 'trial marriage', was called '*servinakuy*', meaning mutual service. The passage to this stage of the relationship was frequently precipitated by the girl's pregnancy. The decision to live together in '*servinakuy*' was not altogether the private decision of the young people themselves. It was an arrangement formally made by both families during visits to the girl's home involving hospitality, negotiation and the exchange of gifts. Strictly speaking it was not a 'trial marriage', since both parties entered the union on the understanding that it was permanent. At the same time it was not as binding as Church marriage, as it could be dissolved for reasons such as infidelity, drunkenness, laziness or total incompatibility. Studies of primitive Andean communities, however, indicate a stability rate of more than 80 per cent.

An economic reason for '*servinakuy*' was the need to save money for the wedding feast, which was a strictly binding social obligation. Also, in a precarious agricultural economy it was desirable that the young man be quickly settled in life in order to divert all his energies to the production of food. Every couple had the ambition to finalise the marriage process with a wedding in church, followed by a three-day feast in the home. Much, however, depended on their ability to pay for such a celebration and on the possibility of the arrival of a priest for the annual village fiesta. For those who migrated to the coast, poverty was the reason most frequently given for not having a church wedding. In the city, as well as in the mountains, the social pressure to entertain family and friends outweighed the priest's encouragement to receive the sacrament.

The degree of guilt experienced by those living in informal unions reflected the age-old conflict between the Christian and pre-Christian traditions. When questioned about their consciousness of sin, they usually replied: 'I suppose it is wrong to live without the blessing of God – a small sin. It's a tradition that helps you to understand your wife better. It would be a bigger sin to marry in the church and separate afterwards.'

This half-hearted acceptance of the Church's moral teaching is surprising after centuries of condemnation of 'living together'. In 1575, priests were ordered to persuade the Indians to give up the custom of trial marriage, which was 'so pernicious and damaging to their conversion'. In 1585, the Synod of Santo Toribio called for severe punishment of those who lived in such a state. One hundred years later, the Bishop of Quito was complaining that the Indians did not think it a sin to live with a woman for some time in order to see if she is 'a good prospect for marriage or not'.

There can be no doubt that the mountain families that migrated to the coast maintained the tradition of trial marriage. Permissive modern attitudes to sex and marriage have strengthened it. In addition, the youth in the urban environment do not have the controls in place that are inherent in the Andean form of marriage. Left without the surveillance of respected elders, the family situation is compounded by hopeless poverty that makes stability far less likely than in the rural environment. Desertion of the family by the father is one of the greatest social problems in the coastal *barrios*. Where any form of permanent employment is at a premium, men are prepared to follow the work wherever it takes them, be it to the jungle or a distant city with a construction company or a transport service. Separated from their wives and families they live for several months on end in work camps or lodgings. Long distance truckers and bus drivers, for instance, have to take lodgings far from their wives. New alliances are made so that it is not uncommon for such men to end up with two wives, two homes, two families, all supported from one pay packet.

The constant search for work leads the braver and younger husbands to the Amazon jungle where the gold mines and logging camps pay wages higher than anything offered on the coast. However, the risks are great because the jungle takes a horrific toll of its exploiters. These men may not return to their homes for two or three years, while their wives live in a kind of emotional limbo, not knowing for sure whether they are deserted wives or widows, or whether some day their man may return with considerable wealth.

Before the mobile phone revolution there was scarcely any means of communication between the jungle and the coast. News of an accident might not reach the coast for several weeks, so it could be all that time before a woman found out she was a widow. As a funeral was out of the question since a body could not possibly be brought back from a distance, she would arrange a wake in the house with candles at either side of the bed or table on which would be laid a few miserable possessions of the dead man, like an old pair of shoes, clothes or a suitcase to represent his journey. Such 'wakes' were not uncommon. They were always a poignant symbol of the wrong inflicted on family life by poverty and the social injustice that caused it.

Second Generation of Missionaries

During the latter half of 1968 the second generation of missionaries began to arrive in Peru either to study the language or, if they already knew Spanish, to begin work on the Cork and Ross mission. The first of this group was a remarkable priest from the Diocese of Cloyne, Paddy Hennessy. He was the only priest from that diocese to work with the mission. Since the Cork and Ross, Cloyne and Kerry dioceses share Co. Cork, it might seem strange that no other Cloyne man came to Peru. Perhaps the explanation may be that Cloyne had been involved with the St James mission long before the Cork and Ross mission was founded. Cardinal Cushing of Boston had family connections with the Diocese of Cloyne and this would attract men from that diocese in a way that Cork and Ross would not. However, what was lacking in numbers from Cloyne was made up in quality and personal commitment by Paddy Hennessy.

Fr Hennessy first arrived in Peru in April of 1968 and worked for four and a half years until 1972 when he was recalled to Ireland. In 1977 he returned to Trujillo to work in the same parish in La Esperanza until 1979. Once again, in 1982 he returned to continue his work until 1985. In all, Paddy worked with the mission for a total of eight and a half years. He always took his missionary work seriously, even though he had quite a humorous personality. Due to the long spread of his presence on the mission he became known to men of different periods who were on site between April of 1968 (before Michael Murphy had returned to Ireland) and June 1985, when a new generation of men had arrived. In his final year in La Esperanza he found himself in the company of young men who had a less self-consciously serious attitude to their contribution to the Third World. With his mature philosophy of 'if you can't beat them, join them', he subjected himself to a minor personality change and became 'the life and soul of the party'. In June 1985, Paddy Hennessy returned to take up a curacy in Fermoy, Co. Cork, where he died just two and a half years later of a brain tumour.

Denis O'Sullivan, a teacher in Farranferris College in Cork, joined the mission in the same year as Paddy Hennessy. Denis was unfortunate in contracting hepatitis just four years later, which necessitated cutting short his six-year term on the mission and remaining at home in Ireland. He did, however, return for a holiday some twenty years later to meet his old friends in the parish of La Esperanza and the teachers with whom he had built up a close friendship.

Also in 1968, Fr Kerry Murphy-O'Connor left the curacy of Bandon to join the mission. His cousin, Cormac, Bishop of Arundel and Brighton and later Cardinal in Westminster, visited the mission during his stay in El Porvenir.

The following year John O'Donovan, who had worked in Rose of Lima Parish, off Biscayne Boulevard in Miami, arrived to serve six years in Florencia. John, with his ebullient personality, brought life and joy to the mission staff, both Irish and Peruvian.

Later that same year, Bishop Lucey's secretary, Fr Tom Kelleher, began his six-year stint on the mission. Of a literary bent, having edited the diocesan magazine, *The Fold*, he maintained a rich correspondence with Bishop Lucey and later wrote an important history of the early days of the mission.

In 1971 Joe Murphy arrived to serve the three years that were allotted to newly ordained priests. Some twenty years later Joe Murphy would return to work on the mission at a dangerous time when terrorists threatened the very survival of the enterprise. That same year John Shorten, one of the oldest volunteers so far, arrived to serve for six years, during which he was appointed superior of the mission.

Denis Costello, formerly a teacher in the Kerry diocesan seminary, arrived in 1972 and worked in El Porvenir for three and a half years. His cynical wit and shrewd observations were often quoted throughout the thirty years that followed his departure. That same

Second Generation of Missionaries

year also saw the arrival of three more recruits. Pat Walsh, a teacher in Farranferris seminary arrived to become the first parish priest of a new parish, La Sagrada Family (The Holy Family), where he built the fourth parish centre of the mission and a large parish church.

Michael McCarthy was a native of Bantry and had a quality of personality that Peruvians would describe as *'simpatico'*. The literal translation of this quality would be 'nice', but much is lost in such a translation. *'Simpatico'* reaches out to encompass a much wider range of qualities than those encompassed by the frigid English word 'nice'. Perhaps a story would best express the difference. When Mick returned home his replacement in the parish of La Esperanza was doing the First Friday calls. Full of the enthusiasm of a new arrival, he encouraged the sick to place a little altar on the bedside chair with a picture of a saint on it. The next month when he returned there was a framed picture of 'Mick Mac' glaring up at him from the altar.

Liam O'Driscoll also arrived to serve his six years in 1972. Later, Liam would become the press secretary of the diocese at home and editor of *The Fold*. In 1990 he would return to Peru with a film crew and a senior editor of the *Cork Examiner*, Tim Cramer, to produce a film and coffee table book to mark the silver jubilee of the mission.

In 1973 two young priests, Bertie O'Mahony and Pat Stevenson, arrived in Peru to work for a period of three years. Later Bertie would return to work for a further six years, during which time he established a house of residence for the local boys who wished to study for the priesthood at the major seminary. From the Diocese of Kerry a new man arrived, Luke Roche, to continue the faithful Kerry support of the mission. Luke worked in Florencia de Mora for six years. Finally, in 1974 Michael Ryan arrived to work for three years in Florencia. Michael later suffered from the dreaded disease of Guillain-Barré syndrome and succumbed to heart failure in 1992 at the early age of forty-eight.

The men of this second generation of missionaries continued the extraordinary building programme of their predecessors. During this period no less than nine chapels were built, five schools were extended, two convents were extended and a new parish centre was built in El Porvenir.

Theology of Liberation

None of the Cork priests, apart from Michael Murphy and Michael Crowley who had worked previously in the country, had any knowledge whatsoever of the Church in South America. Their ideas of conversion were the same as those generally held in Ireland. The way to save souls in South America was by the provision of sacramental services to as many people as possible. For adults, the provision of the sacraments with appropriate preaching would bring them up to the standard of religious practice that was at the time universal in Ireland. Children, just as in Ireland, would be taught religion in school so that they would know the Commandments, the sacraments, the creed and their prayers, all of which would ensure that they would grow into practicing Catholics who would be grateful for the provision of Mass and the sacraments, which had been denied their forebears for so long because of the shortage of priests.

This was a rather naive approach by priests coming from a country where Christianity had been in existence for fifteen hundred years and had been intensively practiced since Daniel O'Connell's time, whereas in South America the reality had been totally different. Unlike the mission of St Patrick to Ireland, the mission to South America had gone hand in hand with a violent conquest of the people. Baptism of the native people had run way ahead of instruction in the faith. Weekly practice of the Catholic liturgy had never been part of the experience of the newly baptised, apart from the few who lived in the coastal cities, where practice was mainly limited to older women.

Farming in a vertical world

Fishing from a raft made of reeds

Flower sellers meet the Cuzco–Machu Picchu train

Dancing the Marinera, a creole dance

A mountain shrine to the Virgin

Bring flowers of the fairest

An improvised garden centre

Celebrating Carnival in a mission playground

Flowers for Teacher

Smiles for the camera

Straw huts after an 'invasion'

Dressed for a fiesta

Travelling with Mum

Mercy Sister Theresa with Bishop Murphy

Trees planted in backyards turn the desert green

Going home from the market

Machu Picchu, lost city of the Incas

Sister Elena visiting an adobe house

Adobe bricks dry in the sun

Sacred heart (top right) above a family living room

Procession of the Virgin passes the mission's first church

Selling food for guinea pigs

Bon Secours Sister Angelita in her special education class

Neo-colonial church in the deprived parish of El Milagro

Running a food kitchen in a private house

Bishop Murphy, showing the strain of the terrorist threat

A traditional Peruvian pageant

Children of the Andes

Llama and girl among the stones of Cuzco

Bishop Murphy of Cork and Archbishop Prado of Trujillo

Near the Gate of Heaven at 12,000 feet

Theology of Liberation

The fact that the Cork mission was going it alone in an area quite distant from Lima, where clerical interactive discussion would have been possible, meant that current clerical pastoral thought had little or no influence on the Corkmen. Frequent social contact with experienced missionary groups like the Maryknoll and Columban Fathers would have helped them to adjust to the new reality in which they found themselves, and familiarised them with the new movement of ideas that, as it so happened, was at that same time emanating from Peru itself and permeating the whole Catholic Church in Latin America. The Catholic thinkers of Lima were presenting a whole new picture of the mission of the Church, a new analysis of the Christianisation of South America and a radically different plan of future pastoral methods. This new stirring of ideas came to be known as the new line (*linea*) or Liberation Theology.

Newly arrived Irishmen were exposed to a certain amount of the new ideas while in language school in Lima. Sometimes lectures were given to the students by local priests or experienced missionaries in order to prepare them in some small way for the new culture in which they would find themselves working. An example of this was the talk given in 1969 by a native priest of Trujillo, Fr Calderon, who had in fact been of the greatest help to the founders of the Cork mission some four years earlier. He conducted a daylong course on the history of the Church in Peru and the challenges facing it in the coming years. He divided his talk into three parts, covering first the years following the Conquest, second the era of the Republic from 1811 to the 1930s, and third the modern era from the 1930s to the 1960s. It was not so much an historical account as his own interpretation of history. He noted how the Spanish had baptised everyone in the country in the space of two hundred years, a practice which he described as 'sacramentalisation' rather than 'evangelisation'. In 1933 there had been a Eucharistic Congress, which ushered in the modern era with its multiplication of institutions: dioceses, parishes, confraternities, boy scouts, etc.

When he came to talk about the current pastoral methods he mentioned what was purely cultural: Mass, processions, feasts; and what was 'mediaeval': giving the minimum to the maximum, i.e.

baptising everyone regardless of the impossibility of subsequent education in the faith because of the shortage of priests and the poor state of religious education in the schools. The few priests available were expected to spread their influence thinly on the ground, trying to give the minimum to the maximum number. In this method the parish is seen as the centre of everything. It is seen as the only portal to salvation based on the teaching that outside the Church there was no salvation. The only pastoral strategy was to get as many as possible to the sacraments because salvation means the salvation of the individual soul by grace. The temporal, as such, has no supernatural significance. Politics is indifferent, but you can use it as a means to an end; the priest is a 'do-gooder'. The country is Catholic, the people have the faith and the challenge is to revive it.

He then contrasted this mediaeval model with the modern reality in which we live – a pluralist non-Christian world. Politics, art, philosophy and science exist independently of religion. A new type of sanctity must be built for all these kinds of people. This can only be done by the influence of small groups steeped in the faith who will carry the gospel to others; groups of people well versed in the faith who do not limit their religious lives to consideration of their own salvation alone. In the formation of these small groups, the accepted strategy of giving the minimum to the maximum will be reversed: the maximum will be given to a minimum number. Institutions will be replaced by movements. Greater emphasis will be placed on the celebration rather than the reception of the sacraments. Evangelisation, according to this new theory, will be attentive to the needs of the people, and it will first study their spiritual condition. The agents for spreading this new gospel will be, first of all, the laity. The priest will play his part but will enjoy no special status. There should be non-systematic catechesis to deliver this message; it should be as disorganised as life itself.

This daylong talk, especially its conclusion, puzzled the newly arrived Cork priests to the point of irritation. While they gained a lot from his explanation of the history of evangelisation in Peru, the conclusion drawn at the end seemed to contradict everything they had been trained to do as priests and seemed to rubbish everything

Theology of Liberation

they were attempting in the young Cork mission. The talk which they assumed would lead to definite guidelines on how to proceed with their missionary activity left instead everything in an open-ended state of indecision. They all felt lost. When Fr Calderon was asked what he had in mind by way of the practical steps that could be taken in advancing the ideas, he gave an evasive answer. In the words of one of his listeners: 'We were all together led on a grand tour and it was an enjoyable experience, but when we came to the cross roads the guide suddenly disappeared.' What Fr Calderon's listeners did not know was that this talk was inspired by the whole movement of Liberation Theology, which was a new way of looking at the mission of the Church and which had by an extraordinary coincidence been founded by a Peruvian priest, Fr Gustavo Gutierrez.

Fr Gutierrez was a priest of the Diocese of Lima who was born in 1928 in Arequipa in the southern Andes of Peru. Honoured in Spain with the Prince of Asturias Award and in France with the Legion of Honour, he is easily the Peruvian priest who is best known internationally. Occasionally to be seen breakfasting in the St James Centre House in Barranco, Lima, he appears to be a shy, rather insignificant little man, minding his own business scanning the morning paper with squinting eyes. If one had not heard of his international fame one would think him some ordinary local priest who dropped in for coffee from his parish. This image belied his stature among theologians and his controversial position among the highest Vatican circles.

His theological thoughts all his life were coloured by the poverty Gutierrez had experienced growing up in his native Peru. As he said: 'I come from a continent in which 60 per cent of the people live in poverty and 82 per cent of that number are in extreme poverty.' His lifelong task has been trying to reconcile the coexistence of such appalling and widespread poverty with the mission of Christ and the power of Christian nations throughout the world.

The Theology of Liberation that he has developed begins with the fact that the gift of life has been the supreme manifestation of God in this world. He sees the existence of poverty as the result of unjust structures, which, in fact, are sinful in themselves. His analysis appears unusual to most Christians, who have always considered sin as a personal matter. To say there is collective guilt in the creation and maintenance of systems of injustice is a new approach. He observes that society in its efforts to achieve progress in the world actually condemns to great poverty those who have the least possessions. It is often that progress in the developed world is achieved at the expense of the Third World countries, which produce the raw materials used to fuel economic advancement elsewhere. He believes that the Church should construct spiritual, intellectual and economic liberty among the socially oppressed.

In 1986 the Catholic Church responded to the poverty in Latin America at the Second General Conference of Latin American Bishops in Medellin, Columbia. The conference described the poverty and injustice that prevailed on the continent as 'those realities that constitute a sinful situation'. It proclaimed Christ as the liberator from sin and all that is oppressive and dehumanising. In taking a preferential option for the poor, the Conference went on to argue very strongly that temporal progress and the growth of justice were essential to the building of God's kingdom. It saw the pastoral role of the Latin American Church as promoting social and political change.

At the same time, Medellin was very clear in its rejection of Marxism and Liberal Capitalism. It sought a system that would make the well-being of the person and the community a priority. Over ten years later in 1979, the Latin American Episcopal Conference met at Puebla in Mexico and confirmed all that it had begun in Medellin. After the Conference of Medellin, the development of Liberation Theology moved forward rapidly on a variety of levels, which ranged from group reflection to popular articles, pamphlets and published books. The inspiration for Liberation Theology was the Second Vatican Council's document *Gaudium et spes*. This document defined human existence socially and referred to the social dimension of sin. It pledged the Church's commitment to the social problems of humanity. It recognised the inadequacy of individualistic morality to deal with these issues. It encouraged theologians to use the social sciences to understand specific conditions and guaranteed them freedom in their efforts.

Liberation Theology generally follows the procedure of *Gaudium et spes* by presenting its doctrine in two steps. The first describes the human situation being addressed; the second presents theological teaching in response to these human dilemmas. One of the characteristics of this method of theology is the stress it puts on the option for the poor. Gustavo Gutierrez's book, *A Theology of Liberation*, while it won worldwide attention, drew some criticism from the Congregation of Doctrine and Faith 'because of its uncritical acceptance of the Marxist interpretation of South American society'. Speaking at a missionary conference held in Maynooth College in the 1990s, Bishop Michael Murphy of Cork and Ross said: 'It must be said that South American theologians made an honest attempt to address the appalling poverty in which their people lived and tried to interpret such a scandalous situation in the light of the gospel. The fact that some of them might have used the same methods as the Marxists in their analysis of history did not necessarily mean that they drew the same conclusions.'

The Jesuit theologian, Roger Haight, would hold that Liberation Theology is now the universal theology of the Church. He cites as the reasons for this gradual appropriation of the themes of Liberation Theology: 1) it is a continuous development of Vatican II; 2) it is an attempt to interpret Christian doctrine against the background of human suffering; 3) it draws together theology and the social teachings of the Church; and 4) by uniting theology, ethics and spirituality, it provides answers to the fundamental questions of why one chooses to be Christian in the modern world. Because of the stand taken by the bishops, the influence of Liberation Theology and the moral support of priests and religious, the Church in Latin America is seen today as the champion of the poor and the moral leader of the people, a situation that contrasts starkly with an earlier perception of the Church as an ally of the rich and powerful.

Feeding the Hungry

Attempts to give food to the hungry in the Third World frequently generates television images of young men squabbling over bags of food, grabbing sacks of flour from trucks, pushing, shoving, trampling one another and then running off into the bush with their booty. A variation on the theme depicts a food drop from the air. Here the humiliation of the recipients is even further exaggerated and compounded by a danger to life posed by sacks dropping from a great height on the heads of the hungry. Such scenes tell more about the failure of organisation by the aid agency rather than the plight of those whom they attempt to help. Such scenes in no way demonstrate the reality of ongoing food aid programmes run under normal conditions.

The Cork and Ross mission organised food aid programmes for several decades without triggering any of the chaotic scenes that developed world television viewers seem to expect. These programmes were so carefully organised and so transparently fair that they enjoyed the confidence of the community they served. Just as there is never a run on a well-managed bank, so the mission programmes were highly effective in relieving distress, while at the same time showing respect for the people whom they helped. The mission staff, both Irish and Peruvian, were fastidious in the equitable distribution of the available resources and fiercely intolerant of any suggestion of corruption. The consistent delivery of huge amounts of food aid, week after week, year after year, was the result of careful planning and strict supervision of the storage and fair distribution of the food supplied.

Feeding the Hungry

The priest in charge of the programme in each parish devoted much time to the work. Much help was given by the Peruvian staff, which included parish secretaries and volunteer helpers who were fully indoctrinated in the importance of honesty and justice in carrying out their work of charity. The food, which consisted mainly of rice, flour and cooking oil, originated in the surplus agricultural production of the United States. Each diocese in Peru took responsibility for their quota of the rations, which they stored in a central depot from which each parish arranged transport to their parish store. The only expense to the mission was the cost of transporting the trucks of Caritas food (as it was called) twice monthly. All the work of unloading the sacks and dividing out the food parcels for the recipients was done on a voluntary basis by the leading men and women of the parish. It took a team of men to unload the trucks and store the sacks and containers in the parish store, a well-built room with barred windows to prevent robbery. This team was drawn from unemployed men who were willing to work hard for a few hours toting sacks in return for a small portion of flour and oil to take home to their families. On the day following delivery of the food a group of lady volunteers spent three hours in clouds of dust filling four kilo plastic bags, ready for handing out to the recipients.

Next morning the queue formed from 7.30 onwards at the door of the parish rooms awaiting their hand out of flour and oil. These women were the poorest of the poor. They were dressed in rags with slight hints of the Andean skirts and shawls, relics of their days spent in their native habitat of the high Andes, but now badly worn and caked with dust. For shoes they had no more than worn flip-flops; many were often barefoot. Most had a baby slung in the shawl on their backs and many had a two-year-old child trailing behind them as well. Each had a tale of misery of their own: abandoned by their husband, no hope of work, several children at school, no earnings, a mud-walled hut without light or water or furniture. Each woman carried a card that entitled her to her portion. This was stamped as she passed into the room. There she was handed her bag of flour and little plastic bag of cooking oil knotted at the mouth to keep it from spilling as she wended her way home through the sand. It was the ethos of the whole operation that every woman was treated with respect. There were always smiles and reassurance for the mother and a cuddle for the child. Week by week they became more acquainted with the parish secretary and her helpers. There was a positive attempt to create a family atmosphere.

The card entitling the people to their food ration was given to them after an interview, during which their economic situation was assessed. Obviously, if their husband had steady employment, such as driving a bus or working as a carpenter, they would not qualify. The priest in charge of the programme in each parish usually met the new applicants. This was a difficult job as the priest found himself in a dilemma. The quantity of food allotted to the parish was limited. If too many drew from it the individual ration would become negligibly small and would not be worth collecting. At the same time cases of critical need had to be helped in some way. Compromises had to be made. The needy had to be helped, so those a little better off were asked to come back after a few months to renew their request when the quota might be increased, or some of the recipients had gone off the list because their condition had improved. The priest took on this delicate task, as it would not have been fair to expect any volunteer to undertake it.

Sometimes bogus applicants showed up who did not live in the parish at all or else had a stall in the market and wanted the food for resale. The priest was usually tipped off by the parish ladies about these people, who were well known to them as opportunists when it came to making money. The *barrios* had a most effective intelligence system; very little went unknown to the local women.

The programme of food distribution was the bedrock of the hunger relief policy of the mission. There were, however, variations on that which contributed to its popularity among the community. One of these was a special treat at Christmas. The treats central to Christmas celebration in Europe such as Christmas cake and turkey was in Peru an Italian concoction known as *panettone*: a light, yeasty, brack-like cake with crystallised fruits and currants boxed in coloured cardboard. Obviously, such a luxury would not come on the Caritas

Feeding the Hungry

programme, so these Christmas treats were purchased with funds from Cork for distribution on the last Caritas day before Christmas. The order for perhaps 2,000 *panettones* was placed with a local bakery well ahead of time and ferried by the sackful in the pick-up truck to the parish store. Included with the *panettone* were a few *bizcochos*: small cakes made of similar sweet ingredients.

On the Caritas day before Christmas rations were doubled for each family and supplemented by the *bizcochos* and *panettone,* and it would lift even the most unromantic heart to see the joy in the faces of the mothers of families heading home with their Christmas trophy. Without this treat from the mission there would have been no hope of anything extra for Christmas in those family hovels.

The Christmas Special was not the only special programme; there was also a weekly one dedicated to those afflicted with tuberculosis. This terrible disease was endemic in the *barrios*, often being passed from an aged grandmother who was a carrier to the teenage girls of the family, who would have shared her unventilated sleeping quarters. Males, of course, of all ages also suffered, and untreated it surely led to death. For these TB patients there was a special day for food distribution. This had the advantage of isolating them from the other recipients as well as leaving more time for attention by a nurse and more privacy for receiving a larger ration of food. The combination of medication and extra nutrition had a very high success rate in curing the victims of this disease and many young girls who would otherwise have gone to an early grave went on to study, marry and live a normal life as mothers of families.

Another strategy in the fight against hunger and malnutrition was the importation of Irish powdered milk, which was purchased at home and shipped out in a 'piggy back' system on freighters carrying other goods to Callao, the port of Lima. The Cork businessman, Liam St John Devlin, who was a director of Irish Shipping, was invaluable in organising these shipments. In a country where fresh milk was practically unobtainable and canned milk was unsuitable for long-term consumption by infants, the Irish milk powder was like gold. For those afflicted with tuberculosis it was literally a lifesaver.

Another subgroup that benefited from the food programme was the mothers of twins. Normally mothers breast fed for two years, but nursing twins was beyond the ability of mothers who were undernourished themselves. One parish had the rather large number of sixteen sets of twins, all of them thriving on the Irish milk. A group photograph of the twins with their mothers was published in Cork's *Evening Echo* accompanying the annual appeal for Peru.

The mission social welfare programmes went beyond the supply of food for the hungry. There was also an educational branch, even though the numbers availing of that service were far less. Adult education classes dealt with cooking and dressmaking. The cooking classes instructed women in the preparation of delicious dishes using the cheapest ingredients locally available. Qualified instructors demonstrated how to use humble ingredients such as vegetables, sweet potatoes, rice and flour. The latter food source was used in the production of fancy cakes that a mother could produce at little cost for family events such as birthdays, which custom dictated should be celebrated for every family member, young or old, in Peru. This valuable initiative brought joy to many a child amid the general deprivation of their youth.

Dressmaking classes were directed by a local tailor, who shared his skill with the poorer women helping them to clothe their children in the school uniform that was both standard and obligatory all over the country at a fraction of the cost of purchasing the uniforms ready to wear. Advance purchase of the material by the mission ahead of inflation provided the material for the uniforms at an almost nominal cost.

At the heart of the whole social programme was the group of volunteer women numbering twenty or thirty drawn from each geographical sector of the parish. Working their district in pairs, these women forged a link between the parish and the people that was an invaluable means of communication for the priests. They visited the homes, encouraged parents to baptise their children, organised local prayer groups and kept the priest informed of illness, domestic need and family problems. In a parish of 40,000 people staffed by two or three priests, such a structure was a basic necessity if any effective help was to be provided for a deprived community. Through those local organisers the Church's presence was felt by all age groups, bringing them to the Lord and the Lord to them.

The prayer groups met weekly and the programme of the meeting was simple. The Rosary was recited as the group gathered in some dim humble living room, unfurnished except for a few benches on which the women sat, surrounded by their younger children sitting on the earthen floor. The reading for the following Sunday was read and discussed, each woman applying the message of the gospel to her own social and family problems. It was surprising to Irish missionaries how conversant these people were with the Bible. It was a South American tradition and one that was exploited to the full by the Protestant Evangelicals in their proselytising activities. The mission also produced a small pocket-sized prayer book containing all the popular devotions, ranging from the prayers to St Martin de Porres and St Rose of Lima to the Stations of the Cross and prayers for the dying. This little book was so successful that it ran to a second edition.

These local prayer groups functioned on their own, but they always welcomed a visit from the priest or nun. The living conditions of these women who welcomed the prayer group into their homes never ceased to shock the Irish sensitivity, even after years living in Peru. On the one hand there was the understanding they had of the Bible spirit and message, perhaps because it was so relevant to their own poverty, and on the other hand the level of poverty that was normal for them. That general deprivation was indicated by small details such as dress and footwear, the condition of the children who continually rubbed their eyes, which only exacerbated the irritation that provoked the rubbing, their emaciated and under-developed limbs, the women whose eyesight was failing and who used the lens of someone's discarded spectacles as a magnifying glass to enlarge the print of the Bible.

In this general misery, biblical parallels came easily to mind: the rabble in the desert fed with bread; the curing of the blind, the sick and the lame; the lepers who cried out for a cure; the old woman 'bound by a devil for fourteen years'. All these types were present in the darkened room, still drawing both consolation and inspiration from the comforting words of Jesus.

The foregoing gives some idea of the range of social services provided by the mission without mentioning the sense of gratitude expressed by the people. This was constantly and elaborately conveyed to the Irish priests and nuns, as though they had provided these benefits from their own money instead of from the funds donated at home. The gratitude was expressed in many ways. Birthdays, as mentioned, were always celebrated and none more so than that of the priest or nun whose date of birth they generally ascertained, no matter how hard one tried to keep it a secret. A whole series of *'fiestas'* would be put on in different houses to celebrate the occasion. A guinea pig would be killed and stewed and garnished with lettuce and sweet potatoes, served with courtesy and ceremony. When the time came for the Irish to return home to Ireland the farewell ceremonies might be protracted over several weeks. Each street, each home of one of the volunteers, insisted on hosting some little party of farewell, so much so that many kept the date of departure absolutely secret to the last minute from the local women and slipped away quietly to Lima where they would catch their long flight home.

The Fall of the Inca

The small airport that serves Trujillo is located some ten miles outside the city on a sandy bluff above a fishing village that is known by its Indian name, Huanchaco. The ribbon of sand that girds the Peruvian coast at this point is the first sight of Trujillo that the visitor gets from the air just before landing. The village is inhabited by Peruvians leading a traditional way of life that predates the days of Inca rule going back at least to the Chimu civilisation, which had created the vast adobe city of Chan Chan, whose ruined walls now separate Huanchaco from Trujillo.

Huanchaco is not a fishing village in the European sense of an artificial harbour crowded with trawlers, but rather a settlement where men still fish as their ancestors did, using crude canoes woven out of reeds that carry only one man, riding astride like a jockey. The comparison with a jockey is indeed apt as the little rafts are known by the locals as 'little straw horses'. Propelled by a single paddle, these little 'horses' ride the rolling wave crests so far out to sea that they cannot be seen by the naked eye.

The village itself houses these gallant fishermen and their families, as well as some city professionals who like to spend the summer months by the sea. A few modest bars and restaurants give the place a semblance of modernity. In the summer season, when city dwellers come to picnic on the beach, temporary straw huts provide the bars and restaurants to meet the visitors' needs. Once the end of March comes and the cold mists of autumn settle on the shore, these huts are folded away and the place goes back to what it had been for centuries before the white man arrived.

Children of the Sun

The prospect of living within a drive of a beach brought an emotional lift to all newly arrived Irishmen. However, they soon learned that in Peru the proximity of the Pacific Ocean meant nothing to the natives. Back home in Ireland, the presence of the surrounding seas has dominated the Irish imagination, inspiring it with the mythical Isles of the Blest and St Brendan's epic voyages. Whether looking westwards over the ocean to a land of opportunity or southeastwards to France or Spain in the hope of political liberation, the Irish have always turned seawards for the fulfilment of their dreams. The Pacific Ocean, on the other hand, in its becalmed greyness, makes no impact on the native Peruvian psyche. No one knows or cares what countries lie beyond that western horizon. No emigrants have ever crossed that monotonous expanse; no ships ever arrived on its western horizon. It remains an irrelevant waste of water, untouched by all save the few inshore fishermen of Huanchaco.

However, if the ocean is irrelevant to the Peruvians, the mighty Andes dominate their daily lives, especially the lives of the migrants to the coast. For them the mountains will always be home. Their food comes from the fertile valleys lost amid the peaks. Their water flows all the way from glacial heights to the streams and canals of the coastal desert. As well as providing the physical needs of food and water, the Andes also feed the Peruvian imagination with the folk memory of the glory of the Incan civilisation, which the Spanish conquistadores destroyed forever. If the foreign missionary does not acquaint himself with that great national trauma – the destruction of one culture by another – his preaching and philosophising will be politely heard and instantly forgotten. Because of this it was always recommended that the newly arrived missionary would visit the mountains as soon as he had completed language school and familiarised himself with his new parish. The best way to begin to understand the people and his place in their lives was to drive to the high mountains from which they had come, and there was no better place to visit than the mountain city of Cajamarca, where the definitive and tragic encounter between the Spanish and the Peruvians took place when the conquistador, Pizarro, defeated and

The Fall of the Inca

captured the Inca god-king Atahualpa. This historical event, which is still fresh in every Peruvian mind, is a tale of courage, innocence, betrayal and infamy.

A visit to Cajamarca brings to life the cunning and perfidy of the Spanish and the unfortunate association of their coming with the coming of the Catholic faith. The conquistador brought the sword in one hand and the Bible in the other. Every Peruvian knows the story of the capture of the Inca king, of the ransom he paid in gold and silver for his freedom and how the Spanish reneged on their promise and killed him when he had paid the ransom. Both the Spanish perfidy and the coming of Christianity are commemorated in Cajamarca. Here beautiful colonial churches stand side by side with the prison in which the Inca king had been held and the square where he had been executed. Visiting these squares and buildings where history was made inevitably encourages one to read that history and, in the case of the history of the conquest of Peru, that wonderful story is beautifully written by William Prescott.

When Prescott set about the task of presenting the story of the Conquest he was fortunate to have a huge deposit of archives to draw upon. The Spanish have always had a penchant for recording everything in chronicles and account books. There was a practical reason for the keeping of exact accounts: the king claimed one-fifth of all the gold and silver plundered in Peru. Any falsification of those accounts could have the most serious consequences for the malefactor. The result was that even in the beginning of the sixteenth century, daily transactions were carefully recorded and finally lodged in libraries in Seville and Vienna and in other great European institutions. The happy result of this bureaucratic tradition was that Prescott had access to eyewitness accounts of the events of the Conquest.

Before the discovery of Peru, the Spanish had conquered Mexico and had reached Panama where a colony was established. Rumours suggesting an El Dorado somewhere south of the equator whetted the appetites of the Spanish adventurers in their thirst for gold. Finally, an expedition to survey the Southern Ocean was organised in Panama when three men came together to form a confederacy:

Children of the Sun

Francisco Pizarro, Diego de Almagro and a Spanish priest, Fr Hernando de Luque, who, as Vicar of Panama, had control of enough funds to make the exploit possible. Once these three men, two soldiers and a priest, had received the sanction of the Governor of Panama, they lost no time in making preparations. First, they drew up a contract by which they bound themselves to divide equally the whole of the conquered territory. Because Fr de Luque had advanced gold bars to the amount of 20,000 pesos, it was declared that he was entitled to one-third of all the land and treasures of every kind: gold, silver and precious stones. The men swore an oath to keep the covenant and, to give still greater effect to the compact, the priest gave Holy Communion to the parties, dividing the Host into three portions, of which each of them partook.

Eventually the expedition reached the Isla de Gallo, off the coast of Ecuador, but the Spaniards found themselves so short of food and threatened by the Indians that it was decided to send Almagro back to Panama for reinforcements. When the Governor of Panama learned of the problems of the expedition, he sent a ship to rescue them and bring them back. When the ship arrived at the Isla del Gallo with the offer of rescue and encouragement to abort the voyage of discovery, Pizarro made the decision of his life in a dramatic manner, which has since made the phrase 'draw a line in the sand' a common phrase. Prescott describes the dramatic moment:

> Drawing his sword, he traced a line with it on the sand from east to west. Then turning towards the south, 'Friends and comrades', he said, 'on that side are toil, hunger, nakedness, the drenching storm, desertion and death; on this side, ease and pleasure. There lies Peru with its riches, here, Panama and poverty. Choose, each man, what best becomes a brave Castilian. For my part, I go to the south.' So saying, he stepped across the line. He was followed by thirteen others.
> (William H. Prescott, *History of the Conquest of Peru*, London: Swan Sonnenschien & Co., 1905, p. 125)

The Fall of the Inca

Today in the Cathedral of Lima, above the tomb of Francisco Pizarro, a mural depicts the dramatic moment and bears the names of those gallant men who crossed the line in the sand and passed forever to fame and fortune.

The rescue ship then sailed back to Panama without them for further supplies and for seven months the fourteen adventurers barely existed on the Isla de Gallo until they saw the white sail again on the horizon. Boarding the ship they sailed southwards along the Peruvian coast, putting in here and there to meet the natives and examine their living standards. Everywhere they landed they were received with the same spirit of generous hospitality, the natives coming out on their balsa rafts to welcome them with their little cargos of fruit and vegetables. Pizarro sailed on southwards, always keeping the mighty snow-clad ranges of the Andes in sight.

In every place he visited, Pizarro heard reports of the great monarch who ruled over the land and held his court in the mountains where his capital was ablaze with gold and silver. Though the white men did not see much evidence of such wealth on the coast, they did observe the developed state of agriculture in the irrigated valleys rich with tropical vegetation.

Nine degrees south of the equator Pizarro's followers begged him to turn back. More than enough, they said, had been done to prove the actual position of the great Indian empire for which they had searched so long. Yet with their slender force they had no power to profit by the discovery. All that remained, therefore, was to return and report the success of their enterprise. They had taken some natives on board and instructed them in the Spanish language so that at some future date they could act as interpreters. They also took some llamas, examples of textiles and ornaments of silver and gold. With these Pizarro set out from Panama for Spain, where he would visit the king and get his approval for the conquest. The evidence impressed the king who made him Governor General of the new province and sent him off in January of 1531 for Panama, where he gathered together three ships and one hundred and eighty men.

Children of the Sun

Back again off the coast of Peru, Pizarro heard that the Inca king was in Cajamarca, high in the Andes. Without hesitation he began his march into the mountainous interior for the first time, eventually arriving at his destination, which he found deserted because the Inca and his army of followers and attendants were camped some miles away. Pizarro took advantage of the fact that the city was empty by occupying the buildings that formed three sides of the huge square. These consisted of spacious halls with wide doors opening onto the square. In two of these halls he stationed his cavalry and placed the infantry in a third. The city was overlooked by a hill on which the Indians had built a fortress. Here he placed the two small pieces of artillery. All were to remain at their posts well concealed until the arrival of the Inca. Only when the signal was given by the discharge of a gun were they to attack the royal procession, slay the Peruvians and take the Inca king, unharmed, as a hostage.

At noon the procession began to approach the city, the Inca borne on an open litter, on which was a sort of gilded throne, the canopy lined with the richly coloured plumes of tropical birds and studded with shining plates of silver and gold. In a gesture of friendship the Inca sent word to Pizarro that he would enter the city with only a few warriors and without arms.

Not long before sunset the procession entered the square and a few thousand filled the square. Not a Spaniard was to be seen. Then a Dominican friar approached the Inca and through his interpreter explained to the Inca the reason for the arrival of the Spanish. His long explanation began with the creation of the world by the one true God, the redemption of the world by Christ, the divine authority of the king of Spain, who had sent them to bring the faith to Peru. He requested that the Inca accept the true faith and submit to the divine power of the king of Spain. The Inca enquired by what authority the friar had said these things and he was given a copy of the Bible. Prescott recounts the following events:

> The Inca took the book, turned over the pages a moment, then threw it down with vehemence, and

exclaimed: 'Tell your comrades that they shall give me an account of their doings in my land. I will not go from here until they have made me full satisfaction for all the wrongs they have committed.' The Friar, greatly scandalised, stayed only to pick up the sacred volume, and hastening to Pizarro, asked him to attack at once, adding, 'I absolve you'. The fatal gun was fired from the fortress, the Spaniards poured into the plaza, horse and foot, and threw themselves into the midst of the Indian crowd. The latter, taken by surprise, stunned by the report of the artillery and muskets, the echoes of which reverberated like thunder from the surrounding buildings, and blinded by the smoke which rolled in sulphurous volumes along the square were seized with panic. They made no resistance. There was no escape from the slaughter. The nobles around their king's litter threw themselves in the way of their assailants in a vain effort to protect their master. The struggle became fierce around the royal litter. It reeled more and more, and at length, several of the nobles who supported it having been slain, it was overturned and the fall of the Indian King was broken by Pizarro who caught him in his arms. (*Ibid.*, p. 198)

The Inca king was taken prisoner and held in what is now known as the Ransom Room, today one of the main visitor sites in Cajamarca. In the days that followed, the prisoner discovered the conquistadores' love of gold and he promised them that he would pay a ransom for his freedom. He marked a line as high as he could reach on the wall of the room and promised that he would fill it with gold to that height. He also promised to fill an adjoining room twice with silver. Word was passed to the farthest reaches of the Inca Empire that the king had ordered the treasure to be brought. Even though the amount of gold assembled never reached the vast amount promised, so great was the amount delivered to Cajamarca that Pizarro acquitted the Inca of further obligation. Then they put

Children of the Sun

him on trial for idolatry, adultery and attempting to excite rebellion against the Spanish Crown. He was declared guilty and sentenced to death by fire. When it was explained to him that if he received Baptism, the painful death by fire would be commuted to the milder form of strangulation by a garrotte, he consented to receive Baptism. The new convert received the name John, as it was the feast of John the Baptist, and Pizarro himself acted as godfather. The Inca then submitted himself calmly to his fate.

When one considers that the details of the execution of the last Peruvian monarch are known by all Peruvians to this day, one can understand the existence of a certain scepticism about the claims of the Catholic religion to be a source of truth and love and justice. Spanish-born missionaries, of whom there are many working in Peru, must find it difficult to distance themselves from the behaviour of their countrymen not only at the time of the conquest itself, but also in the succeeding centuries when the native population was cruelly exploited, particularly in the mining industry. Irish missionaries could, at least, point to the sufferings of their own people at the hands of English colonisers. Fortunately, the people of Peru are not argumentative. Instead they tend to agree with whatever an outsider says, while maintaining all the while a discreet silence about the thoughts that lie buried in their hearts.

1975–1990: Years of Peace and Progress

In March 1975 what might be called, perhaps rather loosely, the third generation of missionaries began to arrive, led by two Maynooth classmates: Michael Murphy and Denis Cashman. Later in the year they were followed by two further college contemporaries: Michael Nyhan and, from the Diocese of Kerry, Tom Looney. In the following year another man of about the same age joined them: Ted Collins from Clonakilty. In 1977 Robert Young came to serve for three years and later would return to continue for six more years. He was followed by Denis O'Leary and Bernard O'Donovan and a newly ordained John McCarthy. Bernard would return to serve during the closing years of the mission.

In the year 1978 the mission ran into a crisis when the supply of volunteers to work in Peru dried up. Bishop Lucey was philosophical about this situation, stating that if it was the will of God that the mission should end through lack of volunteering priests then so be it. By then Michael Murphy was Coadjutor Bishop of Cork and Ross and when the volunteer crisis became apparent he was appointed to take charge of staffing the mission. As an immediate solution to the crisis the rules of recruitment were changed and older men who had served in the early years were allowed to return to Peru for a further six years. Under the personal direction of Bishop Murphy and later Bishop Buckley, there was never again a shortage of recruits until the vocations crisis hit the home diocese in 2004.

The period of the 'third generation' of missionaries was marked by a reduction in the building programme and a concentration on the consolidation of the religious life of the parishes. Excellent youth programmes were established, such as 'Choice', which involved a residential weekend during which the option of living one's life as a Christian was contrasted with the meaningless existence of those who have no faith. Not only did this spiritual experience attract many young people to Catholic living, but it also inspired some young men and women to consider a religious vocation.

All the parish meeting rooms, which had been constructed in the first years, were now put to good use as centres for instruction in the faith for adults and children alike. Each church and chapel had developed its own faithful clientele of daily and weekly worshippers. During this period, the third and final parish, The Holy Family, was established on the fringe of the settlement in La Esperanza. In 1976 a new presbytery and a large parish church were completed and two priests went to live there. Holy Family, in the event, was the last parish on the Peruvian mission to be occupied by the Irish priests right up to the closure of the mission.

The new parish differed in many respects from the three older ones. Here only two priests lived instead of the three or four who occupied the other houses, which meant that one man was on his own whenever the other was away on business or on leave. The new parish had no resident nuns, no medical centre and only one parochial school. There was a meeting room but no sports area in which the youth could play basketball or organise other social activities such as dance festivals or concerts. Yet, in spite of these limitations in infrastructure, a great community spirit and a loyal church-going tradition was developed thanks to the untiring efforts of the priests working in the area and the extensive food aid programme that was put in place to meet the great need of this most deprived population.

The next decade, the 1980s, saw the arrival of thirteen new men. Newly ordained Finbarr Crowley joined the mission in the autumn of 1980, served for four years and then returned in 1988 to begin a further tour of duty. In 1981, Leonard O'Brien, Edward Collins and Patrick Crowley arrived followed by another man from the Diocese of Kerry: Paddy Murphy in 1982. John O'Callaghan, Teddy O'Sullivan, Sean O'Driscoll and Connie Twohig had all come by

1975–1990: Years of Peace and Progress

1984, with three more following in 1986: Ted Hallahan, Christy Harrington and Martin Scully.

During the 1980s some beautiful churches were built to replace schoolrooms that doubled as chapels on Sundays. One of these was sited in the first parish, El Porvenir. The Church of the Blessed Sacrament in La Esperanza and two neo-colonial churches were built in the parish of Holy Family: one in the Christ the King section and the other in El Milagro, the village some miles distant from Esperanza.

By the end of the decade the total number of churches in the mission came to fourteen, served by twelve priests. By then the Bon Secours Order had taken over the running of a maternity hospital, which had been built by the Lions Club of Trujillo. This wonderful development had been promoted by the lawyer, Dr Santa Maria, who had always been a friend of the Cork and Ross Mission. The project capitalised on the long experience of the Bon Secours Sisters in College Road in Cork, where they ran one of the most respected maternity hospitals in Ireland.

The fifteen years between 1975 and 1990 were years of peace and service of the poor of Trujillo by priests and nuns who had the resources to meet their spiritual, medical and social needs, thanks to the continued generosity of the people at home who funded the great work through the annual collection in May each year, and through the many fundraising projects run in all areas of life in Cork, ranging from schools, trades unions and cooperative creameries to parish groups and social functions. The mission had caught the imagination of the lay people at home and the priests and nuns on the mission had little difficulty in putting the funds provided to immediate good use.

Vocations to the Religious Life

The contribution of the Sisters from Cork and Ross to the success of the mission was beyond question. Without them contact with the families, especially with the women, would have been extremely superficial. And today, over forty years later, but for the nuns there would be no Cork presence in Trujillo since the priests were withdrawn.

Two religious orders were involved from the beginning: the Mercy Sisters and the Bon Secours. A third order, the Presentation Sisters, also took part by sending a series of their Sisters to live and work with the Bon Secours over a period of twenty years.

Generally the Sisters were older than the priests. For that reason it was perhaps more challenging for them to become proficient in a new language, in which great accuracy was called for in nursing and fluency in teaching classes. The early arrivals were nuns who had been accustomed to living in communities of twenty to thirty; now they shared a house with three or four. Surviving all of these challenges, they provided services for the people in every area of life, ranging from sewing and knitting to parenting and family planning programmes. They organised talks on the Billings method, craft classes for the knitting of Aran sweaters for sale, and cooking classes that produced nutritious meals using the humblest and cheapest of ingredients. Above all, they put the religious formation of their people as a first consideration.

Wonderful and praiseworthy as all this work was, the decision with the most far-reaching consequences was taken in 1971 by the two orders when they decided to prepare for the introduction of local vocations into their respective congregations. A nun from each community was sent off to be trained in the art of spiritual formation and direction. They attended courses in Lima aimed at producing novice mistresses. When the convents had been extended to accommodate novices and a team of spiritual directors was in place, they proceeded to recruit to their orders. Already they had forged close links with other groups of religious women. Mainly through these social connections along the coastal cities of Peru, contact was made with young girls interested in the religious life. These were invited in small groups to come and live in the convent for a number of weeks, after which they were sent back to their families. After this 'living experience' they were again contacted and if they were still interested they came into permanent residence as 'aspirants'. From this beginning those who wished to remain graduated through the slow process of formation leading to first profession and then, after some eight years, to final profession. The Mercy Sisters ran their noviciate attached to their convent in Florencia; the Bon Secours purchased a house in Lima close to the Columban Fathers. There they set up their noviciate, which was strategically located for the girls who wished to study nursing or education.

The work that had begun in the early 1970s had reached fruition at the end of the 1980s when the Mercy order numbered some twelve Sisters, of whom half were finally professed, while the Bon Secours had fifteen Peruvian professed nuns, of whom four had been finally professed. By then the Mercy nuns had acquired a house in Lima where the novices could be formed in the religious life and from which they could attend the university.

It was these courageous programmes that ensured the survival of the Cork and Ross presence in Peru long after the home diocese was no longer able to supply priests for missionary work. In the short term, however, the programmes of recruitment had spectacular results by bringing the Irish priests and nuns into contact with the cultural and social life of the country at a more intimate level than was possible by ordinary parish contact. The experience of living with Peruvian girls day after day, eating with them and speaking their language gave the Irish nuns a feeling for the people that would otherwise have been impossible. The presence of these white-veiled Peruvian girls helping the priests at Masses, devotions and parish meetings gave the mission a credibility and a sense of permanency that could never be achieved by a mission staffed by foreigners alone. In teaching the faith to groups of children in Saturday and Sunday 'schools', these girls had advantages of age, language and local understanding that no outsider could match.

Apart from making a huge contribution to pastoral work, the novices brought a sense of youthful fun to the social life of the mission. For instance, in the hot summer months of February and March, Peruvians celebrated 'Carnival' in what might seem to be a childish way, but was in fact quite amusing. During Carnival it was the custom to throw dishes or buckets of water over someone for laughs. So, someone might be reading a paper seated on a bench outside a bus stop or garage, and someone might steal up from behind and drench them with water. The expected reaction always happened: the victim gave chase and the perpetrator ran off laughing. Priests in public were, out of respect, saved this ordeal, but not so in the convent grounds where the Peruvian novices often surprised an Irishman with this humorous tradition.

The novices, because they wore a veil that was universally respected, were always addressed as 'Mother', even though they were still only aspirants to the religious. Wisely, the religious orders integrated the Peruvians into their worldwide congregation by bringing them to spend extended visits to Irish convents, to Paris and to Rome where some of them studied. Some were brought to Europe for important occasions such as General Chapters and the installation of a new bishop in Cork.

In the course of the years, the Bon Secours had extended their accommodation both in Trujillo and Lima. By 1987, however, they felt strong enough to make a new foundation some three hundred kilometres to the north of Trujillo in a diocese called Chulucanas in a village called Salitral. Climatic conditions differed substantially from Trujillo because of the proximity to the Equator where there were seasonal rains. These periodic rains delayed their arrival by a week, and even on the day of the Sisters' arrival in Salitral they had to be ferried across a swollen river in a watertight jeep. Initially in fairly primitive conditions, they made their new foundation working in over twenty rural villages and hamlets, some of which could only be reached on horseback. Some years later, the motherhouse back in Trujillo hived off another group founding a new convent in the Cork mission territory, in a most underdeveloped area of the desert where there was neither light nor water. There they lived among the poorest new arrivals from the mountains. All of this expansion led to a marvellous moment in 1996 when all the houses in Peru were combined in an independent province of the Bon Secours congregation with, as the first Mother General, Sister Angelita, who had in fact been their first novice some twenty-five years earlier.

In March 2008 an event took place in Cork that meant that the wheel had turned full circle. Forty-one years after the first four sisters set out for Peru, four more set out to nurse Aids patients in Africa and two of the four were natives of Peru. Bishop Lucey, who himself spent his last years in Africa, would have been pleased to think that the mission he had founded so many years before had produced new missionaries to 'teach all nations'.

The shortage of vocations to the priesthood in Peru was a fundamental reason for the presence of foreign missionaries in that country. For that reason there was always an idea in Bishop Lucey's mind that 'something should be done' to solve this chronic problem in the Church in that part of the world. In the bishop's correspondence in the 1970s with the superior of the mission, Fr John Shorten, he was already hinting that the time had come for some practical steps to be taken to address the situation. The suggestion met with little enthusiasm from the priests on the mission for starting any kind of seminary, because they were well aware that neither the St James Society nor the Columbans had ever attempted entry into this field of pastoral activity. The priests in these two congregations had a longer and wider experience of Peru than the Corkmen. Also, they were to work in the country for indefinite periods, whereas the priests from Cork were strictly limited at the time to a six-year tour of duty on the mission.

Trujillo, in any case, did have a major seminary. This modern building, located a few miles from the city, had been constructed with financial help from North America and was staffed by an international faculty drawn from Spain, North America and South America. There was even an Irish priest on the teaching staff, Fr John B. O'Sullivan of the Diocese of Kerry. A native of Sneem, Co. Kerry, John B. (as he was called) had served for six years with the Cork and Ross Mission almost from its foundation. A hard-working scholarly priest, he had taken a special interest in preparing catechetical programmes not only for the Cork-run parishes, but also for the whole Diocese of Trujillo. In the course of this specific work he had made close friendships with many Peruvian priests at national as well as local level.

Some time after his return to his native diocese in Ireland it became clear that a professor of Church history was urgently needed at the seminary in Trujillo and without hesitation he volunteered for this challenging position. In the event, John B. spent six years working on the faculty of that major seminary. Always both studious and energetic, he not only delivered his lectures there but even wrote a textbook in Spanish for the students, the production of which was funded by his friends in the Irish parish of Millstreet, where he had served as a curate.

Daily life in the Peruvian seminary was extremely demanding for Fr John B. O'Sullivan. Not only did he lecture on his subject, but he also acted as a counsellor to the students, living full time in the college and sharing meals and social life with the students. Spanish was the language of daily life with no break except on his day off when he spent time in one or other of the Cork presbyteries in the city, where he could relax in an English-speaking environment. Sharing the ordinary meals with the seminarians brought its own difficulties for an Irishman with a somewhat delicate constitution, unused to the highly spiced fare so appreciated by the natives.

With such an educational facility available in Trujillo that enjoyed a close association with the Irish missionaries, it would seem superfluous to envisage some other seminary course targeted at the vocations coming from the Cork parishes. Bishop Lucey, however, always liked to have personal control of his own projects. Also, he felt that the impoverished background of students who might come from the *barrios* would make it difficult if not impossible for them to integrate with the general body of students in the seminary.

For those reasons he evolved a scheme whereby boys from the Cork parishes who wished to study for the priesthood would live in a house of residence in the grounds of one of the Cork presbyteries and travel daily to the seminary for lectures. Their formation, spiritual direction and supervision would be in the charge of one of the Cork priests. All financial needs would be met from the Cork and Ross mission fund. An architect was engaged to design a residential block for the students with a comfortable room for each, as well as service and recreational areas. Once opened, the facility welcomed quite a number of young men anxious to become priests.

The Archbishop of Trujillo, however, was never enthusiastic about the arrangement. He felt that it was not desirable that students would live in such proximity to Irish priests whose living standards and funding would far outstrip anything that the native clergy experienced. He felt that it would be more normal for them to participate fully in the life of the seminary as full-time residents. Taking the long view he felt that when the Irish mission would eventually depart these young native priests would have to integrate fully into the ordinary life of the diocese with its variety of living conditions, ranging from the remote mountain villages to the impoverished *barrios* and the well off middle class city parishes.

Whether subsequent events proved the archbishop right or wrong is hard to know for sure. The reality is that most of the young men who began life in the mission residence drifted away back to the secular life to such an extent that the maintenance of the student residence was no longer practicable and those who remained moved into the major seminary itself. Their link with the mission was still maintained through financial subvention of their upkeep and their preparation in parish pastoral activities during vacation periods.

In 1987 the first student sponsored by the Cork and Ross mission, William Costa, was ordained a deacon in the Cathedral of Trujillo. He went to live for his diaconate year with two of the senior Cork priests in the presbytery of the Holy Family parish. A year later he was ordained to the priesthood in the church of that parish in a joint ceremony involving the Bishop of Cork and Ross, Michael Murphy, and the Archbishop of Trujillo. Since then Fr William has worked in the parishes built up by the mission. He became parish priest of the first parish that was handed back by the mission and has continued to carry on the great work begun by the Irish for the following twenty years. Some other native students also completed their course and were ordained after being sponsored from the beginning by the mission. The numbers were not large but their work has been out of all proportion to their numbers, thanks to the extensive infrastructure built with funds from Cork. Their living needs have also been subsidised by a trust fund set up in 1992 fuelled by the Cork and Ross mission fund, which still continues to grow thanks to donations and bequests still coming in.

Compared with the normal Peruvian parish, the ones once established by Cork and Ross enjoy well-built churches, meeting rooms, presbyteries and transport vehicles that would be far beyond the dreams of other impoverished parochial centres.

The Mission in Crisis

It was not by accident that in the second half of the twentieth century the presence of so many foreign missionaries in Peru coincided with the most active communist movement in recent times. Both the communist and the missionary movements, though diametrically opposed in their aims and *modus agendi*, owed their existence to the same underlying cause: the level of poverty among the peasants in the mountains and the miserable living conditions of the migrants on the coast. The treatment of both groups was inexcusable in a world of unprecedented wealth.

From the 1970s into the new century the communist movement in Peru was known as the Shining Path, an extraordinarily secretive movement that eschewed manifestos, public threats and announcements in favour of a type of terrorism of unprecedented savagery. Back in the 1920s, the Communist Party of Peru was founded by José Carlos Mariátegui, who went on to declare that Marxism and Leninism would open the shining path (*sendero luminoso*) to revolution. In the late 1960s a breakaway group of communists came to be called 'The Shining Path Guerrillas', and became known generally as the '*Senderistas*'.

The founder of this group was Abimael Guzman, a professor of philosophy in the University of Ayacucho in the southern mountains of Peru. In the university he developed a following of students, many of whom became teachers in the rural countryside high in the Andes. The aim of the movement was to replace the bourgeois institutions of Peru with a communist peasant revolutionary regime, passing first through the Maoist development stage of 'new democracy'. In the tradition of Chairman Mao, Guzman believed that the movement should begin in the remote countryside and, working from there, eventually achieve victory in the cities, especially in the capital, Lima, a city of twelve million people. One would have expected that such a rurally based movement would court the support of the poor peasants. For a time this is what it did by imposing summary retribution on enemies of the local communities such as robbers and cattle rustlers. But the *Senderistas* went further by attacking others in the communities who committed no 'crime' other than that of being managers of local cooperatives or working as small-town traders in the village markets. These innocent people were slaughtered with horrific brutality. The aim of the movement was to close down the markets and cause social havoc in general. Naturally, this became unpopular with the population, who formed *'rondas'* or vigilante committees to defend themselves against the revolutionaries. This antagonism gradually developed into a type of civil war, which was largely ignored by the government far away in Lima.

The first act of war against the central government was the burning of ballot boxes on the eve of a national presidential election that followed the handing back of power by a military junta to the electorate. So brutal became the atrocities committed on both sides by terrorists and vigilantes that the army moved in after the government had declared the mountainous region to be in a state of emergency. Instead of solving the problem, this move was compounded by the fearsome acts of the army perpetrated in the name of law and order. At the same time horrific scenes of butchery were enacted by the *Senderistas* in village squares where people had their throats cut, were stabbed and burned. The *Senderistas*, when they carried out such operations, insisted, on threat of further reprisal, that the bodies be denied decent burial. Caught between the revolutionaries and the army the peasant population evacuated in huge numbers to the coast, where they swelled the already overcrowded settlements encircling Lima.

In spite of the army suppression, the guerrilla movement pressed on towards the capital carrying out terrorist attacks on electric pylons in an attempt to black out the city. In 1983 the huge Bayer factory in Lima was burned to the ground, causing the loss of millions of dollars and condemning the huge work force to virtual starvation in a country where unemployment assistance was unknown.

The Cork and Ross mission, located five hundred kilometres north of Lima, was well out of reach of this violence, but as the power of *Sendero* increased and took control of huge regions of Peru, the movement progressed northwards and, in the event, this had long-term consequences for the mission. Because of the success of the mission in helping the poor with schools, medical clinics and general social organisation, it was inevitable that it would attract the hostility of *Sendero* with its policy of sowing unrest, deprivation and starvation in the furtherance of its aim to take over the country.

If the *Senderistas* planned to prepare the ground for the sowing of their revolutionary ideas by wrecking the economy of Peru, they found an unwitting ally in the president of the country, Alan Garcia, who ruled from 1985 to 1990. He was elected as the representative of a left-wing workers' party and began well with promises of introducing social integration to Peru. However, his term of office was soon damaged severely by events such as a prison mutiny, which was brutally suppressed: one hundred rioting prisoners were forced to lie face down in the prison square where they were shot by prison police. Garcia also attempted to nationalise the banks. The undemocratic nature of this move was encapsulated in what became an iconic photograph of a military tank battering in the doorway of a bank in Lima. The president's championing of the poor and the marginalised was also called into question by a military action taken against a newly 'invaded' area of desert around Lima, which involved the baton charging of the poor settlers and the burning of their huts.

It was, however, in the management of the national economy that Garcia displayed incredible incompetence. By 1990, his final year in office, inflation had reached 7,649 per cent, thus preparing the way for the severity of his successor's corrective economic measures. During the period of hyperinflation that marred Garcia's final years, the poor suffered most. The situation was so critical in the Trujillo *barrios* that the Cork and Ross mission had to assume a responsibility that in its twenty-five years of existence it never had to take on before – that of using mission funds to purchase food to feed the poor. Up to now the mission had organised the distribution of food donated by the United States and channelled through Caritas, the Catholic relief agency. Now the situation called for emergency measures as the people faced starvation.

No longer was the distribution of food through the traditional system of weekly handouts adequate to the needs of the community. This had to be supplemented by the provision of cooked meals prepared in strategically located private homes, with raw materials purchased by the Irish priests and delivered by pick-up truck to the 'food kitchens'. The purchase of supplies for these kitchens put a huge strain on mission funds, but the critical need for food left the mission with no other option.

It was inevitable that such a successful operation in the relief of poverty and the advancement of social development would attract the attention of the communists. The *Sendero* movement saw such charitable activity as foreign imperialism at work. In their plan, the more misery in the country the better, as it would hasten the collapse of democratic institutions leaving the way open for a takeover of the country. The impressive success of the Cork mission in the relief of near starvation would inexorably attract the attention of the Shining Path movement.

In May of 1991 an event took place some three hundred miles south of Trujillo that set the alarm bells ringing for the Cork nuns and priests, when an Australian nun was murdered along with four other community workers by the *Sendero Luminoso*. Sr Irene McCormack, a religious of the Sisters of St Joseph of the Sacred Heart in her early fifties, had come from her native Australia to work in Peru some four years earlier. Robert Brophy knew her well as a fellow student in the language school. She spent her first two years working with the Columban Fathers in a poor *barrio* of Lima and then, in spite of the threatening presence of the communist terrorists in the mountains, moved to the parish of Huasahuasi in the interior

The Mission in Crisis

of the country on the main highway between Lima, the capital, and Tarma, an important mountain urban centre. In that parish, which was also run by the Columbans, she spent the last two years of her life in the service of the poor, distributing Caritas food aid and encouraging the youth in reading and learning. The zone in which the parish was located was a great potato-growing area, especially of seed potatoes. Both the area's strategic location on a main highway and its agricultural importance for the country would have made it a strategic target for *Sendero* in its overall plan of reducing Peru to bankruptcy. Hunger, however, was prevalent in this productive agricultural area because of the exceptional economic measures employed to reverse the effects of the previous president's ruinous economic policies.

Sr Irene was remembered by her religious colleagues and grateful parishioners as a cheerful, hardworking, kind and holy nun with no political involvement whatsoever, her only interests being the relief of poverty and the promotion of education for the young. It was, however, these particular efforts at improving the lot of the poor that *Sendero* feared more than armed opposition as forces that would ultimately triumph over their atheistic utopia.

The chilling events of 21 May indicated both the clinical efficiency with which the terrorists carried out their intimidation and the exactitude of their local knowledge in targeting their victims. The raiding party of that night knew exactly who they wanted and where they lived. In all, they picked out five people for execution on that evening: Sr Irene, a teacher of the rural community, the ex-mayor of the town, a member of the neighbourhood watch and a delegate of the local development organisation. Each was taken from their own house and rounded up in the town square where a two-hour 'trial' took place.

The raiding party, numbering about sixty, was comprised mainly of young people – 'almost children', according to eyewitnesses. Sr Irene was accused of being a 'yankee'. To this the people replied that she was Australian. 'That does not matter', they said and went on to speak of the North American surplus food she had distributed. As the early South American twilight faded into darkness, the prisoners were ordered to kneel and each was killed by a shot to the back of the neck, Sr Irene being the first to die. Later, as had been her wish, the nun was buried in the town where she had died.

In a letter of sympathy to her colleagues and relatives, Bishop Michael Murphy of Cork and Ross stated he was fully aware of the increasing danger to the missionaries in Peru. His concern would be further increased by the events of August in the same year when no less than three missionary priests would be murdered much closer to Trujillo, one a mere seventy miles away.

On 9 August 1991 a double murder took place in the Diocese of Chimbote, the neighbouring diocese to the south of Trujillo. This second attack on religious indicated that *Sendero* had by now targeted the Catholic Church in their armed struggle to establish a Maoist State in Peru. The attack on two Franciscan priests, natives of Poland, was so similar to the murderous attack on Sr Irene McCormac that it must have been decided at the central command headquarters of the Maoist movement. A subsequent attack on an Italian priest confirmed this theory.

The Polish priests were young men who had worked in the mountainous area for over two years, organising adult religious education with the help of lay catechists, as well as organising the peasant labourers in their struggle for social justice. On the fateful evening, the priests had finished the 7.30 Mass and, as was their custom, held a meeting with their twenty-five lay helpers to discuss the catechetical programme for the coming week. A knock came to the door of the priests' house and they were informed that members of *Sendero Luminoso* wished to enter. The priests replied that whoever looks for the truth and wishes to work for justice was welcome to the presbytery. Fifteen hooded men entered and engaged the company in a cold conversation for about forty-five minutes. Most of the exchanges dealt with religion, the teaching of which they opposed, as it tended to dull the desire for the armed struggle for justice. They were also opposed to the manner in which the peasants were organised to protect their rights. Also, they opposed the handing out of food to the poor of the area.

The Mission in Crisis

While this conversation was proceeding in the parish house, another group of about fifteen surrounded the town and, violently entering the premises of the national telephone company, cut communications with the outside world. A smaller group took the town's mayor from his house and brought him to the presbytery where they demanded the keys of the food store of the town. When this was refused they used dynamite to blow up the doors of the storehouse. Then they commandeered the parish truck and loaded the two priests into it saying they were going on to a nearby village. This was not so, because after crossing the bridge at the entrance to the town they headed for an old mining centre called Pueblo Viejo. A few minutes later people heard the shooting and found the bodies of the two priests lying by the roadside.

On 25 August 1991, *Sendero Luminoso* struck at the Catholic Church once again, this time in the parish of Santa located on the Pan-American Highway, seventy miles to the south of Trujillo. The victim was an Italian priest, Fr Alexandro. This latest murder triggered outrage in both the local and national press. All the commentators agreed that the purpose of this series of murders was to force out of Peru the many Catholic priests and nuns who had come there to work as missionaries. It was also noticed that the Maoists were making a mockery of the communist idea of internationalism by victimising men and women from different nations of the world. Clearly Guzman was accepting the communist teaching that religion was the opium of the people.

Journalists insisted that the people of Peru were not anti-clerical and held foreign priests in the highest regard. To attack priests, whether native or foreign, was completely contrary to the wishes of the public. There was a unanimous call on the Catholic Church to launch a campaign against the subversives from every pulpit in Peru.

Such a call was understandable in the light of the situation all over the country at this stage of the Maoist campaign. So widespread had the subversive activity become that one could say in truth that Peru was experiencing a civil war. In the same month of August, during which the priests were killed, in the space of one week at least ten engagements took place between the guerrillas and the forces of the State. In the district of Huaraz in the central Andes, many columns of guerrillas attacked a police garrison. Once the police were defeated, the Maoists summoned the local people to the town square where they held a public trial of the mayor of that town and of a neighbouring town. Both representatives of the State were accused of collaboration with the armed forces and were immediately shot.

In Laramarte, Ayacucho, at 9.45 at night, *Senderistas* violently attacked an anti-guerrilla police base killing eleven of that elite force, and with the unconditional surrender of the barracks the arms were surrendered to the Maoists, who remained in the town for five hours, during which they destroyed the national bank and burned the town hall. In another town near Ayacucho in the early hours of the night, two columns of guerrillas attacked the army barracks of the district. In a ferocious assault fourteen soldiers were killed and twenty more wounded. In Huamachuco, a rural town in the district of Trujillo, also in the night, a column of guerrillas ambushed a military convoy, killing nine soldiers and leaving fifteen gravely injured. In this attack powerful explosives were used to mine the road over which the convoy was to pass. In the Pucalpa region at three in the afternoon a patrol of marines was attacked with modern arms and potent explosives. Twenty marines died in the attack. In Huancavelica the subversives used forty kilos of dynamite to mine the road the police patrol would use. After the mines were detonated, they attacked the police with rifles and mortars, forcing them to surrender. In Barranco, a wealthy suburb of Lima, terrorists surprised a police patrol, killing three men with powerful firearms. Similar attacks left eight soldiers dead in Puno, twelve dead in Huanaco and twelve peasant civil defence operatives dead in Huancayo.

Back at the Cork and Ross mission in Trujillo, priests and nuns braced themselves for the violent attack that they now knew was inevitable in the light of the breakdown in law and order all over Peru and the series of attacks aimed at foreign Catholic missionaries in the neighbouring Diocese of Chimbote. The flow of this information about these events from the mission back to Cork was

The Mission in Crisis

the cause of serious concern to the priests and nuns of the home diocese; to none more so than the two superiors of the religious orders concerned: the Bon Secours and the Mercy Sisters, as well as the bishop himself. These three carried a burden of responsibility not unlike that of a president in time of war; their decisions were ones of life and death. While all three wished the mission to carry on its great work, no one wished to see coffins arriving at Cork airport from Peru. The critical situation suggested many options ranging from closing down the mission to ignoring the dangers and continuing as hitherto. In between these extremes lay less dramatic choices such as lowering the profile of the operation, reducing personnel, transferring to a more peaceful place in South America and so on.

A permanent mission committee already existed in Cork to support the men and women in the field and to advise the bishop on decisions relating to the mission. On 3 September 1991, this committee met and set up an ad hoc committee to address the new situation in Peru. The ad hoc committee numbered six people, one from each of the orders involved, and four priests, one a founder member of the mission, the other three former mission superiors. They drew up a report within a few days suggesting ways and means of dealing with the crisis. The contingency plan suggested certain preparations to be taken immediately and an evacuation plan, which could be implemented in the event of an attack on the mission.

The preparations suggested were that each Irish person would have their personal documentation for leaving Peru up to date, to arrange that the native Peruvian nuns and the lay parish committees would be asked to maintain uninterrupted parochial service during the absence of the Irish priests and Sisters, the Peruvian teachers were asked to take responsibility for the running of the parochial schools and the native Sisters to run the medical clinics. The first recommendation of the evacuation plan stated: 'Any priest or nun who wishes to remain regardless of danger should be free to do so; anyone who wishes to return to Ireland should be free to do so.' It went on to point out that the superior of the St James Missionary Society in Boston would welcome any priest to their houses in

Ecuador, while the superior of the Columbans in Ireland had offered accommodation in Lima or Chile. Both the Bon Secours and Mercy Sisters had their own accommodation already in Lima.

It is a tribute to the courage of the nuns and priests that none of them opted for the choice of returning immediately to Ireland. Their reluctance to leave is understandable because of the bonds of friendship that bound them to the people whom they had served for so many years, and especially to the lay leaders in each parish whose loyalty had been unflinching, in the case of many, for a quarter of a century. In addition, there was a general feeling of trust that that loyalty would withstand the awesome power of *Sendero* and act as a bulwark against any local following of Abimael Guzman's philosophy.

Life on the mission continued as usual through October and November of 1991. As these months in the southern hemisphere mark the closing stages of the academic year and usher in the long summer vacation, they corresponded to the heightened parish activity in Ireland in April and May when First Communions and Confirmations, as well as class graduations, coalesce to make it the busiest period of the year for every parish. Already the nuns and priests were making plans for summer retreats, courses and, perhaps, either a holiday in Ireland or a short vacation in Lima. As these busy weeks passed, confidence grew and the memory of the earlier murders of foreign religious receded until, in early December, *Sendero Luminoso* struck directly at the Cork and Ross mission for the first time.

The communists selected as their target an outlying medical clinic and food storage centre, which contained medicines for the sick and food for the hungry. The medical centre occupied the inside corner of a large walled-in yard featuring brick walls strengthened by reinforced concrete columns at intervals of about ten yards. In a sense it was the most obvious of the many mission centres to attract an attack because of its location at the very perimeter of the Cork and Ross territory and its proximity to the foothills of the Andes.

The raiders broke into the well-secured building and robbed the medicines, valued at over £1,000 in Irish punts, a considerable amount almost twenty years ago. However, much more significant were the slogans daubed on the external walls of the health centre and the handwritten posters affixed to the walls. In addition, there were printed posters bearing the hammer and sickle, pictures of Chairman Mao, as well as propaganda posters peculiar to the Peruvian Communist Party. The most prominent slogan daubed in letters two feet high read: 'Death to Irish Imperialism'. Four handwritten posters carried quotations from Chairman Mao, from 'President Gonzalo' (the name always given to Abimael Guzman, head of *Sendero*), and statements of policy by the Peruvian Communist Party. A red poster with a yellow star carried the inscription: 'The People's Guerrilla Army'.

This attack was followed by a handwritten letter delivered to one of the convents that purported to come from the northern base of the Peruvian Communist Party. Running to two foolscap pages, it revealed an intimate knowledge of the people who staffed the mission, including the native Peruvian Sisters who were members of the two religious orders. The letter stated that it was addressed directly to the religious women. Claiming a membership of 70,000, together with 30,000 more supporters, the writer was confident of triumph. They went on to claim that they knew the names of the nuns and their families and that these relatives would be kidnapped one by one if they continued to participate in the marches for peace. They threatened to enter the convents, eliminate the superioress and dynamite the building and churches.

Subsequent to the attack on the medical centre, a young man from the same district came to one of the Cork priests to tell him to be careful in case there would be dynamite placed under his car and not to travel alone. He named one of the Irish Sisters and one of the priests, whose names were on a death list. This young man agreed to be interviewed further. It appeared that his family in the Amazonian jungle was in the drug business and had connections with *Sendero Luminoso*. When Bishop Murphy arrived a few weeks later for his Christmas visit and was informed of all these events, he came to the conclusion that this man was an official messenger of the guerrillas, who were now waging a psychological war of nerves in an attempt to get the Irish missionaries out peacefully.

Children of the Sun

The bishop made an even more alarming discovery when he learned that some young people closely associated with the daily running of the mission were attending local meetings of *Sendero*, who on experiencing some kind of personal crisis admitted such involvement and gave the names of another priest and nun, both Irish, who were on a death list. It was then obvious that the mission had been infiltrated and that some Irish priests and nuns were in mortal danger. Bishop Murphy, in a statement publicly released at home in Ireland, summed up the situation:

> The priests and sisters were advised that the threats should be taken seriously, so naturally an element of uncertainty, and indeed of fear, became part of life for them. They were forced to curtail the normal activities of the mission, and to adopt a much lower profile than usual. As the weeks passed, the tension increased, and when I arrived in Trujillo in mid-December, I felt that, to ensure the safety of our people, some difficult decisions would have to be made. I met each priest individually. I also spoke with the local Archbishop. I discovered from these and from other reliable sources that various parish groups had been infiltrated by the terrorists. Death threats had been made against a number of our priests and sisters. Sendero was beginning to control parts of our parishes and were effectively determining what we could or could not do. All the advice I received was that the wisest thing to do in the circumstances was to scale down our mission in Peru.

The obvious way of scaling down the mission was to implement a plan that had existed from the very beginning nearly thirty years previous, vis-à-vis handing back to the local bishop some of the territory entrusted to the Bishop of Cork and Ross at the beginning. It had never been the intention of Bishop Lucey to keep these parishes forever; they were to be developed in infrastructure and in

The Mission in Crisis

spirituality and then staffed by native clergy when they were viable units. As the longest established communities, the original parishes, El Porvenir and Florencia, were the obvious choices to be given back. These would now be returned to the local archbishop and food distribution would be discontinued until the crisis had passed.

The idea of handing back parishes had been in the minds of the Cork and Ross priests for some time, as they felt the longer they stayed the more the locals would rely on their presence. Many felt that there were other areas of South America crying out for help. One of these areas could be selected and a new mission founded. The bishop decided to send four priests from Trujillo to Chile on a temporary basis with a view to identifying a suitable area in South America for a new mission. Under pressure from *Sendero*, the bishop had to make the following decisions in December 1991:

- El Porvenir and Florencia were to be handed back to the Archbishop of Trujillo.
- Four priests would remain on in La Esperanza.
- Four others due to finish their time on the mission in the near future would return home.
- Four others would go to work in Chile and plan a new mission. Their brief was to continue the Cork and Ross missionary dimension in a new location in South America. Meanwhile, they would help in a parish in the city of Valparaíso in Chile.
- The Irish nuns would move to their convents in Lima for a time, leaving the Peruvian members of their communities to run the medical centres and keep the convents open. While the schools would continue to function, food distribution and the running of food kitchens would cease.

When Bishop Murphy published these decisions in the Peruvian press there was immediate outrage that *Sendero Luminoso* could intimidate such a successful missionary operation to such a degree. This anger, expressed in news reports as well as editorially in the Trujillo newspapers, was immediately picked up by the national press in Lima. The blame for the scaling down of a mission that had been so helpful to the poorest of the poor was unambiguously laid at the feet of the communist guerrilla movement. The press reaction was a dramatic validation of the work of the Cork and Ross missionaries, as well as a tribute to the huge financial contribution the people of Cork had made to the development of every aspect of life, from sport to culture to spirituality, all for the benefit of the poorest section of Trujillo over a generation. From their daily news reports of the murderous brutality of *Sendero*, the press, more than any other agency in the State, appreciated the mortal danger in which the missionaries had found themselves in the previous months.

The news of Bishop Murphy's decision had already reached the Irish newspapers through the wire services even before he left Peru for home. The press sympathised with the bishop on the difficult decisions he had been forced to make and unreservedly condemned the forces of anarchy that had threatened the lives of the personnel of a mission that had won the hearts of Cork people for a generation. In the *Irish Examiner*, Tim Cramer, one of the senior editorial staff, wrote:

> It is worth remembering, at this stage, that there always has been and always will be a risk factor in mission work. In the case of the Cork and Ross mission in Trujillo, the risk has been accepted by the priests and nuns themselves. Bishop Murphy, however, has given the necessary wise leadership and decided to minimise the risk, reluctant though some of the missionaries may be to abandon a people who need their ministrations and a country that tugs forever at the heartstrings.

For the Shining Path guerrillas, 1991 had been the most successful year in their struggle to turn Peru into a Maoist State. Through intimidation and murder they had undermined the local officers of State, such as district mayors, and through violent confrontations with the army and the police they had gained control of two-fifths of the national territory and half the population, even extending

The Mission in Crisis

their area of control along the southern coast as far as Lima itself. Some members of the movement were even boasting that they had achieved 'strategic equilibrium', meaning the ability to fight the army head on. With a young active membership recruited from the provincial universities, they were fighting on two fronts: first attacking the peasants who had organised resistance through local defence forces and second the armed forces. The peasant resistance groups, in theory, were to defend their villages until the arrival of the army, who would then overcome the communists. In practice, however, the fight was well over by the time the soldiers arrived to find the butchered bodies of the peasants lying amid smouldering huts that were once their homes.

For a guerrilla force, numbering little more than 10,000 fighters, to wrest control of so much of a country defended by a regular army of 120,000 soldiers was an extraordinary achievement. In addition, their stranglehold on the country brought the economy to its knees. The greatest strength of the movement was the absolute control its leader, Abimael Guzman, held over his followers; ironically this was also to prove its greatest weakness. Charles de Gaulle once wrote about the qualities of a leader: 'There can be no prestige without mystery. In the designs, the demeanour and the mental operation of a leader there must always be something which others cannot altogether fathom which puzzles them, stirs them and rivets their attention.' Guzman was always a figure surrounded by mystery. The only photographs of him that existed were nearly twenty years old. During that time he led the most secretive life, never seen in public, never making a public statement. He had become a mythical figure. Some believed he was dead; others said he had left for Europe and that he was capable of passing through international frontiers at will. His invisibility, coupled with the brutality of his deeds, made him as fearsome as an evil spirit whose wickedness was as evident as his presence was invisible.

With the turn of the year from 1991 to 1992, Guzman, for the first time in his life, let down his guard with catastrophic results for himself and his bloody movement. The circumstances of this event were pedestrian enough, even if the consequences were of national importance. In a relaxing moment he was attending a party held by his supporters, where he drank and danced either unaware or heedless that one of the partygoers was filming the event on a video camera. The crucial tape found its way into the hands of the police who were then able to study not only his appearance, but his gestures and movements, body shape and profile. The clip was passed on to the detective unit of the police set up especially to deal with terrorism, who quietly studied the footage over and over again until the most wanted man in South America was as recognisable to them as a member of their own family.

Along with this priceless source of identification, a second lucky break came when a disgruntled follower tipped off the police that his leader was living in a quiet suburb of Lima. Perhaps the most extraordinary aspect of these events was the secrecy that the detective department maintained right through the investigation. Everyone familiar with Peru and Peruvians knows that secrets can never be kept. Rumours, whispers and leaks ensure that at parish level, city level and national level everything gets put about sooner rather than later. Yet this secret was kept to the very end. In the case of Guzman even the slightest leak would have tipped him off, made his capture impossible and doomed the country to endless years of savagery.

For two weeks the detectives kept the house under surveillance cleverly disguising themselves, some as street cleaners, others as operatives of the national telephone company. Before moving in they had to verify that their quarry was really there. From patient and prolonged study of the man's lifestyle they came to know that he suffered from a chronic skin complaint that necessitated regular medication. Under the disguise of street cleaners they removed the refuse bins from outside the house and found the discarded tubes of the medication used for the complaint. They were then certain their man was inside the house.

By coincidence, one of the detectives lived close by. On the Saturday night of the assault on the house this man staged a barbecue in his garden – not an uncommon Peruvian custom where visitors danced and sang the night away, keeping neighbours awake

The Mission in Crisis

into the small hours. This ploy enabled the police to fill the area with their officers in a manner that did not excite the slightest suspicion among the neighbours. Meanwhile, two detectives sat in an unmarked car opposite the terrorist's house. Their vigilance was rewarded when a girl emerged and went to the corner shop to purchase cigarettes. As she opened the door to re-enter, the police swooped and entered the house without resistance, while the other officers moved into firing positions and police cars, prowling nearby, screamed into the area sealing off the house within a wall of fire power. Neighbours, assuming that it was a raid on drug dealers, never suspected that they were witnessing the political event of the century in their city.

Describing the arrest of Abimael Guzman in one of Lima's daily papers the next morning, the writer gloated:

> The man who could not be captured, the man who could never be found was not only found and detained by captors who were neither North American marines nor 'Blue Berets' of the United Nations, nor elite members of the armed forces, but only simple detectives who did no more than their patient, humble and silent work for which the country owes them eternal gratitude and public recognition. These policemen had re-vindicated their institutions so much disparaged in recent years for the actions of some of their colleagues. Guzman, who had become an idol to his followers, in the end had feet of clay. Without even the personal courage of drawing a gun in order to confront his captors he meekly submitted to the police.

The police on that night drew a massive haul of prisoners taking not only the leader of the Maoists, but up to twenty of their high command. Guzman was subsequently displayed in public in a steel cage on the streets of Lima behind bars that will confine him for the rest of his life. His movement would eventually disappear and later a Commission for Truth and Reconciliation would reveal that in all

Children of the Sun

69,280 victims had died in the civil war, victims of *Sendero Luminoso*, of MRTA (another parallel terrorist group) and of atrocities carried out by the military in response to the armed attacks on their members. Poor peasants, primarily from indigenous communities in the sierra, constituted the vast majority of the victims.

The whole twenty-year long brutal campaign of the Shining Path guerrillas came to an unexpected end with the capture of Guzman. This event might have been expected to take place in some heroic last stand against the forces of 'bourgeois imperialism' with the central character resisting to the last bullet and facing death with gallantry. Instead, it revolved around the search of a trash can in a Lima suburb.

Like many communist movements around the world, the *Sendero* had come to be dominated by one man, rather like Castro in Cuba, Stalin in Russia and Mao in China. While the cult of the personality favoured a movement in many ways, it often proved a fatal flaw when that person lost his freedom and was revealed as powerless as any small-time criminal in custody. The whole Shining Path movement lost its lustre and almost instantly faded into history.

The final defeat of the *Senderistas* was an enormous feat for the government. Here was a man responsible for thousands of deaths, for impoverishing the country for years, for dislodging huge chunks of population from the Andean highlands and forcing the poor into sub-human living conditions in the *barriadas* around Lima; a man who for a time was on the verge of taking over the country, instantly removed from the scenes of activity that he masterminded and his followers dispersed forever. Had he succeeded in his campaign and dislodged the democratic government of Peru, his probable treatment of the people he supposedly liberated would have been analogous to the Pol Pot regime, as Dalrymple, a British commentator, observed.

The fall of *Sendero* meant that the Cork and Ross mission survived, escaping the slaughter consequent of a communist purge of what they would describe as 'oppressive institutions'. In the quiet aftermath of the terrorism, the peaceful handing over of the mission to the native priests was possible and the Sisters of both religious orders, now well strengthened with native vocations, were able to continue and expand their religious and social work without the dread of imminent terror.

The happy outcome of the reign of terror should not obscure the dangers that the priests and nuns lived through for over ten years. In deference to their relatives in Ireland, little was made of the danger to which they were daily subjected. The Lord has to be thanked that no member of the group paid for their courage with their lives.

Cork Priests in Chile

Since the earliest days of Christianity, the missionary has always been a person who travelled from place to place, never putting down permanent roots anywhere. This was the pattern established by St Paul, that first great missionary who travelled widely in the Middle East in what was then known as Asia Minor and is today the country of Turkey. On arrival, Paul preached the message of Christ, and as soon as he had a community of believers he established a local Church and moved on to pastures new, though always maintaining contact through letters, such as his famous epistles to the Church of Corinth, Rome and Ephesus. Usually Paul moved on when he thought the newly established group of believers was strong enough to survive without him, but sometimes he was run out of town, as happened when his negative preaching about Diana threatened the business of the silversmiths of Ephesus.

The Cork and Ross mission was never meant to be a permanent establishment. Yet because of the shortage of native vocations in Peru, and the endemic poverty of the people there, the mission remained in the same place for a generation. Only for the pressure from the Maoist guerrillas who threatened not only the lives of the Irish missionaries, but those of the Peruvian nuns who had joined them, their relatives and the buildings themselves, the mission might never have branched out at all. In January 1992, the Bishop of Cork and Ross took the decision that the profile of the mission should be lowered in Trujillo and that a new mission should be founded somewhere else in South America. He transferred two priests from Peru to Chile, together with two other Corkmen newly arrived from the language school in Bolivia. They were to work in Chile on a temporary basis while scouting out new territory for the next Cork and Ross missionary venture. Until this new area was identified and approved, there would be no formal agreement signed, even though the four priests would take up duty in some parish in Chile immediately.

Many people are familiar with the strange appearance of Chile on maps of the world, mainly because of its peculiar configuration. While other countries like France, Spain and the United States of America roughly correspond to a square or rectangular shape, Chile appears on the map as a long strip on the periphery of the carrot-shaped South American continent, its length being all out of proportion with its width. In fact, from its northern frontier with Peru to the tip of Tierra del Fuego, the country runs for a distance of almost 3,000 miles, while its widest point from the coast to the Andes measures just 200 miles. The country's unique shape is dictated by its Pacific coastline in the west and the Andes chain to the east.

The beautiful sunny city of Santiago, capital of Chile, was built by the Spaniards in a fertile valley within sight of the snow-capped Andes, and is laid out in gracious boulevards with ornate public buildings and churches. Some miles to the west of the capital lies the city's great seaport, Valparaíso (the Valley of Paradise). Both cities are built on seismic fault lines and are susceptible to earthquakes, while prehistoric volcanic activity has surrounded each with steep, shelving hills where the millions of poor who populate the area live in huts that cling to the vertiginous levels on which they are precariously perched. In Valparaíso cable cars help to ferry residents to their homes.

Robert Brophy, superior of the small missionary group, writing home remarked on the confined conditions in which the poor families lived, often two families to a hut, which would lack both water and electricity – tattered wooden buildings and shacks all spilling steeply into this world famous shipping port. To reach their new parish, El Buen Pastor (The Good Shepherd), the priests had to make their way up the steep, narrow, winding streets of the city.

Children of the Sun

From the very top, on which their house was built, they could look across the bay to the elegant seaside resort of Viña del Mar (The Vineyard of the Sea), where the rich of both Chile and Argentina spent their summers. The view encapsulated the chasm dividing South America's rich from its poor.

The Cork priests' new parish had a population of 80,000, served by six simple little churches. The parish had been entrusted to the care of the Irish priests as a result of a meeting between Bishop Michael Murphy and the Bishop of Valparaíso held in Santiago in January of 1992. The time of their arrival in Chile was fortuitous because the Catholic Church was held in high regard, thanks to its consistent resistance to the dictatorship of the president Augusto Pinochet, who had violently wrested the country in 1973 from the democratically elected president Allende. During the dark days of Pinochet's brutal regime from 1973 to 1990, when thousands of people were killed or 'disappeared', the Church had stood by the widows who cried out for justice and news of the whereabouts of the remains of their murdered husbands and sons. In the end, it was the growing power of these groups that brought about the return to democracy in a peaceful manner.

For the two young priests newly arrived from language school, Valparaíso was an exciting introduction to the new culture of South America while for the other men who had left their beloved Trujillo so unexpectedly the change to a new environment did little to distract them from memories of the people 'at home' in Peru. It was clear from their correspondence that their hearts were still there with their friends. Such is the pain of all true missionaries.

In the course of the year in Chile, the priests produced a document outlining the pros and cons of each location for the planned missionary outreach. They considered the question of language – Brazil uses Portuguese; the rest of the continent Spanish – the health risks associated with the jungle and living at great altitude, the political stability of each country, as well as proximity to the parent mission in Peru.

Language ruled out Brazil, even though it offered great scope for missionary work and the presence of the Irish Kiltegan Fathers would have been a helpful support in the initial years of establishment. Argentina had appeal because of its long association with Ireland, its temperate climate and the presence of the Christian Brothers. Similarly, Chile enjoyed a temperate climate and a strong Columban presence similar to that in Peru, which had always supported the Cork mission in every way possible over the years. Ecuador had much to recommend it. Priests from Cork worked there with the St James missionaries and the Augustinians, and its borders touched those of Peru at a point little more than a day's drive from Trujillo. The capital, Quito, though located in the mountains did not have a problem with altitude; Guayaquil, on the coast, had great communities living in poverty and was short of priests, while further up the coastline, the Portoviejo diocese had a mixture of lowlands on the coast and country villages in the Andes.

Any newly arrived missionary group would always need initial backup from sympathetic contacts in their newly chosen country, preferably people of Irish origin who would understand both the language and the practical problems of transferring money through the banks, as well as the complicated procedures of gaining residency as foreigners. In Caracas, capital of Venezuela, Jerry O'Sullivan, a native of Lisavaird in west Cork, held an influential position both with the Catholic bishops and the government. Arriving in Venezuela as a Legion of Mary envoy several years earlier, he settled in Caracas, married and rose to be Director General of the Conference of the Venezuelan Bishops. For a time he had been seconded to the Venezuelan government as National Coordinator of Industrial Diversification – a position of great importance in a country where the entire economy was based on the oil industry. In establishing a new mission, such contacts with the bishops and the government would have been of the greatest help.

In the report that the priests prepared for Bishop Murphy, they stated that they would welcome the participation of Irish Sisters in the proposed mission, similar to that given in Trujillo where the nuns had achieved so much in bringing help to the poor and the sick.

After much discussion and reflection Ecuador won out and Robert Brophy travelled to Quito where he consulted the Papal

Children of the Sun

Nuncio, who recommended a number of dioceses that would welcome outside help. The Diocese of Portoviejo was chosen and an agreement between Cork and Portoviejo was signed on St Patrick's Day, 1993, providing for the establishment of a mission in an area of Manta on the coast to be staffed by four Irish priests, with a possibility of a fifth being added, for a period of ten years. The details of the agreement regarding appointment of priests, the holding of property and the settlement of any disputes that might arise were similar to those of the agreement between Cork and Trujillo, made on the same date some twenty-eight years earlier. In the event, the agreement in Ecuador was as pleasing to both sides as it had been in Peru. In both cases, amicable relations always existed between the missions and the host diocese, not only during the term agreed – after both missions had closed, close relations continued to exist between the Irish and the South Americans.

New Mission in Ecuador

In February 1993, Bishop Michael Murphy of Cork and Ross issued a statement to the press in Ireland announcing the launch of an extension of the diocesan mission to South America from Peru to the neighbouring country Ecuador, which would take effect on the following St Patrick's Day.

Few in Ireland would have known much about Ecuador, apart from the fact that it was located on the equator, which gave it its name. The Republic of Ecuador is located on the Pacific coast of South America, immediately to the north of Peru, with its interior territory reaching upwards to the summit of the Andes and eastwards to the tropical jungles of the Amazon basin. Like Peru, Chile and Bolivia, Ecuador formed part of the great Inca Empire while its capital, Quito, located in a beautiful valley in the Andes, ranked with cities like Cajamarca and Cusco in importance in the life of that Empire. Since 1832, the famed Galapagos Islands have formed part of Ecuador.

The site chosen for the new mission was Manta in the Diocese of Portoviejo, the largest diocese (in area) in Ecuador. Manta itself is a port city of 200,000 people situated just south of the equator with the expected warm and humid climate, which is cooled by the sea breezes from the Pacific Ocean. A growing shanty town, home to 80,000 new migrants from the mountains, surrounds the city in which the poor live in conditions as deprived as those in the other Cork mission in Trujillo, for the most part without priests or churches or any of the religious, educational and social services that such communities require to support a normal, dignified lifestyle.

Children of the Sun

About 80 per cent of the population of the whole city of Manta were without employment and most of those lived in the shantytown.

Bishop Murphy explained that the decision to opt for Manta was made because he and the priests felt that there was a greater need of a missionary presence there than in Chile, where four priests had worked during the previous year. If you measure the wisdom of the choice of location by the religious and social needs of the population then Manta was a wise choice. Perhaps a single statistic gives greater scope: there was only one diocesan priest stationed in the whole city. The Jesuits served one side of the city and the Salesians the other, numbering together no more than eight men, all living in the city centre, many of them old and the remainder involved in schools or other commitments. On the arrival of the Corkmen, the diocesan priest moved to a parish on the coast where he also doubled as chaplain to the Air Force. Two of the Irish priests moved into the house he vacated and the other two rented accommodation in another sector of the allotted area.

The arrival of the Irishmen enabled the bishop of the area to draw up parish boundaries for the whole city, giving his new helpers two parishes: La Paz and San Patricio. The notion of 'parish' in that part of the world was quite different from what is understood by the term in Ireland. In Ecuador, 'parish' is understood in a more flexible way: the priest and the church being little more than 'service stations' where people go for the sacraments. In the two newly formed parishes there was no such thing as parish groups, no sense of community, no parish organisations and no parish meeting rooms. Even though the parish of La Paz had its own priest's house and church, they felt it could prove to be the more difficult to develop since a tradition had already been established whereby the priest was there for sacramental services only and there was nothing in the line of community development, which meant that lay people had no experience of involvement in parish life or taking any responsibility for handing on the faith in a planned way.

The Irish priests immediately got in touch with an architect to remodel the existing house to accommodate parish meeting rooms. Of the two priests living in that parish, one took responsibility for a

New Mission in Ecuador

large scattered community newly settled in the outskirts of the parish. The other two priests rented a house in the newly named parish of San Patricio, a vast area divided by ravines making it very difficult terrain. The fact that they lived among the people did much to establish a bond with their new parishioners and gave them a propitious start in the community. There were drawbacks from a personal point of view, as living in rented accommodation in an area where there was no piped water meant that water had to purchased from visiting tankers, or from local dealers who brought water in on donkey back and sold it by the bucket. Because of the heat and the ever-prevalent flies, all water had to be boiled. Two churches already existed in this area, though they were badly located because subsequent settlements were made in areas far removed from the church. Many areas had no service at all. An immediate need was a parish centre that would include a priest's residence and parish meeting rooms where children could be prepared for the sacraments and adult groups could be organised.

The new missionaries, however, were not entirely alone in their efforts to develop parish life, because the diocese was developing an overall plan whereby catechists would be trained and lay leaders would be prepared for work in every parish in Portoviejo. The mission enthusiastically embraced this plan and became part of it, developing at the same time a close relationship with the archbishop.

It was fortuitous that the founder priests of the new Cork and Ross mission already had experience of working in Peru and Chile, as it brought home to them the realisation that the true missionary is a transient person, someone who comes to set up structures, to create a tradition of parish service and then moves on. The time to be spent in Manta was fixed at ten years. This gave them an understanding, which they would always have to keep in mind, that the area would have to be handed back to the local clergy who would be far less numerous than themselves. Hence the importance of building churches and houses that would be habitable for years to come and building a sustainable parish community that would survive their departure. It would be a vote of confidence in the local

Church that it could take over when they would leave, and that that date would be known to all in advance. The priority was the building up of a eucharistic community, making people aware of the consequence of being part of that community, forming them in an awareness that they are the Church and have to assume responsibility for its life. In a word, they saw the work of the mission as establishing a local Church, forming lay leaders, encouraging vocations for the local diocese and setting up structures that would survive their departure, when they would move on to some other area of need.

At the time of the mission's foundation, the teaching of religion was banned in State schools. They had hopes that this might change, but even if it did it would mean that all religions would be taught in the schools with the result that preparation for the sacraments would still remain the responsibility of the parish. Therefore, the immediate challenge for the mission was the training of catechists and lay leaders.

Early Years in Manta

One year after opening the Manta mission the priests were able to report considerable progress to Bishop Murphy at home in Cork: the new church and classrooms were almost completed; plans were progressing for the building of a new church and a medical centre representing an investment of up to £100,000. To put this amount in context, one might recall that two dwelling houses could be built for that sum in Ireland at that time. They also requested approval of the construction of a smaller £30,000 chapel in an area where there was no religious presence whatsoever. It was also reported that 50,000 deutsche marks were forthcoming from the German bishops' overseas agency to help with the projects. Apart from bricks and mortar the priests were also investing in human resources with the running of training courses for lay people, who would participate in the religious education of both adults and children in the various catechetical courses.

The new medical centre was already providing much needed assistance to the poor and the sick. Two doctors and a physiotherapist were in attendance each day and it was planned to set up a pharmacy later in the year. As the State provided no medical assistance, each patient contributed a nominal amount towards the cost of the medical programme to pay for the salaries of the doctors and the upkeep of the centres. The government had decided not to subsidise hospital care, leaving patients to pay for all their medical attention. Considering that the average salary was about $80 a month and a visit to a doctor cost $20, none of the poor in the shantytown could afford such a visit. The result was that more and more people were coming to the mission looking for help.

One year later, Robert Brophy, who had been the founder and first superior of the new mission, finally left for Ireland having completed a varied term in South America working in three different countries: Peru, Chile and Ecuador. The people of his parish showed their appreciation of what the Irish had done for them by turning out in their hundreds to bid him farewell.

The appointment of a paid full-time pastoral agent was a new departure for the Cork South American mission. The importance of such a move was stressed by Bishop Murphy, who always believed in bringing professionalism to the work of a mission.

While the year 1993/1994 was a year of setting up structures, the main focus in the following year had been on pastoral initiatives. The main buildings were in place but two more projects were proposed for the building of more classrooms. This indicated the growing numbers of people who were attending religion classes. Dental care was added to the medical provision as well as a laboratory for carrying out quick and efficient tests without waiting for the results to be returned from some distant testing centre. The mission also linked in with a programme run by the pharmaceutical companies designed to help the poor. Membership of this programme entitled the mission to buy and sell medical products at reduced prices. The aim was to have these medical centres financially independent of subvention by the mission. In striving for financial independence, the priests were looking to the day when the Cork connection would be ended and the medical centres would have to survive on their own. The numbers of children participating in the First Communion programme had risen to three hundred and fifty, as compared to ninety in the first year. One hundred and thirty catechists were working on a voluntary basis and six youth clubs were attracting teenagers to church activities while adult groups were also in place.

If comparisons could be made between the original mission in Peru and the new one in Ecuador, one difference stood out: the preoccupation in Ecuador with building a self-sufficient and self-reliant Christian community that would survive the departure of the Irish. In Peru, at the beginning both funding and the supply of personnel had seemed limitless, but after thirty years the major change in Irish religious life with the consequent drop in vocations had alerted the Corkmen to the transient nature of their work abroad and the growing certainty that the day would come when the Cork outreach would come to an end.

New men, like Kieran O'Driscoll and Kevin O'Regan, were still arriving in Ecuador. By 1997, in one parish there were three churches with a population of 40,000 people; in the other there were four churches serving 50,000 people. One thousand children were in the First Communion programme and five hundred preparing for Confirmation. Family catechesis was also introduced, where parents attended classes in religion designed to help them to teach their children the faith at home. Impressive as these numbers were, it was still obvious that, taking the population into account, huge numbers were untouched by the parish activities. A programme of home visitation to be carried out by the active Catholics was organised, ensuring that at least five times a year someone knocked on the door of each house in a gesture of welcome and support from the local Church. This might seem intrusive to Irish observers, but in South America where the Evangelists, Pentecostals, Jehovah's Witnesses and Mormons relentlessly knocked on doors, it was an essential strategy to keep people loyal to their inherited Catholic faith.

All was going well with the Cork and Ross mission until December 1997 when, as so often happens in South America, a natural disaster struck the continent's west coast in the form of El Niño, a name given to the periodic change of direction of the ocean current in the Pacific Ocean that brought catastrophic climate change to the region.

Two Ocean Currents

The line of latitude that passes through Dublin lies north of Newfoundland and just to the south of Moscow. Yet Ireland never suffers the harsh winters of these areas thanks to the ocean current that originates thousands of miles away in the Gulf of Mexico.

In the southern hemisphere, the Humboldt Current, originating in the frozen seas that wash the Antarctic icepack, protects the west coast of South America from the tropical heat that one would expect in tropical latitudes. The Humboldt Current flows northwards from the Antarctic into the South Pacific Ocean, unobstructed by any landmass until it meets the sheer, submerged cliffs of the continental shelf of South America a few miles off the coast of Peru.

In 1802, the Berliner, Baron Von Humboldt, discovered a current of cold water running from south to north in the sea off Trujillo. From this discovery he formulated the scientific principle that ocean currents decide the climatic conditions of the land, in this case not only of the coast, but also of the Andes and the Amazonian jungle beyond. When he tested the sea off Trujillo, he was surprised that the temperature was as low as 15°C and concluded that it was the seawater that cooled the air and not, as had always been assumed, the winds that cooled the sea. In the tropical latitudes of Peru, the temperature of the seawater should average 25°C. Instead, it fluctuates between 14°C and 18°C all year round, guaranteeing the coastal area a temperate climate free from tropical rains, and providing a rich feeding ground for fish and for the sea birds and seals that live off the fish.

Two Ocean Currents

One would expect the Antarctic seas where the Humboldt originates to be as barren as the frozen land, but the remarkable thing is that they are extraordinarily rich in nutrients and all forms of marine life. The richness of vegetable matter in the sea accounted for the tremendous variety and number of animals and birds that Captain Cook saw on his voyage of discovery in the Antarctic. Even the Humboldt Current itself, however, with its chilly waters, teeming life and stiff accompanying breezes that blow forever out of the southwest, can have its unreliable moments. These occur a few times in every century when another current, bringing warm water from the west along the equator, forces its way down the coast of Peru and pushes the Humboldt far out to sea.

In March of 1997, a fisherman in the Peruvian fishing port of Chimbote, leaning over the side of his vessel, put his hand in the water and discovered the water was warmer than it should be at that time of year. With the inherited wisdom of centuries, he immediately detected that the great Pacific Ocean currents had changed: the dreaded El Niño current would arrive by the following Christmas. The Spanish translation of 'The Baby Jesus' is 'El Niño Jesus'. The concurrence of the warm ocean current with the feast of Christmas has transferred the name of the Christ child to the current, which has been known for at least a century as El Niño.

The El Niño of 1997/1998 proved to be the most catastrophic in recorded history. The first casualty when the warm seawater flowed southwards along the South American Pacific coastline was the fish that died out, starved of the nutrients of cold seas. The pelicans, left without their rich diet of anchovies, faced starvation and became so disoriented by hunger that they invaded the streets of cities in Chile in flocks that disrupted traffic. The seals that bask on the Peruvian seal cliffs tried to swim southwards to cold waters where fish still lived, only to die in the attempt, or else, like the pelicans, braved their fear of humans to enter city homes in search of food. Inevitably, the tropical air lying over the normally cooler coastline brought spectacular thunder and lightening storms ushering in a deluge that saturated the dry dusty foothills of the Andes. The dusty surface of those hills turned to mud and began to move slowly at first and then

Children of the Sun

with gathering momentum turned into crashing landslides, bringing huge boulders and tons of mud crashing down the mountainsides, sweeping before it towns and streets, highways and bridges. Cataracts of ochre mud and water raced down through villages built with no more durable material than mud bricks dried in the sun. These walls, saturated at their foundations, returned to the wet mud from which they had been made so that gable ends opened like the tail gates of trailers and fell in one piece to the ground, immediately followed by the roof and remaining walls collapsing like the proverbial house of cards.

Such was the force of the landslides that flowed down river beds where once quiet rivers passed that modern reinforced concrete bridges were no match for the energy released by El Niño. They too fell into the rivers that they once spanned. With the collapse of up to fifty major bridges in Peru, communication within the country broke down, supplies of food, gas and petrol were interrupted and living standards in many communities went back to a level of primitive existence such as had not been known since Inca days. Hundreds of miles of paved roadway between the cities in the mountains and the coast collapsed beneath the rushing waters, tossing huge Volvo trucks used for the transport of people, animals and food into the boiling cauldron of ochre water like dinky toys. Far south of the equator in Chile, over 80,000 people lost their homes. Even the Atacama Desert in that country, the driest place on earth, had its arid sands soaked with water, so that flower seeds buried there for hundreds of years germinated and the desert bloomed.

This climatic catastrophe was not limited to South America; it had global consequences. Drought affected the Australian outback with consequential bush fires. Brazil, too, burned in drought. Argentina was flooded and the pacific coast of Mexico experienced unaccustomed hurricanes, one of which flooded the luxurious seaside resort of Acapulco, killing four hundred people in one day. Further north, the Californian coast was deluged with rain and swept by storms. Mountain cataracts rushed to the coast of southern California, sweeping away in places the sands of Malibu Beach. Some weather experts even connected the deadly storm of

Two Ocean Currents

Christmas Eve in Ireland, which left many homes with a cold Christmas dinner, with the El Niño current, 7,000 miles away off the coast of Peru.

Ecuador, even though better prepared for rain than Peru (there is an annual rainy season there), still suffered greatly. The poor of Manta, where the Cork mission was located and who had built their homes in dried up riverbeds, saw their flimsy homes built of bamboo and tin roofs swept away before their eyes, while several of their neighbours were swept to their deaths. Cut off from supplies of food from the mountains and fuel from the city, supply centres faced starvation as well as homelessness. The unpaved streets of their shantytowns were turned into impassable rivers and, later when the rains finally ceased, rutted passages of dried mud. With the stoical faith of the native South Americans, parishioners still plodded through the wet mud and afterwards along the rugged terrain to attend their weekly Mass.

The Cork mission did all it could to alleviate the sufferings of the victims of this natural disaster by providing free medical aid and financial help. Before the arrival of the rains, which they knew would follow the arrival of El Niño, they reinforced the parish buildings with protective walls. However, the year's planned courses in adult education and the preparation of children for the sacraments had to be postponed until normal climatic conditions returned. For the priests themselves the danger of infection from the dreaded dengue fever carried by mosquitoes was ever present and, in fact, one of the priests contracted the illness with the result that he had to return to Ireland earlier than expected. Overall, however, the mission survived and continued to complete its ten-year commitment to the Diocese of Portoviejo.

A New Dawn in Trujillo

In 1992 Bishop Murphy sent off three of his missionary priests, Bob Brophy, John Collins and Eugene Crowley, to look for a diocese in which to establish a new branch of the mission. In the previous year, he had handed back to the Archdiocese of Trujillo the two parishes originally adopted in 1965. El Porvenir and Florencia de Mora, as well as the parochial schools and all the convents occupied by the Irish Mercy Sisters, were now outside the Cork and Ross parishes. All that remained within the Cork territory were two parishes, La Esperanza and Sagrada Familia, one convent of the Bon Secours order and three parochial schools. The remaining five or six priests distributed themselves between the two presbyteries still in the Cork territory.

The terrorist threat gradually receded and the mission began to adjust to its new situation, which in Trujillo was much changed from the days when twelve priests, spread over four presbyteries, worked side by side with four convents of Irish sisters and the Peruvian staff of seven parochial schools. The adjustment would have been difficult for any group, but for the survivors on the mission the difficulty was compounded by the fact that four of the priests were second- or third-time workers in Peru. They had seen the early challenges facing the newly arrived people from the hills being overcome with the passage of the years, when squalid shantytowns developed into reasonably comfortable suburbs serviced by electricity, water and sanitation. They had seen the children of the first settlers advance through education to university standard and some enter professions such as nursing and teaching. Now on the

A New Dawn in Trujillo

uninhabited sands of lower Esperanza, they saw the whole process begin again as new invasions of people from the Andes, displaced by years of terror, started from nothing on the long journey to a developed community. Most of the parish of Sagrada Familia was now made up of primitive settlements without light or water or sanitation. They had no schools and no churches. For young missionaries this would have been a challenge that they would accept, just as their predecessors had done some twenty-five years earlier, but in fact the men on site in 1993 were far from young. Only two, Ted Sheehan and Eugene Crowley, were on their first missionary journey. One of the older men went home to die in 1995; another would be dead in just over a decade. Even Bishop Murphy, who still visited the mission regularly and took an interest in every detail of its running, would be dead by 1996.

New blood was injected into the team in 1996 when Pat Fogarty and Sean O'Sullivan joined John O'Callagan and Liam Hickey in Trujillo, and Kieran O'Driscoll and Kevin O'Regan joined the team in Ecuador, where another 'first timer', Eoin Whooley, was in residence since 1993. 1997 saw the appointment of John Buckley as Bishop of Cork and Ross. His appointment was beneficial to the South American mission as during his years as coadjutor to Bishop Murphy he had acquired a 'feel' for the mission and its people, which would not have been possible for a bishop coming from a different Irish diocese. As coadjutor, Bishop John Buckley had visited the mission and administered Confirmation to many groups of young Peruvians. He knew the missionaries well as many had been his contemporaries in college, while the younger men had been his students when he was president of Farranferris College. Added to this advantageous background was his personal disposition to listen to others and act on their suggestions, which is exactly what he did when he met the mission team on his visit to Ecuador and Peru in May 1998.

In January of that year, the priests working in Ecuador and Peru held a weeklong meeting, during which they reflected on the work of the South American mission with a view to planning its future in the light of the ten-year contract in Manta and the falling number of vocations and ordinations at home. This conference produced a four-page document outlining a well-thought-out plan for the future of the mission in Peru and Ecuador. The priests felt it imperative that the ten-year contract with the Diocese of Manta in Ecuador be honoured and that after the five years that still remained the operation would be closed. They were confident that they were moving in the right direction to meet the goal of establishing the necessary infrastructure, a pastoral programme that was lay orientated and a formation of people that should be self-maintaining as a local church by 2003 when the contract ended.

The situation in Trujillo was somewhat less clear-cut. Since 1991 the mission had consisted of two parishes covering the district of La Esperanza in the northern part of the city. However, the expansion had been such with continuous waves of migration from the mountain areas that what started originally as six parochial 'centres' had grown to eleven, with a population of 150,000 living, for the most part, in primitive shantytowns. This expansion had placed a tremendous workload on the priests of the mission, and with resources having to be stretched between the larger established centres and the newer underdeveloped areas, it was felt that the Trujillo mission, as it stood, could not continue.

The final proposal that came out of the analysis of the Cork and Ross involvement in South America was to hand back the developed section of La Esperanza to the local diocese in 2001 and concentrate all the manpower and funds on the poorest areas of La Sagrada Familia and El Milagro. They were conscious that this proposal impinged on the home dioceses, and so they proposed a general meeting of the priests of Cork and Ross to be held in Blarney in September, at which the proposals could be presented and which would offer an opportunity for discussion on how the dioceses would address a future mission.

While this summary outlines the main proposals, the document itself reflects the extraordinary commitment and enthusiasm of the band of priests remaining in South America. Far from living on past glories, they were facing up realistically to the future, with the poorest of the poor as the central focus of that future. In a sense the mission had gone back to its roots, put down some thirty-three years earlier when it came to the rescue of a people so poor and so marginalised that even among their fellow citizens they counted for nothing. Over those productive years those poor people, with much help from the mission's varied programmes, had advanced to at least a basic level of decent living. With so much achieved it was time for the missionaries to move on and they did not have far to move: just a few hundred yards into the bleak desert where new shantytowns and a hungry, deprived population had settled.

In May of 1998, Bishop Buckley visited the mission and promised full support for the diocesan mission and discussed the meeting of clergy in Blarney fixed for September, which would be facilitated by Fr Peter Hughes of the Columbans, a man with many years of experience in Lima. Reassured by the support of the bishop and the good will shown by all of the Cork and Ross priests at the Blarney meeting, the missionaries in Ecuador and Peru forged ahead with their plans for the immediate future in Manta and for what those in Peru hoped would be stability for at least a further ten years.

Ecuador: An Undertaking Completed

During his 1999 pastoral visit to Ecuador, Bishop Buckley viewed the various building projects completed in the preceding months, blessed the new classrooms in one parish and the renovation of the parish church in another. Even though less than three years remained of the contracted time in Manta, the priests still pressed on with the planned projects for the benefit of the faith of the people, projects that would enable the local priests to carry on the work of service and education begun by the Irishmen.

During the endless flooding caused by El Niño, hundreds of families who had built their makeshift homes in a dried up riverbed had to be relocated. A new ring road to the city of Manta encircled the Cork and Ross parishes and here the flood victims were re-housed in what became one of the fastest growing locations in the city. The location of a new bus terminal within its limits guaranteed continued growth over the coming years. A two-phased plan was proposed by the priests and approved by Bishop Buckley, which envisaged the immediate construction of classrooms and a medical centre, followed by the building of a church in the following year.

On the new ring road where the mission had built a church and seven classrooms over the previous three years, it was proposed to complete the centre with the construction of a concrete area about the size of a basketball court, which could be used as a recreation area for the youth who would otherwise be left to play football on some rough sandy street, and where cultural events such as concerts and dance festivals could be organised. Such consideration for the whole lifestyle of a poor community had always been typical of the

Ecuador: An Undertaking Completed

Cork priests, who never confined their input to strictly 'religious' matters, but instead took into consideration the wider aspirations of the whole human person. A similar entertainment complex was approved, which was to be added to an existing church/classroom centre in another area.

Finally, the Santa Ana community situated on the southern side of the parish was selected for the building of five classrooms and a multipurpose room, which could double as a Mass centre and large meeting room. In this deprived area, the missionaries had up to then borrowed the State school for these purposes, but they feared that this arrangement might not last when the local clergy took over. The investment in the training of lay helpers was now paying off as those trained over a two-year period felt confident enough to take part in the different programmes aimed at the teaching of the faith to children and their preparation for First Communion and Confirmation.

The news that Ted Sheehan, who had served in Peru, was coming to work in Ecuador was welcomed. His arrival would complete the team in Ecuador until the return of the parishes to the local archdiocese in the year 2003. However, such was not to be the case, because one man returned to Ireland in 1999 to be replaced by another Peruvian veteran, Christy Harrington. One year later in 2000, Bishop Buckley again visited Manta and found the building projects completed. In a sense it was also good news to hear that, in a sector known as Maria Imaculada, the church built some years before was inadequate to cater for the numbers of parishioners attending Mass. The bishop approved the building of a new church on an adjoining site, the deconsecration of the existing chapel and its conversion to use as a community hall. All of this development meant that a shantytown was converted into a growing community taking pride in its development and placing the Church at the heart of the community, giving it a cherished place in the hearts of the people.

By March 2003 the ten-year contract was completed and one parish was handed back. At the request of the Archbishop of Portoviejo, two of the Irish priests agreed to remain on in the other

Children of the Sun

parish until the month of July. With their departure for Ireland, the contribution of Cork and Ross to the poor of Manta in Ecuador came to an end.

Two years later Bishop Buckley sent two of his priests to represent him at a celebration to mark the Golden Jubilee of the ordination of the Archbishop of Portoviejo. They were delighted to find the two parishes where the Cork priests had served now staffed by a resident priest. All of the churches and classrooms were in full use; a young local priest, Fr Patricio, as it happened, was making full use of all the facilities, including the pick-up truck left by the Irish priests, and serving the people in a way that would have been impossible but for the facilities established by the mission. There was also a great sign of hope for the future in the number of seminarians attending the Mass of celebration to mark the archbishop's jubilee. The local seminary had up to sixty young men at various stages of preparation for the priesthood. As well as this, the medical centres developed with such enlightened planning had survived the departure of the Irish and their financial backing and were functioning as self-financing services providing hope to the sick and the poor.

The Last Years of the Mission

Once the decision to hand the local diocese back to the parish of La Esperanza was made, a whole process of documentation of the buildings and the property had to begin. An inventory of all the buildings had to be drawn up, as well as an inventory of their contents, so that a receipt could be obtained from the diocese on the handover. Without this full documentation the Irish priests could be exposed to accusations of asset stripping if any of the furnishings and sacred vessels of the churches disappeared. The buildings themselves had to be surveyed by an engineer to ensure that they conformed to all the building regulations. Otherwise, in the event of collapse in an earthquake, the Irish could be held responsible by the State authorities for substandard construction. Legal title to all the properties had to be finalised. As these legal processes can be long drawn out in every country, in Peru, with its tradition of Spanish legal processes, the challenge was enormous for the Irish priest who took responsibility for the task.

The employees of the mission in that parish also had to be taken care of in compliance with the law of the land, which specified redundancy compensation calculated on the number of years of service and on the income earned during those years. As some of these parish secretaries and housekeepers had been employed for up to thirty years, during which inflation had sometimes run into extraordinarily high percentages and currencies had even changed, this task called for the services of a lawyer experienced in employment law. It was also felt by the priests that every building should be in top repair on being handed over, so they had all of the buildings painted and brought up to their original condition.

While this was going on in the older parish developments of the poorest areas, the parish of Sagrada Familia was rapidly advancing following the well-tried pattern established over the years. Even though the newly settled areas of Sagrada Familia were within minutes of a community of twenty years standing, they might as well have been located hundreds of miles away. The new arrivals from the Andes had no bond whatsoever with those who had migrated twenty years earlier. They would not have known any of them personally and, with a sense of inferiority connected with the lack of education and the ignorance of the customs of the coastal environment, they would have kept to themselves and remained within their newly erected shacks of straw matting and mud bricks. As natives of the interior of the country, church-going would have been alien to their way of life, since a visiting priest was a rarity in the Andes and a resident priest was unknown outside the larger mountain cities. Only when a church was built right in the heart of their primitive encampment did they begin to build up a relationship with the priest and begin to see Sunday Mass as part of their normal way of life. The way forward for the missionaries was to acquire some land from the housing ministry and construct meeting rooms that could double as a chapel and begin to run classes for the children and provide a basic medical service. A church-run complex such as this was essential to give the new community a sense of identity and provide the priests and nuns with a base from which they could be of use to such poor and dislocated people.

The wisdom of this approach was proved by the extraordinary success of the Cork and Ross mission over the previous twenty-five years. And so the five remaining priests, three of whom were first timers in Peru, set out to meet the needs of their new parishioners by establishing new centres, confident that they would be in the area for at least a further ten years. The last years of the century were occupied in the acquisition of building land and the construction of three new centres. As the building of the centres proceeded, some locals would form a committee of helpers, some indeed trying to fundraise (raising, in effect, little more than a nominal contribution), a practice that gave the local community a sense of ownership of their developing parish. The buildings were simple, usually of mixed use: meeting rooms downstairs, a chapel upstairs. The minutes of the priests' meetings record the urgency and enthusiasm shown in advancing this programme of parish development. Over a five-year period, three centres were developed, bringing the number of Mass centres from eight to eleven, with Masses programmed at regular intervals and the steady building up of a faith community among the poorest of the poor. It was against this background of development that serious concern developed among the priests in regard to the future staffing of the mission. Funding from Ireland was not applied solely to parish building, but was also used in wider social development work in helping State schools to buy furniture and build school extensions. In Mayfield in Cork, a fund had been set up as a memorial to Fr Con Twohig, who had died early in life as curate in that parish. Some of that fund was used for social aid.

Another imaginative project was the part funding of a public market in the deprived village of El Milagro some miles outside Trujillo. Already this village had its fine church built by the Cork and Ross mission in its central square. Contact was made with Irish Aid, a fund administered by the Minister of State for Overseas Development at the Department of Foreign Affairs, and the sum of £27,654 (Irish punts) was approved. This money would be jointly administered by the Pastoral Council of El Milagro and CICADESCO and amounted to over half of the total projected cost of the roofed market, with its counters, water supply and all the other equipment of a modern public market. By December 2002 the project was completed and two pitches, or sales areas, were donated to the pastoral council, who subsequently rented them out to provide a source of ongoing income for the maintenance of the church and parish centre. This was a far-sighted strategy for the survival of the parish when the Irish priests were gone.

Side by side with all this energetic work in the building of parish centres and the building up of a Christian community was one worry hanging over the mission. This becomes clear from the recorded minutes of the priests' meetings. Even though two of the five survivors were coming to the end of their contracted time in Peru and would soon return home for good, there was no definite news of replacements from home. Bishop Buckley was by then making annual visits to Ecuador and Peru. In August 1999, the bishop arrived for a special purpose: to bid farewell to the retiring Archbishop of Trujillo, Emmanuel Prado. He wished to acknowledge publicly the contribution this fine bishop had made to the Cork and Ross mission over a period of many years. However, this pastoral visit was a landmark for another reason: the surprise announcement that one of the priests at home on holidays would not be returning for health considerations and that he would not be replaced. The news came as such a shock to the others that they held another formal meeting with the bishop on the following day, when the bishop explained that because of the declining number of priests at home and the impossibility of finding a volunteer, he was left with no alternative but to reduce the number to four. Other dioceses had been approached for help, but the result had been negative.

The priests made the case that already in the recent past their numbers had dropped from six to five, while the Mass centres had increased by three. In response to the analysis of the situation, the bishop promised to try again to find volunteers on his return home. However, by March of the following year he wrote to say he had failed in this endeavour. When the Bishop of Cork and Ross visited Trujillo again in November of that year, he spoke of the state of the home diocese and in particular of the challenge faced by declining numbers of clergy. Many parishes had seen the numbers reduced, other parishes had been forced to amalgamate, and the trend was that the numbers of the clergy would continue to decline sharply in the foreseeable future. In this context, he spoke of the difficulties he encountered in finding volunteers. He spoke of the possibility of establishing a new mission project in some other Latin American country that might be more attractive to possible volunteers. This suggestion was dismissed by those present because of the needs of the existing location and its historical association with Cork. It was

The Last Years of the Mission

agreed that the bishop would communicate with each priest in Cork and Ross, inviting them, confidentially, if they were interested.

During his September visit in 2001, Bishop Buckley revealed that two priests under forty-five years of age had indicated their willingness to volunteer, as did several of 'the old guard' who had worked previously on the mission. He spoke of the realistic possibility of continuing with three priests until the end of 2005, after which any priest who wished to serve on the missions could do so with the St James Society or the Columbans.

Just over a year later in January 2003, Bishop Buckley phoned from Ireland to say that in spite of the best efforts of the diocese, there were no volunteers for the mission and that he had decided, in consultation with the Cork and Ross mission commission, that the operation should be closed either in June 2003 or January 2004 if Sean O'Sullivan and Pat Fogarty were willing to stay until that time. Both agreed, adding that they would prefer to remain on until the feast of St Patrick in 2004, by which time they would have all the necessary legal procedures completed for the final handing over of the mission to the local archdiocese. By January 2004 final arrangements for the departure of the Cork and Ross missionaries were made by a commission of local clergy formed by the Archbishop of Trujillo, Monsignor Cabrejos Vidarte, as a practical expression of gratitude to all the Irish who had contributed to a great undertaking. The following programme was agreed and fully implemented:

- A commemorative booklet outlining the history of the mission and its contribution to the archdiocese would be written.
- The remains of Archdeacon Tom Duggan would be exhumed in Lima and reinterred in a special tomb in El Buen Pastor parish church, which was the first church built by the mission.
- A special open-air Mass of thanksgiving would be celebrated on 29 February 2004.
- A civic St Patrick's Day parade involving all the parish groups, schools and institutions founded by the mission would take place in the central square of Trujillo.

- The Medal of the City would be bestowed on the same day by the provincial council of government, which would be followed by an official lunch of gratitude. Bishop Buckley indicated that he would bear the cost of the event.

In the event, this programme was carried out to the last detail. Bishop Buckley and Archbishop Cabrejos concelebrated the open-air Mass along with over forty priests in a newly laid out park named 'Parque Mission Irlandesa', where a ten metre-high Celtic cross had been erected by the city as a monument to the contribution of the mission. A huge crowd of parishioners as well as the local dignitaries attended. The fifty-five Irish priests who had worked on the mission were represented by Canon Michael Crowley, Canon Michael Riordan and Fr Tim O'Sullivan, who were among the earliest volunteers back in the 1960s.

Dr Luis Santa Maria, a long-term lawyer friend of the Irish missionaries, by then a congressman in the national parliament, presented the Medal of the Congress of Peru to Bishop Buckley. On 1 March, both bishops concelebrated a Mass at the reinterment of Archdeacon Duggan in the church of El Buen Pastor, at which Canon Michael Crowley preached.

A photographic exhibition mounted by former teachers of the mission schools was opened in a colonial building in the old city of Trujillo. On St Patrick's Day, Monsignor Kevin O'Callaghan, Vicar General of Cork and Ross, accepted the Medal of the City, an event which was followed by a civic parade in the central city plaza, which included the hoisting of the Irish flag and the playing of the Irish national anthem by a military band. There is a certain poignance about the final entry in the mission annals, which is here quoted in full:

> The final Mass of the mission was celebrated by Pat Fogarty and Sean O'Sullivan on the night of Friday, March 19th, 2004, in the open air patio of Cristo Rey. Amidst scenes of great faith and sadness the final curtain was drawn on the 39 years of service to this noble

people. During the Mass, Pat Fogarty presented Padre Miguel Escobar to the people of the parish as their new parish priest, encouraging them to offer him the same unconditional support they had given us.

Epilogue

Mass of Thanksgiving in Cork

On 23 September 2004, Bishop John Buckley celebrated a Mass of thanksgiving in the North Cathedral, Cork, in the presence of the Lord Mayor of the city and the Mayor of the county. Bishop John Magee of Cloyne and Bishop Bill Murphy of Kerry joined in the celebration along with priests of the dioceses, many of whom had served in South America. Sisters of the Mercy, Bon Secours and the Presentation orders, including Irish and Peruvians, participated in the liturgy along with lay people from Peru and Ecuador who had been associated with the mission over the years. Many parishes throughout Cork and Ross were also represented. The liturgy, which was both multi-lingual and multi-cultural, reflected the spiritual and personal bonds that linked two Catholic communities that had come to know and love each other over half a century and whose association would continue into the future, thanks to the ongoing presence of the Irish Sisters in South America.